BECOMING
AND
BEING
A
WOMAN

BECOMING AND BEING A WOMAN

Ruth F. Lax, Ph.D.

JASON ARONSON INC.
Northvale, New Jersey
London

This book was set in 11 pt. Bell by Alpha Graphics of Pittsfield, New Hampshire and printed and bound by Book-mart Press of North Bergen, New Jersey.

Library of Congress Cataloging-in-Publication Data

Lax, Ruth F.
    Becoming and being a woman / Ruth F. Lax.
      p.   cm.
    Includes bibliographical references and index.
    ISBN 0-7657-0050-6 (alk. paper)
    1. Women—Mental health. 2. Women—Psychology. 3. Women and
psychoanalysis. I. Title.
    RC451.4.W6L385 1997
    616.89'0082—DC21   96-46470

Manufactured in the United States of America on acid-free paper. Jason Aronson Inc. offers books and cassettes. For information and catalog write to Jason Aronson Inc., 230 Livingston Street, Northvale, New Jersey 07647. Or visit our website: http://www.aronson.com

To my patients who taught me

and my mentors from whom I learned

Contents

Acknowledgments

Most of the essays in this volume are based on papers published in analytic journals that were previously presented at various conferences. I thank my discussants and audience participants for their enriching comments.

Most significant, however, in writing these essays were my discussions with friends during which I could voice my puzzlements, thoughts, and the ideas evoked by the analytic interaction with analysands. Their life stories, conflicts, and attempted modes of resolution stimulated my lifelong wish to learn and understand, and my wonderment at the manifold ways in which the human mind works and reveals itself.

I especially thank Dr. John Herma who not only encouraged my wish to write, but whose constructive criticism taught me how to write; Dr. Edith Jacobson who while discussing my papers always brought up some of her cases and thus taught me by her splendid examples; Dr. Milton Horowitz whose helpful critical remarks were couched in a sense of humor that enabled me to see my writing in a realistic perspective.

I also gratefully acknowledge the helpful critical comments on early drafts unsparingly offered by Drs. Anne Appelbaum, Martin Bergmann, Raquel Berman, Elsa and Harold Blum, Bill Grossman, Otto Kernberg, Helen Meyers, Warren Poland, Owen Renik, and Ted Shapiro. To each of them my deep-felt thanks.

Graciela Abelin and Maria Bergmann, my special dear friends and encouraging critics, were and are of particular significance to me. Their availability and their patience when listening to my doubts gave me a sense of a reliable, friendly presence. Both raised questions and offered suggestions I welcomed and appreciated. Their comments sharpened my thinking. My thanks to them are manifold.

I acknowledge with appreciation the facilitating efforts and enhancing contributions of Judith Cohen, Catherine Monk, M'lou Pinkham, and Norma Pomerantz, members of the editorial staff of Jason Aronson Inc.

Very special thanks to my assistant, Virginia Baker, without whose good will, patience, availability, and resourcefulness this manuscript would not have been completed.

I acknowledge with thanks and appreciation the cooperation of *The International Journal of Psycho-Analysis, The Journal of the American Psychoanalytic Association, The Psychoanalytic Quarterly,* and *The Psychoanalytic Study of the Child.*

Introduction

The chapters in this book present an evolving conception of female psychosexual development based on analytic child observation, the findings stemming from child analysis, and, most important, the analysis of women.

Chapter 1 is an evaluation of psychoanalytic views pertaining to female psychosexual development, femaleness, and femininity. Freud's theories and the effect of his ideas on the understanding of women's psychic structure, psychosexuality, and their inner world are critically examined. The special significance and effect Freud's patriarchal bias had on the manner in which his followers analyzed women and the goals they set for the analysis of women are presented. The intellectual and societal contributions that led to a reexamination and rethinking of Freud's theories, and the effect the new findings had on the subsequent therapeutic approach with which women were analyzed are explored. Current, important investigations leading to a more accurate understanding of women's psychosexuality and their psychic structure are emphasized and discussed.

Chapter 2 is a report on pioneering work and findings. I was the first pregnant analyst who observed and reported on the analytic processes of my patients that took place during my pregnancy. I noted and described their transference manifestations and my countertransferential reactions.

Mother's reaction to having birthed an impaired infant is discussed in Chapter 3. The effect on the bonding process of the baby's defect and mother's narcissistic hurt are explored. The "child within," for so long a part of mother's bodily and psychic self-representation, this fantasy of a perfect being narcissistically and libidinally endowed, is destroyed when birth reveals its defects. For the mother the defective infant becomes the source of narcissistic mortification.

Analytic findings indicate, however, that reactions of attenuated severity to those described above may occur even when a newborn child is perfectly normal but does not coincide with mother's image of her expected, hoped-for fantasy baby. A mother under such circumstances experiences a sense of disappointment. This may be followed by a depression of various degrees of severity.

The *Rotten Core*, a specific type of self-pathology described in Chapter 4, originates as a reaction to a depressed mother's lack of libidinal availability for the child. A child perceives and experiences the unavailable mother as rejecting. The internalization of such an interaction with mother results in a specific kind of identification with the aggressor. It leads to an internalization of the depressed mother, who becomes the intrapsychic malignant introject. The *Rotten Core*, a psychic substructure, represents on the most primitive level the fusion of the "malignant" (angry-rejecting) maternal introject with the "bad" (rejected) aspects of the self. In patients with this pathology, the *Rotten Core* and the "good" self do not merge into a consolidated and integrated self-representation. This is due to the preponderance of hostility in the interaction between mother and child which accounts for the persistence of defensive splitting.

The formation and the consequences of *Rotten Core* pathology are presented to account for the specific split in the self-representation that gives these patients the subjective awareness of a duality of their selves. Developmental consequences of *Rotten Core* pathology are discussed.

Chapter 5 explores the development of the girl's psychosexual feminine self-image during the preoedipal and early oedipal phases and examines the accompanying primary and secondary genital feelings and anxieties. The connection between the little girl's discovery and pleasure in self-exploration and masturbation and the related anxieties about being "closed up" are discussed. The nature of the corresponding object relationships is presented, particularly the narcissistic significance of being like mother.

A little girl develops two different types of genital anxieties as a consequence of her erotic feelings. These occur during different developmental subphases. The first relates to the girl's fears that her genitals will be mutilated; the second develops during the negative oedipal phase when the girl recognizes the significance of the penis she lacks. There is a temporal sequence in the development of these fears, but once both come into play, their vicissitudes commingle and the dominant focus depends on the various factors impinging on the girl's life.

Clinical material presented in Chapter 6 leads to a discussion of beating fantasies that varies from Freud's model. In women the beating fantasy is a multidetermined, multilayered fantasy of forbidden gratification and mandatory, deserved punishment. It thus represents a compromise formation. Analysis of my patient's version of the beating fantasy indicates that mother was experienced as judge, prosecutor, and executioner, who did not condone the fantasied incestuous tryst with father. In the "average expectable environment" (Hartmann 1958), the girl's usual interactions with father during the positive oedipal phase, and the phase-specific libidinally fueled elaborations of these interactions in fantasy, culminate in incestuous desires the girl *knows* are prohibited by mother. The fantasied role girls assign to mother as the punisher in the oedipal drama is equivalent to the fantasied role boys ascribe to father as castrator. For both sexes, anxiety about the safety of the genitals spurs the internalization of parental prohibitions, the repression of oedipal wishes, and the subsequent structuralization of the superego. Mother establishes the "oedipal law" for the girl analogously to father's doing the same for the boy. It thus is the mother, not the father, who establishes the girl's moral foundations.

Identification with the "judge, prosecutor, aggressor–mutilator mother" will become at first the "thou shalt and shalt not" aspect of the superego. Identification with mother's successful womanliness may merge with the idealized mother image of the preoedipal phase and become incorporated in the feminine ego ideal aspect of the superego. Based on the injunction against incest, these internalized identifications form the core of the female superego. Such a resolution is optimal, though perhaps infrequent.

Fran's story and the conflicts that dominated her inner world are described in Chapter 7. Born and raised in a patriarchal family setting, motivated by narcissistic and libidinal strivings, Fran developed discordant identification systems that neither fused nor modulated each other. The structure of her conscious wished-for self-image with its autonomous tendencies was based on an Older Brother fantasy with which she identified. Her submissive self-image was determined by an unconscious ideal modeled on her mother. Enactments determined by the unconscious maternal ideal led to object choices that evoked masochistic behavior, experienced by Fran as destructive to her conscious ego aims.

Fran's incompatible identifications evoked continuous psychic conflict that contributed to splits in the ego ideal. Fran struggled with the riddle: "What and how should a woman be?"

In Chapter 8, five clinical case vignettes illustrate the relevant genetic factors contributing to the development of deviant ego structures of certain masochistic women who unconsciously provoke their self-defeat. Analyses revealed that these patients developed concomitantly two disparate wishful self-images, each based on different internalizations, antithetical to each other and differently cathected. Both persisted in the ego as permanent substructures. The maternally derived wishful self-image may have had a degree of consciousness during some part of the oedipal phase but subsequently became totally repressed. It was ego-alien since it conflicted with aspects of the paternally derived, conscious, wishful self-image that had become the avowed level of aspiration, namely, assertion, excellence, mastery, a desire for autonomy, and certain ethical principles that became these patients' narcissistically significant values. The conscious wishful self-image had become during the process of maturation sufficiently depersonified to function partially as an ego ideal. However, the existence and the disruptive effects of the maternally derived, unconscious wishful self-image interfered with the development of a complete and harmonious ego ideal necessary for integrated, cohesive character formation. These patients' self-representation had a faulty structure because it contained two diverse, yet permanent, self-images—one conscious, the other unconscious—that were split off and that could therefore neither modify each other nor fuse.

Nonintegrated parental introjects—respectively, the cores of these patients' conscious and unconscious wishful self-images—persisted in their psychic structures. This contributed to the formation of their noncohesive superego in which primitive, harsh, and sadistic elements predominated.

The menopausal phase of a woman's life, discussed in Chapter 9, occurs at mid-life, a time that most women experience as stressful. For homemakers, still the majority of women, child-rearing tasks are ending, children become autonomous, and the home feels empty. The menopause appears like the focal point of psychological changes, stimulated in about 75 percent of women by physiological changes that occur in varying degrees of severity. Women at that time start to fear, and many perhaps even experience, the beginnings of aging. The various psychophysiological concomitants of this phase add to a woman's vulnerability and have a profound effect on her psychic reality. Women may frequently use intensified activity, cosmetic surgery, attempts to "reinvent" themselves, and so on to fortify the *denial of the intrapsychic responses* to their awareness of the end of menstruation, which signifies the "change of life"—to the recognition of their changing body self and their decrease in peak functioning. All these losses may evoke a sense of narcissistic pain and mortification. For some women this is a time of conscious self-assessment; for others, an escape into various forms of denial.

An acknowledgment of the physical and psychic changes enables a woman to mourn for and renounce unattainable goals, wishes, and hopes of her youth. She can then attain an adaptive resolution. When this occurs, a woman's libido tied up with the past is freed to fuel creative outcomes following the menopausal phase. In successful cases the mourning process is accompanied by a working through that results in greater self-tolerance and self-acceptance, thus enriching object relations.

The last phase of a woman's life is discussed in Chapter 10. Aging is a process that may take many years. For many women who worked through the menopausal phase, this is a successful period filled with gratifying, often creative activities.

The integration of feminine and masculine strivings enables older women to be both assertive and nurturing. For many women aging is most successful when they are involved in youth-oriented activities.

Some older women seek treatment to attain a sense of inner peace. They hope the resolution of childhood conflicts will help them to reach this goal.

Irrevocably, as the years pass by, failing health and strength eventually indicate true old age. The capacity to accept the final decline with tranquility is a rare gift and blessing.

1 Freud's Views and the Changing Perspective on Femaleness and Femininity: What My Female Analysands Taught Me

In his thinking about a girl/woman's development, Freud emphasized the role of anatomy, biology, and constitution, neglecting the significance of familial and social contributions even though he had postulated the principle of complemental series of intrapsychic and external influences in his general theories of psychic development. Freud's (1933) writings on feminity are an attempt to elucidate how a girl becomes a woman. According to Freud, crucial in this process is the girl's discovery of genital differences. The significance of this discovery for the girl sets in motion general and unique consequences. Comparing herself to the boy, she observes that he has a penis whereas she perceives herself as having nothing. She thus experiences herself as lacking. This psychic recognition evokes a traumatic shock culminating in a profound narcissistic mortification.

By implication, Freud's (1925) postulation that for a girl/woman, anatomy is destiny establishes male genital anatomy as the norm and the female's as a deviation from this norm. According to Freud, the anatomic lack of a penis signifies to the girl that lacking is to be her destiny.

Not having a penis, the girl experiences herself as already castrated. This sets in motion various consequences. Enraged at mother for being deprived of the penis, the girl turns to father who becomes her new love object and from whom she hopes to obtain a penis. This change of object brings to an end the preoedipal homosexual phase (Freud 1933).

Freud emphasized that a woman's castration complex is central to her feminine personality development. Since she experiences herself as already castrated, the girl, in contrast to the boy, has no incentive and does not feel impelled to give up her incestuous wishes toward father. This leads to deficient superego and ego development and a meager capacity for sublimation. The girl/woman was seen by Freud as swayed by emotions and therefore unable to uphold moral standards. Having discovered certain characteristic, though not exclusive, differences in the unconscious infantile fantasies of women and men, Freud (1933) ascribed these to biological predispositions that would inevitably determine the functioning of the respective psychic structures of each gender. He maintained that the differences in unconscious psychic content would affect the principles by which the psychic conscious and unconscious structures are governed.

Freud (1937) maintained that penis envy is unanalyzable, constituting the biological bedrock of women's sexuality. Female masochism, passivity, depression, and a meagerly developed superego pervade the female character in varying proportions. The girl, having discovered her genital inferiority and being unaware of having a vagina, gives up active sexuality. She stops clitoral masturbation and, following the oedipal phase, enters latency, remaining sexually dormant until puberty. At that time, the transfer from clitoral to vaginal sensitivity occurs. This is the pubertal "awakening." Ideally, the girl is now ready for a man. Freud (1933) ended his lecture on femininity, commenting,

I have *only* been describing women insofar as their nature is *determined* by their sexual functioning. It is true that this influence extends very far but we do not overlook the fact that an *individual woman may be a human being in other respects as well.* [p. 135, italics added]

Helene Deutsch, Lampl-de Groot and Marie Bonaparte accepted Freud's views and developed his position further. Lampl-de Groot (1965) stated

The purely feminine love orientation of the woman to the man leaves no place for activity. Feminine love is passive, a narcissistic process; the purely feminine woman does not love, she lets herself be loved. . . . It is well known that many women also retain some . . . activity in their relations to men and love them with real object love, that is, with "masculinity." [p. 41]

In spite of the awe Freud inspired and the admiration with which his findings were received, serious challenges to this theory of femininity were expressed even from within his own circle during the decade from the mid-1920s to the mid-1930s. Thus, Abraham (1920), discussing the manifestations of the female castration complex, stressed that masturbatory gratification not only facilitates resolution of penis envy, but it also enhances future genital gratification. In his letter to Freud of July 21, 1924, Abraham (1965) discussed the early awareness of vaginal sensations in girls.

Jones, Klein, and Horney maintained that there is an inborn biological drive that propels girls to heterosexuality, and that girls are aware of their genital anatomy and experience vaginal sensations during the preoedipal phase. Thus, they disagreed with Freud's assertion that the castration complex propels heterosexuality. They regarded penis envy as a defensive manifestation.

Jones (1922) maintained that femininity is innate and that the girl's masculine position reflects a retreat from disappointed incestuous feelings for the father. In a subsequent paper (1927)

Jones postulated the fear of "aphanisis," that is, complete extinc-
tion of the capacity for sexual enjoyment, as the central anxiety
of both sexes. According to Jones, father's refusal of the girl's early,
receptive, vaginal-sexual wishes, an aspect of her incestuous
longings, leads to subsequent guilt feelings, the fear of aphanisis,
and the formation of the superego. Jones stressed intrapsychic
factors but also recognized the role of social prohibition.

Horney (1924, 1926), who was most vocal in her disagreement
with Freud's theories of femininity, described them as an expression of biased male fantasies. She maintained that a girl's wish to
be a man is a defensive flight to ward off oedipal fantasies and
related fantasy fears of vaginal injury by father's large penis.
Horney (1924) considered penis envy as based primarily on the
girl's perception of her real disadvantages as compared to the boy.
She considered the views expressed by her male colleagues about
the value of the penis comparable to those of little boys.

Ruth Mack Brunswick (1940) understood penis envy in girls
as an expression of a desire to possess the omnipotent mother and
all her attributes.

Edith Jacobson's (1976) article, originally published in 1937,
is the only one I know to have expressed at that time an alternate
view to Freud's pronouncements on penis envy and the female
superego. Jacobson suggested that the catastrophic reaction to the
discovery of anatomic differences between the sexes, which Freud
described, is *not* inevitable. To the contrary, a girl may develop a
fantasy of an internal penis accompanied by an active erotization
of the vagina, which is valued in and for itself. This path leads to
the formation of a feminine ego ideal. Subsequently, superego
formation is not linked to father in a dependent, masochistic manner. Instead, the superego formation is based on greater female
self-esteem and autonomy. In the 1976 note to her 1937 paper,
Jacobson suggested that such an ever-increasing group of women
be considered as "female vaginal" characters rather than "masculine" women (p. 537). This unique revisionist article was not trans-

lated and published in English for forty years. It finally appeared in the *Psychoanalytic Quarterly* in 1976.

Horney (1924, 1926), Jones (1927), Jacobson (1936), Brunswick (1940), and Deutsch (1944, 1945) asserted that the wish for a child in girls is preoedipal. This wish is based on a maternal identification and also on a desire both to obtain a child from the mother and give her one. Father's role in procreation at this time is not understood by the girl and he plays no part in this girl–mother dyad.

Freud was dismissive of dissent. Consequently, until the 1960s, none of the articles that expounded views different from Freud's influenced or altered the adherence of mainstream analysts to his basic tenets. This acceptance of Freud's views was of immense importance because it profoundly influenced analytical technique with female patients as well as the goals of treatment for women. Of great significance in this respect was Freud's (1937) pronouncement regarding penis envy:

> We often have the impression that *with the wish for a penis and the masculine protest we have penetrated all the psychological strata and reached bedrock, and that thus our activities are at an end.* This is probably true, since, *for the psychical field, the biological field does in fact play the part of the underlying bedrock.* The repudiation of femininity can be nothing else than a biological fact, a part of the great riddle of sex. [Italics added; p. 252]

Freud (1937) believed that the ultimate difficulty in the analysis of women lay in their refusal to give up their wish for a penis— their deepest envy and lasting shame. He stated that

> at no other point in one's analytic work does one suffer from an oppressive feeling that all one's *repeated efforts have been in vain,* and from a suspicion that one is *"preaching to the winds,"* than when one is *trying to persuade* a woman to abandon her wish for a penis on the ground of its being unrealizable. [Italics added; p. 252]

Freud was pessimistic; he believed it may not be possible to complete the analysis of a woman successfully.

Based on Freud's ideas of feminine development and conflict, it was expected that analytic treatment would be more difficult and complicated for a woman than for a man. Because of women's dependence and the unresolved attachment to their fathers, it was assumed that termination with a male analyst would present special difficulties. The masochistic impulses characteristic of many women might result in a sadomasochistic bind with their analysts. This could lead to unending analyses. The analysis of shame was considered an especially important aspect of the analysis of women. Freud (1933) regarded shame as a particularly feminine characteristic that has as its unconscious purpose the concealment of genital deficiency. Thus the analysis of shame leads to the painful disclosure of penis envy and to all the perplexing problems associated with it.

The female patient, compared with the male patient, was seen as less aggressive, less defiant, more dependent, and more compliant. A woman was likely to form a stronger and less wavering object cathexis to her male analyst. She wanted to be the kind of patient her analyst wants, and she wanted to be loved. The development of an erotic transference with the male analyst was considered commonplace. This depiction of female patients was not challenged, and the causes for her actually being this way, if indeed she was, were not questioned or examined. During these years, there were few articles on countertransference. Analysis was considered gender blind. The analysis of a female patient with a female analyst was not examined or specifically discussed. Notions about the "neutral" analyst who represented a blank screen or a mirror were generally accepted.

This relatively serene period, during which analysts were usually idolized and sought after and analysis was regarded as a solution to all psychic problems, came to an end with the rumblings of the liberation movements. During the late 1950s and the 1960s, militant feminists began the now well-known attacks on Freudian psychoanalysis. Freud's theories of femininity were examined from without and a similar process began within the psychoanalytic establishment. Women in the literary and academic worlds voiced their dissatisfaction with the Freudian understanding of femininity and with the second-class position of women in society.

Some female analysts began to listen to themselves in a different way. These analysts permitted themselves to remember and reexamine their own analyses. They recalled the squelched feelings that accompanied their experiences. Consequently, they carefully scrutinized their countertransferences to assure as open-minded a listening to their patients as possible.

My 1969 article about the pregnant analyst (see Chapter 2) was the result of such listening without preconceived notions. It meant listening to the patient and myself, empathizing with and analyzing both of us. Obviously, I was not the first pregnant analyst, but I was the first pregnant analyst who observed and reported on the analytic process that went on during the pregnancy. I also carefully examined my countertransferential reactions. My article stimulated further investigations of this topic, which until then had been treated as a taboo.

The reanalyses of female patients illustrate the impingements of Freud's theory on the analytic treatment of women. Findings demonstrate that the preconceived views regarding penis envy, castration, superego inferiority, and the disapproval of aggression have had far-reaching consequences. These views influenced and interfered with listening to and hearing the female patient. As an example, I present the following:

> One of the first patients I reanalyzed in the early 1970s was a woman in our field. She was suffering from a character neurosis and chronic neurotic depression. She spent many hours telling me about her first analysis. Though she had read the works of Horney and was taken by her point of view about women, she nonetheless went to a male, orthodox, Freudian analyst. She now tried to understand why she had done so. May was in her mid-twenties when her first analysis began. She described herself as having been a "so-called rebellious type," idealistic, and passionate. She had read some of Freud's articles and was fascinated by the unconscious as a concept and as a dynamic

reality. She thought of Freud as "a great discoverer" and considered the analytic process as "a personal journey of discovery." Analysis was "a key" that would reveal to her the sources of her unhappiness and the unconscious motives that led to her frequently self-destructive behavior in relationships with men and in her academic pursuits.

Soon after she started treatment, May's analyst told her that she was engaged in "a battle with God" regarding what she considered the injustice in the treatment and position of women in the world. May was angry with her analyst for not acknowledging that she was right (i.e., justified) in her complaints. May wanted to convince Dr. K.; she wanted him on her side.

Knowing something about May's life history, I felt that she had reenacted in the transference with Dr. K. the battle fought with her father as a child. May had lost this battle. In her analysis with Dr. K., May was desperately trying once again. Significantly, only in her analysis with me did May recognize and acknowledge the defeat she experienced with her father. As a child, May was regarded by her father as a replacement for a son never born. She was thus granted all the privileges of a boy. This made May feel triumphant. She believed the path to everything she wanted to achieve lay open. However, May's father did not acknowledge May as a girl whose birthright included the same privileges as a boy's. She was treated as an exception, not as one rightfully entitled.

In the transference with Dr. K., May continued the battle she had lost with her father. She wanted her analyst, whom she admired and loved, to empower her as a woman. She did not want to be given privileges as if she were a man. This battle lasted for almost eight years. Many of May's other conflicts appeared successfully analyzed. Nonetheless, in her analysis with me, as May recalled the experience with Dr. K. and its outcome, she expressed her feeling of defeat, saying, "Dr. K. did not acknowledge that I have the same rights a man has."

May spent hours telling me about her anger and frustration with Dr. K., whose only response to her complaints regarding her male peers' attainment of positions to which she aspired was to say "penis envy" over and over again. "Yes," May exclaimed, still with anger,

> I was envious of them, but not of their penises. I was envious of what
> they could attain because they were born men. I could have done this

work just as well as they, but I was excluded because I was a woman. When there is a choice between a man and a woman in our society the man gets the breaks. I wanted Dr. K. to acknowledge that it "wasn't fair," that I was justified feeling discriminated against. I did not want to hear about "narcissistic mortification." I felt he was telling me, "Stay where you belong." He never acknowledged I had equal rights. Rights not privileges. I now know I did not want to be an exception looked upon as a freak.

May regarded Dr. K. as kind and honest. She felt that he liked her and was concerned, yet she felt misunderstood. "Dr. K. seemed tolerant but steeped in the conviction that a girl/woman should stop 'hitting her head against the wall,' that is, stop trying and complaining about how 'things are' and accept and reconcile herself to her fate as a woman" (*sich damit apbfinden*, [to submit to it]).

May's analysis with Dr. K. stumbled on what Freud (1937) considered "the bedrock—the unresolvable penis envy" (p. 252). May said, "I left my analysis with Dr. K. feeling I have to apologize because I did not want to put up with 'a woman's fate,' and that this meant I am filled with this terrible penis envy."

As a result of our work, it became clear to me that May consciously and unconsciously perceived Dr. K.'s penis envy interpretation as an accusation of being greedy and rebellious, filled with murderous rage and evil. She felt that Dr. K. was saying, "You should atone and not assert yourself." May eventually understood the unconscious motives that led to the selection of Dr. K. as her analyst. "I wanted someone like father to acknowledge the betrayal, to apologize, to say I was wronged and my demands were justified even if they could not be fulfilled. That would have been enough to take away the pain, to help me go on trying." May cried a lot during her analysis with me.

Following the analysis with Dr. K., May continued to live out her unconscious self-defeating patterns. She entered and stayed in an exploitative and ungratifying marriage. She curtailed her assertiveness by giving over the management of the estate to her husband, who made it his own. In her academic pursuits, when on the verge of great success, May did something that made such success impossible. She somehow always failed, perhaps more so in how she viewed herself than in reality. She had two children and felt her analysis with Dr. K. had enabled her to be a good mother.

The ferment of the 1950s and 1960s changed in the 1970s to a productive period of increased inquiry. An examination of analytic concepts and crucial aspects of the analytic process and technique began. There was recognition that what we observe in patients is influenced by our own psychic set and our own perceptions, which must therefore be scrupulously examined. Making interpretations according to what we have learned to expect is inadequate. Interventions have to be dynamically oriented and directed to the specific patient. They have to be responsive to the particulars of each patient. Stereotypical notions about women's biological destiny and its influence on pathology and character were scrutinized and reexamined. Women were listened to in analysis, not told how it is and should be.

Under the pressure of "outer reality," represented on the one hand by the critical attitudes of feminists and on the other by many new analytic discoveries and findings (see Barnett (1966), Blum (1976), Chasseguet-Smirgel (1976), Clower (1976), Fliegel (1973, 1982), Kestenberg (1956), Kleeman (1976), Masters and Johnson (1966, 1970), Schafer (1974), Sherfey (1966), and Stoller (1976), among others), the staunchly held Freudian tenets of female psychosexual development began to be revised. As is well known, the clitoris is not a male organ and the disproved "transfer theory" was spoofed in the movie *Manhattan*, when, during a cocktail party, a vacuous, beautiful woman announced, "I told my analyst I had an orgasm last night, but he informed me it was the wrong kind."

Schafer's 1974 paper was a landmark that scrutinized and critically examined Freud's propositions about femininity from metapsychological and analytic points of view. It also considered women's silent complaints from a social point of view. The significance of this article rests on its open acknowledgment of the patriarchal bias that pervades Freud's theories of female psychosexual development. Most important, Schafer suggested that the writer on women's issues examine and state her or his bias.

In a theoretically astute article, Grossman and Kaplan (1988) concluded that

> the idea that development is easier for one sex or the other belongs to the dichotomous fantasies of sexual rivalries and privilege that are part of the developmental mythologies of gender. In fact, such mythologies of sex advantage and disadvantage constitute a significant anchor for narcissistic resistances in the clinical situation. [p. 366]

Knowing how the "real world" impinges on women, it must be recognized and acknowledged that these so-called mythologies of gender have determined the reality in which women live. They have resulted in the warping of the psyche of thousands of women and men. The consequences of mythologies of gender are daily realities. Psychoanalysis cannot simply dismiss these realities as "anchors for narcissistic resistance in the clinical situation" (Grossman and Kaplan 1988, p. 366). They are realities of privilege reinforced by adherence to gender stereotypes prevalent in a given society.

It is well known that the birth of a female child into the patriarchal world we live in is quite a different event from the birth of a male child. It still is, in most families, an unwelcome event. A *New York Times* (1991) study conducted in the United States found that 95 percent of families expecting a baby hoped it would be a boy. The *New York Times* study in China (1992) reported that female fetuses are aborted and female children sold for adoption. Studies indicate that female infanticide is practiced everywhere in Asia and Africa. A female child's primary object of identification, her mother, is frequently devalued because she is a woman, and she in turn devalues her daughter, who is unwanted. Thus the societal-cultural gender stereotype is transmitted from generation to generation. The usual difference, conscious and unconscious, in the attitudes of mothers and fathers to the children of each sex is by now acknowledged and recognized as a crucial factor in the children's development. A female child's infantile psyche encounters and introjects a set of object relations and social relations that gives rise to the formation of the early "infantile mythology" in which the male is superior to the female. The female child, whose mother does not acknowledge and confirm her genitals and sexuality (Lerner 1975), ascribes her lowly status as due to "her having nothing" (i.e., not having a penis). The girl uses this observable fact to account for her so-called deficiency.

In a given society, specific gender stereotypes are designated for females and males. Society treats the members of each gender differently. The stereotypical gender modes are enacted in daily object relations that transmit to the child of each sex the proscriptions, prohibitions, and expectations applicable to each. This leads to the identification by each sex with gender-specific stereotypes. Society, via childrearing practices, imposes gender stereotypes on each sex. It is thus responsible for and must account for the stereotypes adhered to by its members.

A successful analysis of men and women includes exposing and working through their pathological conformity to socially accepted gender stereotypes. This is a very difficult task. It is made almost impossible when the analyst and analysand share the same gender stereotypes and consider adherence to them a sign of normality and health. In such a situation, the defensive position of the analysand becomes reinforced by the conscious and unconscious attitudes of the analyst, a member of the same society. Behind such a wall of conformity may well remain the analyst's unconscious sadistic and/or masochistic impulses. Failure to analyze conformity to socially accepted gender stereotypes will affect the analytic process and the analytic interventions of the training analyst and his or her candidate, the future analyst. The adherence to the stereotypes will be perpetuated.

Until recently, Freud's theories of female psychosexuality were taught uncritically in most analytic institutes, that is, without adequate consideration of dissenting views. Consequently, most analysts were trained in a manner that prepared them to regard Freud's views as a description of objective (i.e., external) reality, thus perpetuating the pathological conformity to Victorian gender stereotypes. The pathological warping of a woman's psyche was considered "normal" because women were regarded as *biologically constituted* for masochism, chronic depression, and inferior mentality (Deutsch 1944, Freud 1933). Such views resulted in an insidious analytic pressure on women to accept their lot and status. It should be noted that these so-called normal conditions for women were regarded as pathological in men and referred to as "feminine masochism."

Freud and his followers did not apply the same analytic tools to the analyses of women and men. For instance, though the body ego was considered the kernel of the ego, Freud (1923a) did not acknowledge its specific uniqueness in the developing girl. Likewise, though he recognized that every child believes "everyone must be like me" (1905), by disclaiming the girl's knowledge of all her genitals and the effect of their pleasurable exploration, Freud could disclaim that the girl, like the boy, assumed everyone was like her (Mayer 1985). Thus Freud could maintain his proposition that all children believe everyone had a penis.

The patients I have seen in reanalyses, and those whose reanalyses I have been supervising, suffered predominantly from a depressive, masochistic character neurosis. All were professional women, some in our field, mostly married and with children. They were chronically dissatisfied with themselves. Their complaints, though sometimes displaced on outer reality, dealt primarily with conflicts of their inner world. These resulted from the lack of integration of their maternal and paternal introjects, which precluded satisfactory internalization of subsequent selective identifications. My work taught me that it is essential to unravel the sources of women's feelings of denigration and debasement. Most frequently, these are rooted in identifications with a mother whose psyche was pathologically distorted by the acceptance and adherence to the conventional female gender stereotype. Such mothers, chronically depressed, masochistically subservient, self-debasing and defeating, could not be emotionally available and supportive to their daughters and serve as adequate models.

The unraveling of these childhood experiences is most painful for the patient, evoking narcissistic hurts and a sense of shame. In addition to anger, frequently expressed toward their mothers, these patients discovered they also pitied their mothers and felt ashamed of them. To the extent that they could permit themselves to experience such feelings, and also analyze their spurious childhood sense of superiority stemming from identifications with father, these patients felt self-shame and self-pity. In anger directed against themselves as well as their mothers, the patients questioned whether any solutions were possible. None of these patients suffered from any sudden trauma. Being daughters of such mothers and of fathers with stereotypical masculine values formed the matrix of their chronic trauma.

These patients, like May, needed acknowledgment that they as girls/women did indeed experience discrimination. Such factual acknowledgment without value judgment provided them with an awareness that they were heard. No longer having to battle for acknowledgment enabled them to express their real unhappiness, their pain, and pent-up rage at the mother who had not been sufficiently strong in her womanhood to help them express joy and pride in their girlhood. These patients eventually also expressed their rage at their fathers, who did not respect or cherish their mothers and thus did not cherish them, even though they may have loved them. Some of these patients felt, as May did, like exceptions. Others felt relegated to "being girls who were expected to behave accordingly." These patients spoke with anger and sorrow about having felt that they had "no innate right" to seek their own goals and achievements the way boys sought theirs. They vented their rebellious fury when speaking with rage about parental expectations and demands that they behave like girls should.

In the course of their analyses, these patients revealed that each one of them had fantasies, disguised in different ways, of being or becoming a boy (see Chapter 7). The patients now felt ashamed of these fantasies, realizing that such wishes indicated their acceptance of the stereotype of male superiority. Analyzing these fantasies led to the discovery of specific aspects of their childhood sexuality. These patients, as little girls, explored all their genitals and experienced strong sexual feelings. They experimented with different ways of masturbation, sometimes lying on top of pillows pretending to be a man. Some played doctor games. All reported having erotic fantasies. These had mother as the foremost love object during the negative oedipal subphase and father during the positive oedipal subphase.

I learned that each patient also had fantasies of rescuing mother. The central theme was winning mother's love, gratitude, admiration and the exaltation of the girl for her heroism. The girls, while fantasizing, felt very proud, basked in their glory, and believed they had won mother's love forever. In addition to other meanings, these fantasies obviously had an important restitutive role for the girl. The most significant aspect of these fantasies, however, was the change in mother's fate. Somehow, mother was "liberated to be happy." Making mother happy was a very important theme. Analyses revealed that the patients felt in some way responsible for their mothers' "miserableness." None of them knew for sure how or why mother's miserableness came about. Eventually, each patient with great shame revealed that she believed mother would have been happier, really happy, if she (the daughter) had been a boy. Father would also have been happy. Maybe father would then have respected and cherished mother. Lengthy silences followed the revelation of this secret belief. The patients at this time became despondent and depressed.

The patients believed that their mother, because of her own lack of self-acceptance, devalued them since they were girls, that is, because of their genitals. These genitals, however, were their source of pleasure. The girls were confused because they knew their mother had the same genitals and assumed, therefore, that mother's genitals also were a source of pleasure for her. Why then did she devalue them?

When dealing with these painful and, for them, shameful topics, my patients would frequently interrupt themselves and ask, "Do you know what I mean? Do you know how it feels?" My unspoken confirmation was a sufficient response. It was also a necessary one for the development of trust and for the strengthening of the therapeutic alliance. It promoted a reexperiencing, in the transference, of the positive aspects of the sense of sameness with mother. Identification with my analytic attitude helped these patients tolerate the pain and shame associated with their fantasies, including fantasies about my possessing superhuman qualities. Thus the patients, during this phase of the analyses, accused me of having it all and of being unwilling to share it with them— of wanting to keep the ways by which I achieved success a secret because I wanted to lord it over them. They envied me. I became at this time the embodiment of the unresponsive, withholding mother who did not understand. Simultaneously, I also was the focus of everything they hated and everything they hoped for. The expression of these varied, tangled emotions was essential for these patients, as were their reversible regressions. I could, however, in nonverbal ways, give these patients comfort when they felt on the verge of desperation. I absorbed and contained both their rage and their loving feelings. I continued, during periods of relative calm, to analyze the antecedents of their emotions, their fantasies, and especially their sense of worthlessness.

My analytic aim for these patients was to achieve a psychic separation from the parental introjects, a distance from the fateful familial interactions so fraught with conflict, love, anger, and pain. My goal was for the patients eventually to recognize that by introjecting the stereotypes they had made the distorted societal value systems their own. This task was easier when the patients had some female love object with whose competence they could identify, especially if this love object also confirmed their competence. Self-affirmation also occurred if the patients discovered something in their mothers that they continued to admire throughout their lives and that they recognized as part of their own being. My task was facilitated when the fathers acknowledged them as competent girls with a right to autonomy and a pursuit of their own ego interests. Parental supportive congruence was of utmost significance, but it was rare indeed.

It was important for these patients to recognize and analyze that they unconsciously viewed their identification with their father, which promoted autonomy, independence, assertion, competitiveness, and a drive toward achievement, as resulting in forbidden, unfeminine, character traits. This occurred even when fathers encouraged such attitudes in them. Continued analysis revealed that behavior based on paternal identifications evoked unconscious conflict and anxiety. It made the patients feel "unwomanly," that is, different from their mother, whom they believed to be father's love object (see Chapters 7 and 8). These patients felt caught in a dilemma unconsciously experienced as unresolvable since it was based on their internalized, unintegrated, mother–father roles and interactions that they unconsciously accepted as models. Thus they saw as their only choice either to be like mother—devalued yet loved by the man—or to achieve, be valued like a man, but not to be wanted as a woman by the man. The resolution of this unconscious dilemma required a lengthy analysis of the pathological compliance with conventional gender stereotypes of femininity and masculinity. (see Gitelson 1954, Kaplan 1990, Rangell 1974, Reich 1958, and Winnicott 1960).

2   The Effect of the Analyst's Pregnancy on the Patient: Transference and Countertransference Manifestations Evoked by the Analyst's Pregnancy

When I began to evaluate my experience with patients during my pregnancy, I discovered to my surprise that almost nothing had been written about this topic (Hannett 1949, LeBow 1963). Such silence in the usually rich psychoanalytic literature, which abounds in articles on every possible subject and which deals with the pregnancy reactions of analysands during their analysis, struck me as rather singular. I wondered why women analysts, many of whom must have been pregnant while practicing, did not report on their experiences as these related to their pregnancy. Birth, on which so many fantasies, wishes, and fears center, is a universal theme, vibrant in every human being. As such, the pregnancy of the analyst, ipso facto, must constitute a unique experience for the analysand. It is consistent therefore with analytic theory to expect that, for the patient, the analyst's pregnancy has a special significance of a highly charged stimulus and evokes deep-seated childhood conflicts, fantasies, and wishes. My 1969 paper broke the taboo of silence on this topic and stimulated a number of papers written since.

The patient whose analyst becomes pregnant while he or she is embroiled in the transference neurosis has a singular opportunity to reexperience many of the pregenital and oedipal struggles. However, as has been discussed by Freud and many others, since there are variations in transference reactions, which depend on differences in the aetiology of the particular neurosis, it is to be expected that there will also be differences in the patient's reactions to the analyst's pregnancy. It is likely that specific historic events in the life of the patient and differences in character constellation also evoke individual transference variations.

The analyst's pregnancy, however, cannot be viewed as constituting a special event only in the life of the analysand; it must also be considered in terms of its effect on the analyst. According to G. Bibring (1959), pregnancy should be considered a normal psychic crisis that affects all expectant mothers, no matter what their state of mental health. Thus it is likely that the pregnancy will also stir in the analyst, as it does to a larger or smaller extent in other women, some echoes of typical childhood conflagrations. This, most probably, will make the pregnant analyst more sensitive to the onslaught of conflict manifestations in the material presented by her patients.

Consequently, it is obvious and understandable that the pregnant analyst might be more vulnerable than she would otherwise be to the different transference reactions of her patients and that these will evoke a variety of responses, conscious and unconscious. Thus the possibility of an increase in countertransference reactions during pregnancy has to be recognized, since only then can it be dealt with analytically.

There is a third technical and theoretical point that becomes apparent when one considers the pregnancy of the analyst. A personal event in the life of the analyst that cannot be hidden from the patient intrudes into the analytic situation. The so-called anonymity and neutrality of the analyst is interfered with. The patient now knows something definite about what goes on in the life of the analyst, and witnesses over a period of months the unfolding of this process. In terms of classical concepts of analysis one can certainly not speak about the pregnant analyst as the "blank, projective screen." One can raise the question, however, of the extent to which one can speak of her as an "optimal projective screen."

Thus a situation that occurs during the pregnancy of the analyst offers the opportunity for making special observations about transference and countertransference, and raises questions of a technical and theoretical nature about the so-called anonymity of the analyst.

I have abstracted several case histories, highlighting factors in the psychogenetic background that contributed to the patients' pathology. The defensive reactions evoked by unconscious conflicts became exacerbated in the transference neurosis during my pregnancy. I was impressed by the fact that each patient responded to my pregnancy with a reactivation of those aspects of infantile conflicts that were most significant for the development of this pathology. The patients recreated the childhood situation, and I was cast in the role in which the patient originally experienced the mother. It made a great deal of difference whether the patient was an only child or had siblings. The most striking difference, however, occurred between neurotic and borderline patients. The latter became aware of my pregnancy much sooner, reacted to it with much greater intensity, and had a tendency to act out the conflict. As would be expected, the borderline patient found it much more difficult than the neurotic to differentiate between transference and reality aspects.

Case 1

Vera was a beautiful young woman in her late twenties, a borderline schizophrenic. She suffered from acute anxiety episodes during which she had terrible and frightening fantasies. Vera was studying for a master's degree in social psychology. Her back-

ground was in social work and she had held a teaching position
at a university in Latin America. Vera came from a middle-class
family; her mother, of African descent, was the second wife of her
father, who, according to the patient, came from whiter, more
patrician stock.

Vera's childhood story unfolded rapidly in treatment. Her half-
brother lived with an aunt because he did not get along with her
mother. Pablo, an older brother, had died. He was adored by
everyone, had been almost white, and was considered "all perfect."
Vera, however, had had very ambivalent feelings toward him. Consequently, his death at age 13 had been very traumatic for Vera,
who was 10 at the time. While she too had adored Pablo, who represented her narcissistic ideal, she also hated him because of the
narcissistic mortification his "excellence" caused her. In fantasy
Vera identified with Pablo; in reality Pablo was her protector.
Owing to this psychic configuration, Vera for a long time imagined that he only pretended to be dead and would return one day.
She refused to believe that her brother had been buried.

Vera claimed she had a twin Paula, who supposedly was mother's
favorite, the strong baby. Vera at birth was the weakling. Because
of the difference between them, mother raised Vera herself and
gave Paula to a foster home. Paula died within the first half-year.
According to Vera, this was because mother did not raise her. I could
not establish whether this story was a fantasy or reality.

Vera was symbiotically linked with the mother, whom she both
loved and hated. She described mother as a spider whose hands,
like a web, were always around her. However, almost in the same
breath, in ecstasy, Vera would tell how soothing and understanding mother's hands were, how mother rocked her to sleep no
matter how anxious and tense she may have been.

Mother was a primitive, superstitious woman, the daughter of
a once-leading courtesan in town. Vera had doubts about her own
paternity and frequently believed she was the daughter of the black
man with whom mother had run off before her marriage. Though
Vera's incestuous impulses toward father were very strong, she

did not utilize her ideas about the black paternity in her spinning of family romance. The fantasy about the negroid paternity was additional proof for Vera of her inferiority and played a significant role in conflicts centering on her self-image.

Vera's universe was divided into "angels" (the whites or whitish ones) and "underdogs," who were no good (the blacks or blackish ones). Vera's doubts about her paternity were raised when she considered whether or not she had entry to the universe of the "angels." Most of the time Vera felt outside this universe and strove desperately to enter it. These attempts, however, were mostly in fantasy. In reality, as a child, Vera alternated between almost cataleptic plasticity, during which she would sit, stand, do anything mother told her just as if she were a puppet, and outbursts of rage. Vera envied her white brother, who "could do everything" and had entry into the universe of the "angels." She hated her starched dresses; she feared the ghosts and spirits her mother, who practiced voodoo, claimed to see. At times Vera felt she also saw the spirits.

Vera's weird anatomic fantasies and her distorted body and self-image were related to her mother's childrearing routines. Once a week mother used to purge her by giving her a mixture of various laxatives to get rid of the "bad stuff" in her and "all other impurities." Vera would rebel, vomit, and a battle would ensue till she finally "swallowed and kept down" her medicine.

There were other pathology-inducing factors in Vera's childhood. From birth, and at least till the age of 9, Vera had slept in a room with her parents and was exposed to the primal scene. Her reaction was vehement. Vera became very excited by her parents' sexual activities, masturbated violently, rocked her bed to disturb them, entered their bed, put the covers over herself, and attempted to choke herself, hoping that finally upon her death they would notice her and be sorry. Eventually Vera developed asthma and bad coughing spells, which disturbed her parents. She was cured in early puberty by a "kind doctor who came to me and gave me injections."

Vera's feelings about sex were extremely confused. She wanted it, feared it, and knew it was forbidden by mother. Vera feared mother would disown her if she knew Vera indulged in sex. These views were further complicated by the fact that as a child Vera was told by her mother that father had extramarital relationships. Mother was very disturbed by father's infidelity and threatened to leave him. Vera's fate was always uncertain. Mother threatened to take her away, or threatened to leave her with father. Finally Vera was made responsible for the fact that mother remained with father "in spite of it all." Mother impressed on Vera that sex was bad and damnable, and Vera concluded, in spite of realistic evidence, that "angels" did not indulge in sex.

When Vera's treatment began she was involved in numerous promiscuous and self-destructive relations with men. She entered these relationships primarily to avoid loneliness. They had for her the significance of getting something, of being fed. Vera never used contraceptives, she never became pregnant, and she was convinced that she could not become pregnant.

When I became pregnant, Vera had been in treatment for about two years. Her reality testing had improved and she was frequently able to recognize many of her distortions, projections, and interjections. The transference, on the whole, was a positive one. I represented her "good mother" and she was the "dutiful and obedient daughter" who was trying to please. Her behavior was very seductive, and homosexual elements were apparent. She projected those onto her best friend from whom she always expected amorous advances.

Vera recognized my pregnancy unconsciously long before any other patient became aware of it and even before I realized that it was noticeable (some time during the third month). This unconscious recognition was revealed in a dream. Subsequently Vera's behavior became much more turbulent. Her relationship to Jim, a Greek refugee, became more intense. She began to talk about marriage and eventually, in the latter part of my pregnancy, succeeded in maneuvering Jim into marrying her.

Though my pregnancy became more apparent, Vera persistently denied it. I tried in many ways to help her become consciously aware of what her unconscious had known for so long. Finally I told her that I was pregnant. Vera became extremely angry with me and said: "Now you show your shame and everyone can see the terrible thing you have done." According to Vera, the pregnancy was my punishment for having indulged in sex: I was marked.

Subsequently, Vera's reality testing decreased. Projective and introjective mechanisms were employed to cope with conflicts centering on pregnancy wishes. Vera had fantasies of oral impregnation, in which mother and I were equated with the feared and hated impregnator. During this period the transference was negative and turbulent. Because of the unconscious transference identification with me, which was based on the symbiotic links with mother, Vera experienced me as a dangerous temptress. My pregnancy was unconsciously experienced by Vera as an invitation for her to become pregnant.

In the next phase Vera greatly feared that she would lose me after the baby was born. My attempts to reassure her were to no avail: she was convinced I would die in childbirth. It became apparent that this fear was a repetition in the transference of an experience Vera had had with her music teacher. Whereas mother had been experienced as a caressing, spiderlike person who permitted Vera no freedom and thus forced her to escape into fantasy, the music teacher had been experienced as a loving, compassionate person who had helped Vera understand herself and reality. The relationship with the music teacher had ended abruptly when the latter married, became pregnant, and stopped teaching. To Vera this had been a painful rejection, ending the only positive relationship she had had in childhood. For Vera the music teacher had died. After this episode Vera gave up music and became even more dependent on mother.

Vera's reaction to my pregnancy was further complicated by the fact that she also strongly identified with my yet unborn baby.

If I continued to work, Vera assumed the baby would be neglected and would experience this neglect as a rejection. During this phase Vera began to deal with her need to cling to mother and the conflict she experienced because of her simultaneous wish to separate and be free to play and have fun.

Though she recognized her ambivalent feelings and the many negative aspects of her relationship with Jim, Vera married toward the end of my pregnancy. Shortly thereafter, to her great surprise, Vera discovered that she was pregnant. She claimed that she did not know how this had happened or why, because she had never been pregnant before, though she took no precautions.

After she became pregnant, Vera's anger toward me increased. She expressed the wish to terminate treatment and tried to use her pregnancy as a "legitimate" excuse. When we analyzed these feelings, it became apparent that Vera's expectation of being abandoned by me frightened and enraged her. Thus she planned to leave me to avoid the pain of a possible separation initiated by me. Jackel (1966) points out that the wish for a child may be used to counteract separation fears.

Vera's pregnancy had many meanings. It expressed an identification with mother and with me in the transference. At the same time the pregnancy was also an act of defiance. Simultaneously, Vera had done what mother had done, and also what mother had forbidden. By marrying Jim, Vera married an "angel," as mother had. Vera was narcissistically gratified by having a white man. Further, since Jim represented father in Vera's unconscious, her incestuous oedipal longing was finally fulfilled. The intensity of the infantile, incestuous wish, however, made sex with Jim forbidden. Vera was in continuous turmoil.

Because of the nature of Vera's psychopathology, my pregnancy exacerbated her separation fears and consequently increased the defensive symbiotic longings for fusion. Simultaneously, the conflicts related to these wishes intensified. The interlocking relationship that existed between mother and Vera was in toto transferred to me, at times almost reaching the proportions of a transference psychosis (Little 1958). Vera's nuclear conflict, her inability to separate from mother, came to the fore with extreme vividness during my pregnancy. Vera's reality testing, which had until then enabled her to distinguish between mother and me, decreased. Insisting that I would undoubtedly abandon her upon the birth of my baby, frantic and enraged by this conviction, Vera engaged in spurious, independent behavior. She married an "angel" and became pregnant. These actions indicate an intense identification with mother (and me in the delusional transference [Little 1958]). Vera's simultaneous identification with mother and child served as a protection against separation dread. Vera now was mother and had a child—she also was the child who had a mother. While she was pregnant, the symbiosis Vera longed for was complete and perfect; she and the baby within were inseparable.

Case 2

Whereas Vera was clinging and appealed via the helplessness of a little child who needs mother to succor her, Janet was excessively demanding and greedy. Treatment with me was Janet's second attempt at psychoanalysis. She was a big, ungainly woman in her mid-twenties, recently divorced, and desperately lonely. Her pathology was very complicated and did not fall into any specific nosological classification. Probably a borderline, Janet functioned on a very superior intellectual level. There were many hysterical and obsessive character traits, and she suffered greatly because of masochistic tendencies that involved her in self-punitive and self-derogatory situations.

The following highlights of Janet's developmental history elucidate the pattern of the transference neurosis that developed during my pregnancy. Janet was an only child of a very unhappy marriage. Her father, who had died suddenly while Janet was in her early teens, had been a successful professional man who engaged in extramarital relationships and ostentatiously indicated his preference for his daughter over his wife. He confirmed this by leaving Janet the bulk of his estate. The unconscious fantasies and the guilt feelings that this provoked in Janet can be surmised from the fact that she succeeded in squandering her sizable estate in a very short time. When Janet started treatment with me, she was penniless.

Consciously, Janet hated her mother, was consumed with feelings of guilt and remorse, had tremendous outbursts of rage, envied her mother, berated her, and admired her for being a beautiful woman. Janet had always indulged herself in every way she could. She overate and overspent, gave in to impulses and later regretted it. Typically the self-indulgence, though initially gratifying, always had a self-defeating result. Thus she was fat, which she bemoaned, slept with men who took advantage of her, spent too much money on clothes she later did not like, and so on. Impulse control was almost negligible.

It seems that, as a child Janet was alternately overindulged and neglected. Thus she came to equate "getting" with being loved, restriction and control with being unloved. Further, Janet's father, with whom in many ways she strongly identified, frequently came home drunk and behaved in an uncontrolled fashion. Janet used this behavior as a model for her temper tantrums, in which she engaged whenever frustrated.

Janet's self-esteem was very low. She had feelings of self-hate and self-depreciation, despised herself, and derogated everything she accomplished. She felt she had a "Rotten Core" that could not be eradicated. At best, the Rotten Core could be covered up and hidden. Janet's behavior had the quality of a vicious cycle: she did things that demonstrated the existence of her Rotten Core and subsequently berated herself mercilessly for what she had done. Soon, however, Janet would repeat the same pattern. The struggle between impulse and superego was evident. The compulsion to repeat, clearly detectable in Janet's behavior, gave her the subjective conviction that unhappiness, doom, and destruction were her destiny.

Presenting symptoms were prolonged depressive episodes, which increased during the two years after Janet's divorce. During these bouts of depression Janet felt that her destruction was unavoidable. She was incapable of completing her studies and worked as a typist. She was exploited on her job, without friends, and involved in a sadomasochistic relationship with her mother.

At the time of my pregnancy Janet had been in treatment for about two and a half years. She now held a semiprofessional position, was an "A" student in a doctoral program, and lived on her own. In spite of these gains, her core conflict remained untouched. Janet was in the midst of acting out a triangular love affair in which she was "the other woman." Dreams indicated that this behavior was related to her oedipal conflict, namely, her wish to "steal my father from mother." Janet understood the meaning of her dreams, but was unable to use these insights, and repressed them.

When Janet noticed my pregnancy, she reacted with rage and fury. She burst into a torrent of accusations, stating: "You have everything and I have nothing and this is unfair." She claimed she would like something sharp to pierce through my belly and kill the baby. She felt that if the baby were killed, I would concentrate on her and not on the future baby—I wronged her. Janet felt sure that I would interrupt her analysis before curing her because I would devote my time to the baby. The fear of being abandoned was the first reaction. Soon after, however, feelings of envy became prominent. Janet moaned: "How can you manage everything, baby, practice, husband, household, hospital? It's unfair, I cannot manage anything." Somewhat later she stopped the careful use of contraceptives. She reported "two accidents." Janet insisted: "I have as much right to have a child as you."

In the next phase Janet's exaggerated positive feelings toward me predominated. She complimented me on being pretty, wished I were *her* mother, and told me she had to tell all her friends and acquaintances that *her* analyst was pregnant. She was excited and agitated. These manifestations covered underlying depressive feelings. Comparing herself to me, Janet felt she was a "barren woman with no flowering part in her, nothing to grow, a piece of wet mud, a piece of shit." Lamenting, she said: "Being pregnant is being a woman and *not a thing*. During this period Janet reexperienced feelings of rage toward mother and wishes to kill her. These were related to her feeling that her childhood experiences were the cause of her "ruined life." Simultaneously, Janet's fear that she might be pregnant increased. She raged at me because she believed I wanted her to have an abortion, and accused me of being selfish, of wanting to deny her a child. Janet's relationship with her married boyfriend intensified. She now behaved as if she were in love with him and wanted him to marry her. This change coincided with the boyfriend's wish to withdraw from the relationship. Eventually Janet had sufficient insight to recognize that the feelings and wishes about her pregnancy related to her envy of my pregnancy.

Finally Janet consulted a physician, who found her three months pregnant. (I was three months pregnant when Janet "noticed" my pregnancy.) Her feelings about her pregnancy were ambivalent. She found it almost impossible to differentiate between a fetus and a baby, and felt that an abortion meant the destruction of a child. These ambivalent feelings were related to her knowledge that her mother had wanted to abort her. Mother was unhappy that she had failed in provoking a miscarriage. With this in mind, it is understandable that Janet unconsciously identified with the unwanted fetus. Thus the possible destruction of the fetus within her represented to her unconscious an attempted destruction of herself. The rejection of the unborn child became a rejection of herself. Janet oscillated between states of anger and depression.

By coincidence, after an evening in which Janet repeatedly had intercourse with her boyfriend, she began to bleed and had a miscarriage. Though well cared for in the hospital and by her mother, Janet came back to treatment very upset and depressed. She complained that something was missing from inside her. Her boyfriend terminated their relationship.

As a reaction to her loss, Janet went on a buying binge. She ran up a sizable bill, which made paying for treatment almost impossible. She also began to overeat. Despite these attempts at gratification, the depression increased. Some further regression followed, with oral aspects of greed and envy predominating. Janet felt deprived, and raged and stormed at me, feeling that everything I had was at her expense. She engaged in a competitive struggle with me for the "treasures" of life. In this struggle Janet experienced me as having inordinate power and herself as powerless. Not paying for sessions had the unconscious significance of depriving me and defying me. Janet's rage was not provoked by fear that I might give to my future child rather than to her, but by my having what she did not have and wanted to have. To Janet this meant that I took from her.

Janet's reaction led me to the conclusion that she experienced my pregnancy primarily as a narcissistic injury rather than a potential object loss. This was consonant with her regressive state, the borderline features of her psychic makeup, and her strong oral fixations. In Janet's case the envy of my pregnancy, and the transference storm that followed exacerbated the vicious cycle of narcissistic mortification and injury. This evoked an increase in hostile aggressive impulses, first turned toward the envied object and eventually centered upon the self, thus intensifying Janet's feelings of self-devaluation.

Case 3

Doris came into treatment feeling she had "to be saved." She was suffering from an obsessive-compulsive character neurosis with strong masochistic trends and certain borderline features. The psychogenic factors salient to this presentation relate to the birth of a brother when Doris was 2 years old, and to the ensuing prolonged separation from mother and father, which gave her a feeling of being abandoned. Apparently, mother's illness following the birth of the brother resulted in a lengthy hospitalization. During that time, Doris stayed with an aunt and was never visited by her father. In her early twenties, Doris had a prolonged affair with a married man during which she became pregnant. She gave birth to a boy whom she gave up for adoption. At the time Doris started treatment she had "no feelings about it."

Doris had been in treatment with me for about four years when she remarked on my pregnancy. I confirmed her suspicion and she said, "I am so happy for you." Upon inquiry, Doris's suppressed feelings came forth. She said with great anguish: "It isn't the same. Someone else is in the room now. Something has been taken away from me. Before, it was that I spoke to you and then it came back to me, and it was like a circle and there was contact between us— and now it has been taken away from me."

I attempted subsequently to analyze Doris's feelings at the time of her mother's pregnancy and after the birth of her brother. There was a dearth of actual memories but material came up in terms of transference manifestations. In the first phase Doris was silent during the sessions. Finally she admitted to persisting fantasies that I would give birth to a monster, or that something terrible would happen to the baby. She described the baby I would have in gruesome terms, concluding: "You will turn away from it in horror." Analysis revealed that this fantasy represented an unconscious wish: "Were my brother a monster, my parents would not have loved him better than me." The analysis of this fantasy enabled Doris to deal with her feelings of rivalry toward her brother, which until now she had completely denied. She had coped with the guilt related to murderous wishes toward brother by overvaluing him and denigrating herself.

Further analysis revealed that Doris considered all men her enemies, and that she gave her child away because he was a boy. She responded to the existence of her brother with a sense of narcissistic mortification, since she considered him more beautiful, more talented, and, most important, possessor of a penis. All these attributes, in Doris's mind, made brother superior and herself inferior. Doris believed that these qualities caused her parents to love brother more than her.

After these feelings had been worked through, the most traumatic aspect of brother's birth came to the fore: her sense of being abandoned. Doris now was desperate and depressed. The dependency need and fear of enforced separation came vividly to light. She expressed it by saying: "I felt I was one with you and what I thought would bounce back from you to me. Now, you have the baby all the time and I am here only for my sessions. So the baby is here and not I. You don't like me any more, now that you have your baby. I can't count on you." These feelings and similar ones that related to fears of being abandoned and emotionally displaced accounted for many stormy sessions. Negative and hostile transference manifestations appeared. It became quite clear that all of these feelings related to the traumatic object loss Doris had suffered at the birth of her brother. Eventually it was possible to connect her feelings expressed in the transference with this childhood event. For Doris the birth of a sibling, a situation traumatic in itself, had become more difficult to bear because of the subsequent prolonged separation from mother and father. The suddenness of the disappearance of both parents, for which Doris was not prepared, which she could not comprehend, and which was never explained to her, confirmed her fantasies of being abandoned and deserving this fate.

Following the transference storm during which Doris reexperienced her feelings related to the birth of brother, she admitted that she had tried as long as possible to deny her awareness of my pregnancy. Finally, after I confirmed her suspicions, she felt upset and dejected but said to herself, "I *have* to accept it. There is nothing I can do." By telling me how happy she was for me, Doris tried in the analytic situation to behave as she had as a child. At that time Doris tried to be the model child. She was outwardly good, voiced no complaints, and hid her anger and murderous wishes behind the facade of being "mama's little helper." Doris learned from her childhood experience that compliance was the rewarded behavior pattern. Doris's expectations in the analytic situation were based on her childhood experiences. When the appropriate transference situation arose, patterns surfaced that lay at the roots of her character neurosis: she tried, once again, to stifle her anger and, by a suffering compliance, gain acceptance and approval.

The following vignettes illustrate the striking difference between my male and my female patients in reaction to my pregnancy. It is important to note that in their psychopathology, the male patients did not vary greatly from the female patients described above.

Case 4

Danny, an obsessive-compulsive character neurotic, had been in treatment with me for four years at the time of my pregnancy. He was a well-functioning, professional man in his early thirties. Danny came from an unhappy family in which mother and father lived separate lives, though under one roof. Till the age of 10 Danny was greatly under the influence of his mother, a hysterical woman who in many ways used him as a surrogate for the husband. Danny was her confidant and her source of narcissistic gratification. Father was a cold and distant man, frequently absent from home. He seemed to Danny hostile and overcritical.

For months, Danny, usually exceedingly observant about the minutest detail, appeared completely unaware of the visible changes in me. His dreams indicated, however, that he was aware of my pregnancy. Their manifest content dealt with car collisions and squashed bumpers, balloons, and the like. When, after weeks, Danny was finally able to analyze a dream in which primal scene material predominated, he painfully blurted out, "So you are pregnant." It was a question and a statement, a painful recognition. Subsequent material was very unclear. There were indications that an unconscious struggle continued to keep repressed some material relating to mother, which possibly referred to a pregnancy terminated prematurely. While this process went on, transference feeling oscillated from positive to negative. Then the pattern typical for Danny's pathology set in: Danny intellectually acknowledged the fact of my pregnancy and repressed all feelings related to it. Material about the pregnancy always appeared close to the end of the session and thus there was never enough time to deal with it analytically.

Case 5

Bob came from a petit-bourgeois background. He grew up amid constant squabbles and bickering. On a conscious level Bob's relationship to his parents was overshadowed by a fierce rivalry with his younger brother. Bob, an obsessive-compulsive, rigid character neurotic, came into treatment because he felt professionally and socially unsuccessful, and because he felt incapable of having an affectionate relationship with anyone. He had been in treatment with me for almost two years at the time of my pregnancy. For months Bob ignored the visible changes in me.

When I was six months pregnant, in connection with some schedule change, I mentioned to Bob that I planned to work through July and to take off August and part of September. I added, however, that it might be necessary for me to stop working earlier, in July. Bob was silent a long time and then told me about an incident that had occurred several weeks before. A friend, whom he esteemed, did not invite him to his engagement party. Bob felt hurt and slighted. He then began to berate me because I was going to take a long vacation and this might have a bad effect on his treatment. When I asked him whether he knew why I might have to stop working in July, he said "no." When I referred to my pregnancy, he said he knew about it but did not comment on it because "it is your problem and not mine."

In the months that followed, every attempt to elicit his feelings about my pregnancy or to connect his feelings of being rejected with reactions to my pregnancy failed. In Bob the mechanism of isolation was so strong that all his reactions were completely compartmentalized.

Case 6

Paul, a brilliant young scientist working on a secret government project, was an obsessive-compulsive with masochistic and paranoid character traits. Some borderline features were also present. Paul was sexually totally impotent. This caused him great suffering. In day-to-day life Paul was a victim of his fantasies.

Paul came from an unhappy home. His father was a physician, his mother a frustrated housewife. She was in constant competition with father's sisters, who lived with them and dominated the household. When Paul was 5 years old, his mother gave birth to a daughter. According to him, mother thereafter rejected him. Paul maintained he was raised by his aunts, spinsters who claimed to abhor sex. The youngest of the spinster aunts was very beautiful, and Paul displaced upon her some of the incestuous feelings he had toward mother. Paul was extremely jealous of his sister, whom he considered both parents' favorite. He abdicated in her favor. Sister grew up bossing Paul. She succeeded where he had failed. Sister was able to free herself from father's tyranny and leave home. Paul remained in the sadomasochistic family bond.

Paul reported his conscious fantasies fairly frankly. Their repetitive theme concerned the death of father, after which mother beat Paul to force him to have intercourse with her. Variations of this theme accompanied masturbation.

When my pregnancy became quite visible, Paul began to complain that there was something queer in the office. This went on for a while. He scrutinized the furniture, commenting on it. Concomitantly with this preoccupation, Paul elaborated on his theory that "sex is nonexistent because no woman would permit sex." Both these preoccupations became quite repetitious. I finally suggested that the "queerness" perhaps did not relate to the office furniture but to something about me. Paul was silent, then said: "I thought about your pregnancy but it could not be. I denied it, I don't know why."

From subsequent material it became clear that Paul had had a complete amnesia for mother's bodily changes during her pregnancy. He used the denial of pregnancy to reinforce his thesis that sex was nonexistent. Recognition and acknowledgment of the process of pregnancy would have necessitated his admission that in reality other men (i.e., father) were potent, and women (i.e., mother and his analyst) did permit sex. Understood in terms of his unconscious conflicts, the acknowledgment of my pregnancy caused Paul to reexperience the childhood trauma caused by mother's pregnancy. Because of the nature of his psychopathology and the extent of the regression, the recognition of my pregnancy not only evoked in Paul a fear of object loss, it also was experienced as a narcissistic mortification.

Discussion

The reactions by male and female patients to my pregnancy showed marked differences. The pregnancy appeared to be a much more exciting stimulus for the female patients than for the males, who showed a relative paucity of responses. They denied my pregnancy for much longer than my female patients. Finally, when recognition became unavoidable, following a relatively minor turbulence in the transference, the male patients used isolation as the main defense mechanism. By contrast, the female patients acknowledged my pregnancy much sooner. It evoked a profound transference storm and visibly influenced the course of the transference. Though the extent differed, identification was the main defense mechanism.

Since, nosologically, the patients did not differ markedly, and since my pregnancy reactivated similar conflicts in both groups, the cause for the differences in the responses of male and female

patients was probably due to the different psychosexual development patterns of boys and girls. Whereas, at ages 2 and 3, children of both sexes can identify without any intrapsychic conflict
with the parent of the same or opposite sex and act out in play
and fantasy the respective roles of each, the increase in reality
testing and the acknowledgment of sexual differences begin to set
limits to this process. The differences between the sexes affect
patterns of identification and delineate possible areas of narcissistic injury and/or mortification. Within the transference setting,
my pregnancy reevoked not only sibling rivalry conflicts, oedipal conflagrations, separation dread, and an increase in hostile
feelings, but also the conflicting aspects of the wish to identify
with mother. Though identification with mother is primary for
both sexes, the narcissistic vicissitudes and vulnerabilities subsequent to it are different for boys and girls. Thus my pregnancy
provided a different set of circumstances and evoked a different
set of specific intrapsychic responses in men and women patients.

The women reacted to my pregnancy with an exacerbation of
childhood conflicts that manifested themselves in the transference.
Strikingly, their reactions in fantasy and when acting out corresponded to childhood wishes and childhood defensive patterns.
In all three patients there was a partial regression, caused only
by what the pregnancy symbolized for them and evoked in them.
Irrespective, however, of the specific nature of the particular intrapsychic conflict of a given patient, identification was employed by
all of them as the main defense mechanism. Consideration of this
fact suggests that the unconscious selection of identification was
determined primarily by the opportunity that this defense mechanism afforded for narcissistic gratification and compensation.

In the male patients who to some extent identified with me, as
all patients do with their analyst, my pregnancy aroused dangerous repressed impulses related not only to the usual oedipal temp-
tations, but also to infantile wishes to be able to have a child like
mother. The frustration of these longings, in which, no doubt,
homosexual aspects were present, reevoked infantile feelings of

narcissistic mortification and possible injury. Since feelings related to pregnancy envy could not be gratified or compensated via identification, suppression and isolation were employed to contain the intrapsychic conflicts. (Lax 1995a).

On the basis of theoretical assumptions it could be expected that patients would show feelings of anxiety and guilt related to the discovery of my pregnancy, since pregnancy, par excellence, relates to childhood preoccupations with secrets of the bedroom. In the patients I observed, however, possibly because pregenital factors played such an important role in their psychic makeup, this was not the case.

When one takes into account G. L. Bibring's (1959) findings that pregnancy is a period of relative psychic disequilibrium for every woman, one has to assume that this is also a period of greater vulnerability for the female analyst. Consequently, the various transference reactions of patients specifically directed at the analyst's pregnancy must affect her unconscious infantile conflicts in this area. These factors no doubt increase the possibility of countertransference reactions.

My discussions with colleagues indicate that countertransference manifestations are evoked by particularly intense transference reactions. However, the specific form these countertransference reactions take is related to the infantile conflicts of the analyst in question. Thus a variety of different responses came to the fore. Some pregnant analysts anticipated with discomfort the patient's discovery of their pregnancy and thus found themselves delaying the patient's verbalization on this topic. They appeared to fear the hostility they anticipated. These analysts discovered that their discomfort, which was related to the expected attack of the patient, was connected with their own childhood rage and disappointment when a younger sibling was born.

Some analysts caught themselves being blind and deaf to veiled allusions made by male patients related to their condition. These analysts recognized the "blind spots" via persistent thoughts such as, "It really isn't so obvious," or "Can they think I have simply

gained weight?" or "Do they think I just follow the change in styles
and wear shifts?" Self-analysis regarding these blind spots revealed the rearousal of conflicts about femininity in the analyst.
These related to self-image problems and wishes to be "flat like a
man," which during childhood served as a basis for a narcissistically gratifying masculine identification. The pregnancy—and the
concomitant physical changes confirmed by others—was a visible proof, shattering this now unconscious infantile self-image.

Envy of the pregnant woman, a dominant theme in the transference reactions of many patients associated with feelings of
intense greed and deprivation, evoked in some analysts excessive
concern for their patients and in others feelings of anger. Both
reactions were related to problems similar to those with which
the analysts had to cope in their own childhood.

A number of analysts who had been pregnant informed me that
in their cases the patients "really did not know" because it did not
show since they carried a certain way." I was very suspicious of
such statements since they reminded me of the Victorian conviction that children really are blind to the changes in their mothers' bodies, and that they do believe in the stork. Further persistent
inquiries revealed that, during their pregnancies, these analysts
began to embroider large tablecloths or knit afghans. Thus their
laps were always hidden under big piles of handiwork. Though
this is only a speculation, I believe that self-analysis would have
revealed that these analysts unconsciously feared being robbed,
and that these feelings were probably related to infantile fantasies of a similar kind toward their mothers.

Reminiscing about their first pregnancies, some analysts recalled that they became aware during this time of feelings of guilt
toward their patients. These seemed related to fantasies of stopping work entirely and to wishes to devote all their time to the
mothering of the coming baby. The guilt feelings were found, upon
self-analysis, to originate in intense infantile sibling rivalry conflicts (Little 1960, Orr 1954).

Examples of countertransference attitudes could be multiplied and many more transference reactions could be enumerated. To do so would illustrate the manifold reactions that pregnancy can evoke.

Another theoretical and technical consideration raised by the patients' reactions to the analyst's pregnancy relates to the injunctions concerning the so-called anonymity and neutrality that the analyst is to maintain. The theoretical considerations leading to the formulation of these postulates are well known and need not be discussed here. There is no doubt that it is beneficial for the treatment process if the private life of the analyst does not impinge upon the patients and does not interfere with the unfolding of the transference patterns. A question has to be raised, however, about the extent to which this is possible, and about the procedure to follow in cases where it is not. Obviously, pregnancy is not the only condition of which the patient inevitably becomes aware. Serious prolonged illness, a marriage or divorce occurring while the patient is in treatment, the presence of a child where the office and living quarters are together, and so on, are occurrences in the life of the analyst that frequently cannot be kept from the patient.

In these and many other instances the analyst represents a specific reality stimulus to the patient rather than a blank projective screen. Nonetheless, the analyst can function as an "optimal projective screen" if he or she can facilitate the patient's response to the occurring reality situation in a manner determined by the patient's specific psychic constellation. This can occur only to the extent to which the analyst has worked out her or his own infantile psychic conflicts related to a given reality situation and thus is not threatened by the infantile psychic reactions of the patient as manifested in the transference. It is important in this connection to note that the silence with which an analyst may respond to a patient's correct observation about her or his life situation may be experienced by the patient in terms of an infantile parental prohibition to ask questions. Such reaction on the part of the patient would intensify the conflict manifested in the transference. The patient's characteristic psychic constellation usually determines the reactions to a specific reality situation involving the analyst. Careful scrutiny of the countertransference is the analyst's best guide to the appropriate analytic stance.

The cases presented in this chapter demonstrate that a specific reality situation involving the analyst may interfere with the sequence with which the transference unfolds but need not necessarily interfere with the unfolding of a pattern of infantile conflicts characteristic for a given patient.

Addendum

The image of the pregnant woman/mother has received relatively scant attention in analytic literature.[1] This is indeed surprising and puzzling since the body image is an important concept in developmental theory, and the body image of the boy/man with erect penis has been analytically considered in terms of its effect on the female and male self-image and on each gender's emotional reactions. It has thus become a familiar focus for analytic investigation of male and female analysands, especially regarding gender differences with emphasis on narcissistic enhancement and depletion. However, equal attention has not been given to the image of the pregnant woman, the embodiment of fertility, procreative power, the conscious focus of attention for children and adults: the stimulus for an unending trove of unconscious fantasy.

Of interest is a strikingly analogous process in the field of art. Thus, subsequent to the so-called prehistoric period during which

---

1. I am indebted to Dr. R. Balsam whose paper, "The Body of the Pregnant Mother and the Body Image of the Daughter," presented November 1, 1996 at the Scientific Meeting of the New York Freudian Society, alerted me to this fact.

sumptuous figurines of pregnant women with big bellies, buttocks, and hips were utilized via sympathetic magic to endow the earth with fertile procreativity, the image of the pregnant woman disappeared from representational Western art. As far as I know, there are only two exceptions: Giotto's painting in Padua of the Virgin Mary, and Elizabeth, mother of John the Baptist (early fourteenth century) who are comparing their pregnant state, and the Madonna del Parto, the pregnant madonna to whom infertile women prayed for a child. In contrast to this phenomenon, the image of the grown man with erect penis, the symbol of power and destiny, has been celebrated in art through the centuries and up to the present.

I believe similar reasons account for the relative sparsity with which the image of the pregnant woman is dealt with in analytic discourse and artistic representation. In the Western world, throughout the centuries, pregnancy was shrouded in secrecy. Some languages have euphemistic expressions to refer to it. In English we speak of a woman's being "in a family way"; in German she is "under other circumstances"; Yiddish uses the same expression; the French refer to the pregnant woman as being "in waiting"; the Poles say she is "expecting"; and so forth.

A woman's clothing, until quite recently, was designed to hide her protrusions and changes of shape, as if the pregnant form revealed something to be ashamed of. Indeed, many women were ashamed of their body during pregnancy and would "hide" in their homes, visiting only with family and leaving the house as rarely as possible. As this chapter indicates, the pregnant woman-analyst was shrouded in secrecy even in psychoanalysis. Was this analytic secrecy a compliance with a societal taboo? What was the secrecy about? I discussed the analysands' transferences evoked by my pregnancy and my countertransferences. I will now suggest some reasons for the secrecy surrounding pregnancy.

A woman's growing body and characteristically changing shape during pregnancy announced to the world indulgence in sexual activities which, so long forbidden, were to be kept secret, especially from the children. This was the reason for all the familiar stories about the stork, the cabbage patch, and other tales. Even when legally sanctioned, unconscious oedipal wishes and fantasies stirred by pregnancy throw a shadow of guilt on sexual intimacy. This accounts for cases of men who can't have sex with their wives once they become pregnant, and thus for the unconscious they represent mother, and, likewise, for the cases of women who lose interest in sex once they become pregnant. One could speculate that these reactions may be expressions of atonement for unconscious oedipal guilt, or of renunciation.

The practice of couvade suggests yet another reason for the secrecy. A man can't be pregnant. In the couvade ritual, however, the man simulates birth pains. The newborn is secretly brought to him and the man is the one congratulated on the birthing. Similarly, rebirth of the boy from the initiator/father (Roheim 1945) is the essence of many initiation rites. Thus some men may experience a woman's pregnancy as being shown up. This hypothesis is supported, I believe, by the now popular phrase "We are pregnant." Who is the we? Is being present in the delivery room and being helpful, the same as giving birth to the baby? A man's statement: "She bears my child," (not ours) reveals his need for reassurance because of unconscious uncertainty regarding paternity, and of the envy that the act of creating the new life takes place within the woman. Is the preponderance and the predominance of icons of malehood, and the absence of icons of women's procreativity related to issues of gender power? It is, after all, a man's world.

Fear of the evil eye (conscious or unconscious) is also one of the contributing reasons accounting for the secrecy with which most women guard the pregnancy during the first trimester. The evil eye may unconsciously represent the envious mother, now an older woman, who no longer can bear a child. It may also express the fear of punishment when the pregnancy, unconsciously, is too closely connected to oedipal wishes.

We have evidence of children's envy of mother's pregnant body and their knowledge that "a baby is there" from children's games during which they play out being pregnant by stuffing pillows to give themselves breasts and a big belly. We also are familiar with their wish to be like the pregnant mother from their fantasy that by "eating a lot" they will get a big belly and thus they will "make a baby."

Though fascinated by mother's pregnant body, boys and girls somehow know it is a harbinger of the rival to come, whom they anticipate with fear and hatred. Thus, in most cases of adult analysis, the focus is on the arrival of the sibling and the reaction to this event. Few analysts, to my knowledge, inquire about the analysand's memories of mother's pregnant body. It is likely that the anger, the sense of betrayal, and the loss of trust that pervade the child's reactions following the birth of a sibling contribute to a withdrawal of admiring cathexis from the image of mother's pregnant shape, and contribute to its repression.

3 The Birth of an Impaired Child; Aspects of Mother–Child Interaction; Mother's Narcissistic Trauma

Recent psychoanalytic studies, and especially the work of G. L. Bibring (1959) and G. L. Bibring and colleagues (1961), indicate the extent to which pregnancy sets off a process of psychic changes in the expectant mother. Though these sequelae cause a temporary state of disequilibrium, they nonetheless are necessary to prepare the woman for the birth process and the advent of the child. Of great significance during this period are alterations in the woman's object-libidinal and narcissistic equilibrium. During pregnancy a marked shift toward libidinal concentration on the self occurs. This specific type of narcissism, which cathects the expanding self-representation, enables the pregnant woman to feel that the growing body within her constitutes an integral part of herself. The physical symbiosis of pregnancy is augmented by the woman's daydreams about her future child, which she molds in fantasy in accordance with her wishes and ego ideals. In this sense the infant-to-be becomes, during pregnancy, uniquely mother's own, physically and mentally existing within her.

This maternal experience of total union is, however, eventually disrupted by the motility of the fetus, which follows a rhythm of its own. The awareness of apartness from the being within, a process culminating with birth, establishes the physical separateness of the infant. To a large extent, however, this event does not disrupt the unique mother–child bonding. A form of mother–infant symbiosis continues even though the child is now regarded as an object in the outside world. The infant, consequently, continues to be cathected with a fusion of narcissistic libido and object libido.

Winnicott (1956) describes the "primary maternal preoccupation" as a condition of total absorption with the infant during which a withdrawal from all other interests takes place. This state, which Winnicott refers to as a "normal illness," occurs for the "ordinary devoted mother" right after birth and lasts for a few weeks, enabling the mother, from the very beginning (p. 302) to adapt to the infant's needs with heightened sensitivity. Such an ideal of mother-infant interaction, however, does not occur, as Winnicott and others have observed, for *all* mothers, or even for the same mother with *all* of her children. It is important to examine when the primary maternal preoccupation fails.

Analytic work with women reveals that the kind of libidinal investment a mother makes in her child will depend on the extent to which it is unconsciously regarded as an extension of the self and on its unconscious symbolic meaning. There will be differences, for instance, depending on whether the child unconsciously represents a wished-for aspect of the self or an aspect the mother wishes to deny in herself; whether the child is looked upon as a gift from a beloved parent or a manifestation of a dreaded punishment; whether the child represents for the mother a hated or a loved sibling; whether he or she reminds mother of a cherished relative or one who was scorned, and so on (Coleman et al. 1953). The unconscious significance that the infant and growing child has for the mother will determine the shifts in the fusion of narcissistic-libidinal and object-libidinal cathexis, the balance that will prevail as well as the amount of aggression directed toward the child. The libidinal balance will be significantly affected by the extent to which the mother–infant symbiosis becomes resolved and by mother's psychic maturity. These factors will be reflected in the optimally evolving process of boundary formation between herself and her child.

Concurrently with fantasies about the wonderful baby she will bear, the pregnant woman also harbors anxious thoughts "that something will go wrong." There are fears that the baby might be misshapen, retarded, born with one of the senses lacking, or undeveloped. These are thoughts and feelings most expectant mothers try to push away, and regard as intrusions "out of nowhere." Yet the numerous superstitions and old wives' tales regarding practices that will assure the health and safety of the baby-to-be attest to a pervasiveness of such fears in the pregnant woman, be they vocal or dormant. Since such fears are not related to reality clues, they must be determined by the psychic makeup of the pregnant woman, and relate to intrapsychic conflicts stirred by the pregnancy.

When all aspects affecting the significance of pregnancy and the birth of a child are considered, it is understandable that the birth of a defective child constitutes a uniquely traumatic event for the mother. Because the child was experienced during pregnancy as an integral part of the self, the procreation of an impaired child profoundly affects the mother's self-image. It causes a severe decrease in the magnitude of positive, self-directed feelings. The damaged child is experienced by the mother as a narcissistic blow. Conscious and unconscious feelings of self-devaluation ensue, resulting in a profound sense of worthlessness. The fears experienced during pregnancy about the well-being of the child now come to mind. Silently or aloud, the mother of such a child asks: "What is wrong with me that I gave birth to such a child? Why has it happened to me? What have I done?"

Since the true meaning of these questions lies in the unconscious, answers in terms of objective reality understanding are insufficient.

The little girl, as is well known from psychoanalytic investigations and amply described in the literature (Deutsch 1944, Freud 1917a, Isaacs 1927, Kestenberg 1956), suffers a narcissistic blow following her discovery of genital differences. This hurt, in our culture, can be aggravated by reality factors. Frequently, because the little girl's mother devalues her own femininity, she may consciously or unconsciously react to the child with similar feelings. If these attitudes are shared by father, the girl's feelings of inferiority are aggravated. Thus the birth of a defective baby rekindles the dormant, repressed, unconscious conflicts because the child, impaired in reality, represents to the mother's unconscious her infantile damaged self. Subsequently, in the course of her psychosexual development, the girl may make many attempts to compensate for her narcissistic wound and to resolve conflicts related to the acceptance of femininity. The wish for a baby from father is one of the early attempts to compensate for penis envy feelings.

However, irrespective of the degree to which a woman may have resolved her conflicts regarding gender wishes, accepted and taken pride in her femininity, a residue of these psychic struggles always remains in the unconscious. The impact of the birth of a defective child can be fully understood only when this genetic background is taken into account. Whereas the birth of a healthy, vigorous baby could have compensated for mother's unconscious sense of impairment and could have served to fulfill in a psychodynamically acceptable way mother's unconscious childhood longings, the birth of an impaired child evokes in the mother a hopeless sense of failure. The mother feels, consciously or unconsciously, as if she created what she always felt she is, rather than what she hoped to become or be. Thus the impaired child represents her own fantasied unconscious impairment. With the birth of a defective child all of mother's dreams about her baby—all her pent-up hopes and fantasies that accompanied the pregnancy—are destroyed.

The following dream illustrates an emotional reaction experienced by a mother of an impaired child: "I was hungry and they brought me something to eat. Millions of tiny eggs like roe-spawn, but all I wanted was one big, healthy egg."

Vignettes from the analysis of Mrs. A. illustrate some of the points made. Mrs. A. had been in treatment for three years and married for approximately one and a-half years when she decided to become pregnant in spite of being tremendously ambivalent about it. Her marriage was unhappy but offered Mrs. A. the opportunity to act out aggressively toward her husband whom she envied for being a man, and whom she unconsciously wished to destroy since he represented her rival-brother.

Mrs. A. claimed she was delighted when the results of the amniocentesis revealed she would have a baby girl, but she simultaneously announced that her husband was disappointed because he wanted a son.

Mrs. A. had an uneventful pregnancy but was tormented by thoughts and fantasies that the child would be either physically or mentally defective.

She had the following dream during pregnancy: " I had a baby but it was a snakelike thing—slimy. I did not want to have it put on my belly, and did not want to bond with it." *Associations:* "If there was anything wrong with the baby, I would want to discard *him*—not look at *her.* It was penislike in the dream. . . . I think of myself as rotten to the core. Sometimes I think my husband, Dave, will like the daughter much better than me. Sometimes I think the baby is really me."

When Mrs. A. saw me one month after the delivery she was quite depressed. The baby was born with a deformed hand: two fingers were missing. Mrs. A. was afraid this was a sign of other defects. Even though she was reassured by the doctors that the baby was "all right," Mrs. A. persevered in her beliefs, which were really a projection onto the infant of her self-devaluating attitudes and her perception of herself as a defective being.

Following a visit with a friend who had a baby boy, Mrs. A. reported having a dream in which her daughter, Nancy, *was* a boy. Mrs. A. was shocked by this dream. Her associations led to the recognition that she looked upon Nancy's defective hand with missing fingers as a displacement for her daughter's lack of a penis. Mrs. A. finally became able to speak about her disappointment that Nancy was not a boy. This led to her recognizing once again how very much she wanted to be a boy, and how envious she was of her brother and how he angered her. Then Mrs. A. reported in passing that she had seen a lovely hobby horse and bought the kit to make one for Nancy. I wondered what came to her mind. Mrs. A. was silent for quite a while and then asked me to give her a hint. I said, "What does one do with a hobby horse?" Mrs. A. was again silent and then burst out laughing. "You mean I want to give Nancy a penis—to make one for her." The next session Mrs. A. reported the following dream: "I had a nose job but it was without my permission." Her associations were in terms of feeling bereft; *something had been taken from her* without her permission. Mrs. A. went on to say, "It marks *me* for life to have a child who has a part that is defective. I feel wronged. Nancy's defect is there. I can't get rid of my feelings. I also feel I am missing something. I hate myself for making comparisons between Nancy and other children, but I can't stop myself. I see Nancy as defective. I used to always make comparisons between myself and my brother. I also see Nancy sometimes as a lovely little girl. That's what my mother used to tell me. I never believed her. I mean it made *no difference* to be a lovely girl . . . I *was still* a girl and my brother was a boy."

Lussier (1960), while discussing the analysis of a boy born with deformed and dwarfed arms, describes his mother's feelings of shame at his birth, and her wish to keep his malformation hidden. The "skeleton in the closet," a phrase we are all familiar with, expresses eloquently the mortification experienced by mother and family because of the existence of an impaired child and the wish to keep this shame hidden.

The birth of a defective baby brings into painfully shocking awareness mother's failure to achieve the pervasively reinforced narcissistic aspirations for the child present during pregnancy. For the mother, the impaired child once again evokes the failed unconscious wish to repair her own damage. The irrevocable fate that befell her and her infant makes the woman feel helpless, hopeless, inferior, and weak. Reality irreversibly shattered her most cherished hopes and dreams without, however, altering the important goals of her ego ideal. Consequently, a breakdown of self-esteem ensues in which the self and the product—the baby—are devalued. Edward Bibring's (1953) understanding of the dynamics and structure of depression is applicable throughout this chapter. His discussion of the mechanism of depression enables us to understand the inevitability of the woman's depressive reaction following the discovery of her child's impairment. According to Bibring depression is due to an intrasystemic conflict within the ego, namely, a tension within the ego itself. This occurs whenever the ego experiences "a shocking awareness of its helplessness in regard to its aspirations" (p. 39). The highly charged narcissistic aspirations expressed in the fantasy about the wished-for baby when confronted with the reality of the defective baby result in mother's acute awareness of her inability to achieve her hoped-for goals. This may bring about a partial or complete collapse of the mother's positively cathected psychic representation of her self-image. The narcissistic mortification evoked by the discrepancy between the ideal and the reality product may cause a withdrawal of narcissistic libido from the self. This is experienced as a depletion of narcissistic supplies, a narcissistic shock, an injury to the psychic self-representation. Intense feelings of shame and a depression may follow, the emotional correlate of the changes in the narcissistic equilibrium of the mother. The severity of the depression will depend on the extent of withdrawal of narcissistic libido and the additional cathexis of the self-representation with destructive aggressive impulses.

It is of interest to note that the actual magnitude of the child's impairment is not necessarily the criterion on which a prediction could be based as to the extent and severity of the subsequent depressive reaction in the mother. Analytic work with mothers of defective children indicates that this is so because the severity of the depressive reaction depends on the extent to which the mother (1) unconsciously perceives the child as an externalization of her defective self, and (2) is simultaneously symbiotically linked with her child. The recognition of the degree to which these two factors affect the mother–child interaction is essential for the understanding of the numerous permutations that ensue as a result of intrapsychic attempts by the mother to resolve the unconscious conflicts rekindled and aroused by the birth of a defective child.

Observations indicate that the type of maternal behavior is determined primarily by the mother's psychic structure, the extent to which she resolved her identification and involvement with her own mother, and the degree to which she has worked through conflicts centering on penis envy and femininity as well as the characteristic manner in which she attempts to deal with conflict situations. Environmental factors, and particularly the attitude of the spouse to mother and child, are of utmost importance. They usually significantly affect mother's narcissistic equilibrium. The father's accepting and supportive attitude may contribute to help mother maintain the narcissistic libidinal cathexis of her self-image. Such an attitude by the father may also mitigate against the conscious and/or unconscious rejection of the child. Consequently various patterns of mother–child interactions can be observed. These encompass the entire gamut from oversolicitude to complete rejection of the infant, from apparent blindness and insensitivity to the child's handicap to an exaggerated over-magnification of the defect, from demanding for and giving to the child extraordinary attention to hiding the child to forestall the discovery of its defect, from granting the child the prerogatives of an exception to treating the child as the scum of the earth.

Certain generalizations can tentatively be made. Denial of the reality of the child's defect frequently bordering on negation seems to occur in cases in which acceptance of this reality might lead to the possible psychic breakdown of the mother. This is illustrated by the case of a young mother who several days after the birth of her child was informed that he was a dwarf. She reacted at first with disbelief, which was followed by a relatively brief, but extremely intense, interlude of despair. Subsequently, mother adopted the attitude that she knew her child would grow to be normal "if it were properly nourished." Thus she devoted herself to the child, fed and overfed him, and solicited confirmation from family and friends that he was beautiful.

Analytic findings suggest that women who in their childhood denied the permanence of genital differences, and had a fantasy— subsequently repressed—that they would grow a penis by magical means, hold the conviction as mothers of impaired children that some magical means will obviate the defect, and the child will develop normally. Such attitudes are frequently supported by family and friends, who assure the mother that her child will "grow out of it," and by pediatricians, who speak of different "rates of maturation." These reassurances contribute to mother's persistent denial of reality (Forrer 1959).

Rejection of various degrees, culminating in the actual giving away of the infant where this is not necessitated by its physical condition, is a reflection of the mother's need to emphasize her separateness from the child who symbolically represents her unconscious defective self of which she wants to be rid. This type of mother, because of her narcissistic vulnerability, cannot tolerate the continuous mortification caused by her impaired child. The defective child in such cases is also rejected because it cannot serve as a narcissistically gratifying object, as a fulfillment of mother's narcissistic needs.

The following illustrates an extreme case of rejection. A beautiful, highly narcissistic young woman gave birth to a baby girl with a large nevus on one cheek. Upon seeing the child for the first time, the mother turned away, saying, "She's ugly—it can't be a two-faced monster" (referring to the normal side of the child's face and the deformed one). The mother subsequently refused to have any contact with the baby. She did not feed or see the child, nor did she want to speak about her or listen to any explanation of her condition. This mother openly spoke about her wish for the baby to die, and behaved as if the infant no longer existed.

The overprotective, oversolicitous, smothering-the-child attitude and the neglectful, indifferent attitude are opposite ways mothers use to cope with the hostile—and frequently murderous—impulses they harbor toward their impaired children. Analysis indicates that these attitudes reflect unconscious feelings of self-hatred projected upon the child, which represents the unconscious, negatively cathected psychic representation of the self-image.

Analytic investigation indicates that disappointment, grief, despair, and narcissistic mortification are the underlying reactions to the birth of a defective child. Thus, far from being overvalued as a love object, the defective child is devalued by the mother who also devalues herself. To the extent to which an unconscious, negatively cathected self-image determines the woman's feelings about herself, the damaged child will serve as a confirmation and reality basis for such feelings.

Depression, a feeling that can be conscious or unconscious, has many different facets: sadness, mourning, helplessness, and hopelessness as well as a feeling of worthlessness are some of its aspects; rage, bitterness, and anger turned toward the self or outward are some of its other manifestations. However, the conscious and unconscious guilt feelings and shame that many mothers of defective children have, which can be related to their conscious and unconscious hostile and murderous impulses toward these children, are *not* the primary causes for their depression. Analysis of these women revealed that they had already suffered, prior to the birth of their impaired infant, from an unconscious chronic depression caused by an excessive amount of unconscious aggression directed toward a split-off and devalued part of their self. Following the birth of the defective infant, these feelings became externalized and directed toward the child who, as a self object, unconsciously represented the devalued aspect of their self.

The symbiotic link between the mother and her defective child has certain specific characteristics. Self-hatred projected onto the child, unconsciously perceived as an externalized defective self, is the mortar that binds this relationship. The strength of the symbiotic link that binds mother and defective child is determined by the extent to which the negative feelings toward the self dominate mother's personality. Only when—and to the extent to which—mother's unconscious depression resulting from the narcissistic injury caused by the birth of the defective child is alleviated can the process of separation between mother and child begin to take place. The mother of an impaired child is enabled to separate out from the symbiotic entwinement with her child when, as a consequence of intense therapeutic effort, an intrapsychic change takes place that enables her to recognize and accept her apartness. This occurs when mother can achieve self-fulfillment by attaining goals syntonic with her own ego ideal. *Owned* feelings of self-esteem attained from gratifying reality situations enable the mother of an impaired child to view herself and the child separately. When this takes place, the impaired child stops being mother's source of narcissistic mortification. Mother now experiences feelings of grief, sadness and hurt *for* the child when she considers its fate. The impaired child, no longer a self object, evokes mother's empathy and becomes the focus of her loving concern. Such apartness enables the mother to help her impaired child achieve maximum functioning by planning for it realistically. The following clinical vignette illustrates some of these points.

Peter, an 8-year-old boy who dragged his left foot and suffered from a mild spastic semiparalysis of his left arm, due probably to a birth injury, was referred for treatment with symptoms of soiling when he was with mother, extreme negativism, and temper tantrums. During the initial interviews, mother did not mention her son's impairment. She seemed preoccupied with the behavioral symptoms and complained about them. This attitude was mirrored by the boy, who ignored the existence of his damaged extremities. Both mother and son began individual psychotherapy. As the extreme bonding between mother and child loosened, mother's denial of her son's handicap decreased, and she brought painful material related to it to the sessions.

This attitude was paralleled in Peter's sessions. He was now able to acknowledge the damaged parts of his body and to express his anger and pain about the impairment. As treatment continued and the boy's separation and individuation firmed, the power struggle between mother and child decreased, and so did Peter's soiling and negativism. It became clear that Peter's symptoms, in part at least, were a call for help. They were an expression of his need for mother to include his damaged extremities in her acknowledgment of him. The symptoms also expressed Peter's anger that mother failed to do so. As a result of psychotherapy, Peter participated very actively in a course of rehabilitative physiotherapy. He learned to ride a bike, roller skate, and use his left hand as a support so that he could participate in shop at school. The acquisition of these skills contributed toward his increased self-acceptance. His belligerence and defensiveness decreased. These changes helped to improve Peter's relationship with his peers. The boy eventually found gratification in his own activities, and developed his own interests. Toward the end of her own treatment, the mother returned to work, which gave her a sense of independence and personal gratification. Satisfied with her own life, mother now found it easier to accept and acknowledge the limitations of her son. This enabled mother to be empathic and to plan realistically for Peter's optimum functioning. Such a maternal attitude made Peter feel more accepted.

Analysis of mothers of defective children indicates that the specific manifest patterns of their behavior are coping devices and reflect attempts at conflict resolution. Psychoanalytic work with their children, however, amply demonstrates that irrespective of mother's overt behavior, her unconscious attitude toward the child is the determining factor that has the most decisive and pronounced bearing on the child's feelings and attitudes toward itself. The early complete dependency on the mother for survival, which is the biological basis for the child's symbiosis with her, sensitizes and attunes the child to introject mother's attitude and feelings from subliminal cues. The latter reflect mother's true attitudes. Sensitivity to mother's attitudinal feelings is especially acute in the impaired child who, less able to fare for himself than the normal one, needs his mother all the more, both emotionally and physically. Usually, however, because of the unconscious effect of the interaction with her own mother, the mother of the impaired child is unable to care for her defective child in a fully giving manner. Thus the impaired child, from the earliest moments of its awareness, experiences mother's unconscious attitude as lacking in total and unconditional acceptance. Analysis has demonstrated that the unconscious maternal attitude, introjected into the psychic self-representation, eventually becomes the child's unconscious nucleus of self-awareness and self-feeling. Further, these early feelings about the self, usually not accessible to consciousness and arising from internalized rejecting and devaluing maternal attitudes, are most important in influencing the child's developing psychic self-image. These feelings form the unconscious kernel of the negatively cathectic split-off self-representation in the adult psyche. Psychoanalysis of children has demonstrated that lack of maternal acceptance, admiration, even of loving overvaluation, affects the developing self-image in a crippling way. This is especially the case of the impaired child, who needs so much more than its healthy peers for its support and receives less than the latter for its sustenance because the mother experienced the child's birth as a narcissistic injury and is therefore herself narcissistically depleted. The situation is complicated further by the fact that the handicapped child probably has greater needs and is more demanding, perhaps even more clinging and less independent, than its healthy peer. All these factors set up the conditions for a self-perpetuating vicious circle of rejection, demand, rejection, guilt, shame, anger, rejection, self-abasement, anger, guilt, and so on, with mother attempting to satisfy her child's needs but being unable to do so. This was amply reflected by an impaired child in a nursery school who wistfully asked a beloved teacher: "What kind of mummy is she, my mummy, if she can't even cure me of my limp?" The analysis of impaired children reveals that they always, unconsciously, blame their mother for their impairment, harbor angry feelings toward her, and consider themselves shortchanged.

It is interesting to note that even when the behavior of the mother appears to be guided by sound reality factors, analysis of the mother reveals that her behavior toward the child is also motivated by an unconscious wish to heal her own narcissistic wound by attempting to minimize and/or compensate for the actual impairment of the child. In these cases mothering is based predominantly on the unconscious paradigm, "I shall be to my child the mother I wanted to have, not the mother I had, who created the condition that resulted in my narcissistic wound" (Benedek 1959).

Discussion

Childbirth, the most significant event in a woman's life, is fraught with wishes, hopes, and fears. The infant to be, whose existence within its mother's body is symbiotically linked to her, becomes, as the pregnancy advances, the focus of her fantasies and emotions. The "child within," whose existence the mother sustains, of whose existence she is most intimately aware, becomes libidinally and narcissistically endowed, her object of love and aspiration.

Frequently, what the mother wished for herself, and did not achieve, she hopes her child will attain. The mother experiences and relates to the child within as to a part of herself, and hopes this part of her will achieve her hopes and her goals. The child within is both a physical and a psychic reality. However, since the child within is symbiotically linked to the mother, since it is mother's body that accommodates it, since mother bears it and births it, the psychic sense of a dual unity predominates even after birth. When a mother thinks and says "*my child*," she experiences *my* as *part of me*.

These factors, which constitute the psychic reality of a pregnant woman, account for the enormity of the trauma resulting from the birth of a defective child. The fantasy of the child within, for so long a part of mother's bodily and psychic self-representation, this perfect narcissistically and libidinally endowed being, is destroyed when birth reveals its defects. The shock to the mother is overwhelming. Frequently the reality is at first denied because the pain cannot be absorbed. The infant, to the mother, still feels like part of her, and its pain is the mother's hurt. Fantasies, in which magical undoing and assumed guilt are intermingled, preoccupy mother. The defective infant becomes a source of mother's narcissistic mortification. For the mother, because of the symbiotic link, the child's defect reveals her defect. Analysis of mothers of impaired children indicates that they unconsciously feel that their defectiveness caused their child's impairment. Thus mother's unconscious guilt remains unmitigated, which may account for her chronic depressive condition following the birth of a defective child.

Unless worked through analytically, the impaired child, because of the unresolved symbiotic link, constantly stirs mother's unconscious psychic sense of self-deficiency. This may stimulate in the mother an impulse to undo her own and her child's defect. Experienced as part of the self, the child is a narcissistic "love–hate" self object. Ambivalence may predominate in the relationship, repressed by the mother, yet evident in overprotectiveness and clinging, which is usually mutual.

As analysis indicates, reactions of attenuated severity to those described above frequently occur when a newborn child does not coincide with mother's image of her expected, hoped-for baby (Solnit and Stark 1961, M. Sperling 1950, 1970). A mother may then experience a sense of disappointment, followed by a depression of various degrees of severity. The discrepancy between the newborn and the hoped-for baby may be due to the child's sex, its looks, size, temperament, feeding response, and so forth, factors tangible and intangible, yet related to mother's unconscious hopes, which make her feel that the infant does not fulfill the criteria of the wished-for child. The extent of the depression, narcissistic in origin, depends in such cases primarily on mother's psychic makeup, in which reality factors play only a secondary role.

Mother's disappointment in her healthy, normal child who does not measure up to her fantasized, narcissistic self object, and her depression associated with its birth, indicates that Freud's (1917a, 1933) postulate regarding the penis = baby equation, and the usual simplistic assumption that a healthy baby will ipso facto satisfy mother's narcissistic needs, is not necessarily borne out.

A mutually satisfying mother–child interaction is interfered with by the extent to which mother's conscious and unconscious subjective wishes become a source of her disappointment in the baby, whom she therefore cannot respond to as narcissistically gratifying. Mother's depression, a reaction of varying magnitude and duration, stems from the degree to which she finds the baby consciously or unconsciously unacceptable. Mother's mood and her affective state influence her patterns of mothering. All these factors, which are reflected in the earliest interplay between mother and child, invariably affect the child's unconscious self-feelings and thus influence the forming kernel of its self-awareness. The child's early self-representation will be negatively cathected to the extent to which mother's attitude, because of her depression, is nonresponsive to and nonaccepting of the child. Mother's conscious and/or unconscious rejection of the child reflects the narcissistic injury caused by the disappointing and unfulfilling qualities the child has for her. In such cases mother will frequently project onto the child aspects of her split-off, devalued self.

4   The Rotten Core: Legacy of Mother's Depression

A Mythic Expression of Identification with the Aggressor

The Balinese myth about Rangda, the bloodthirsty, child-eating demon queen (Covarrubias 1974, Hoefer 1974), illustrates the universality of certain early mother–child interactions, and highlights the vicissitudes of identification with the aggressor that may result in a split of the self.

In one version of this story the queen, Dewi Kunti, for reasons unknown, had to sacrifice Sadewa, one of her sons, to Rangda. This made Dewi Kunti very sad since she was a good and loving mother. She could not bring herself to sacrifice her son. However, when the witch, Rangda, entered into Dewi Kunti, she became bewitched and transformed into an angry Fury. In this state Dewi Kunti commanded her Prime Minister to take Sadewa to Rangda's forest. The Prime Minister, who loved Sadewa, did not want to sacrifice him and was saddened by this terrible command. However, the witch, Rangda, also entered into him. This transformed the

Prime Minister, and he became angry and violent. He took Sadewa to the forest, tied the boy to a tree in front of Rangda's abode, and abandoned him. Shiwa, the most powerful of all the gods, took pity on Sadewa and gave him immortality. When Rangda arrived, eager to kill and eat Sadewa, she was unable to do so. Admitting her defeat, Rangda asked Sadewa for redemption so she could go to heaven. Sadewa granted her wish and killed her, thus enabling her to go to paradise.

Rangda's most important disciple, Kalika, begged for a fate identical to that of her mistress. Sadewa, however, refused. In the ensuing battle Kalika was twice defeated, but when Kalika transformed herself into the powerful Rangda, Sadewa could no longer vanquish her.

In the Barong, the dance–drama enactment of this story, the dagger dancers attack Rangda. The attack fails. Rangda, the embodiment of evil, cannot be destroyed. Finally, to give vent to their anger and, I believe, helpless despair, the dancers, who are in a ritual trance, turn their daggers upon themselves and in a frenzy repeatedly stab themselves.

Vicissitudes of the child's early fantasy and reality interactions with mother and father are dramatically depicted in this tale. The different personages in the story represent split-off good and bad objects. The destructive element predominates, changing the good mother and also the good father into raging, unfeeling demons. Mother, however, is seen as the prime evildoer since she—as Rangda (the bad mother)—not only demands the sacrifice of the child, but also—as Dewi Kunti (the seemingly good mother)—agrees to sacrifice her son. Thus expression is given to the early experiential struggle in which mother is perceived as a potential destroyer. Father—as Prime Minister—at first is seen as weaker than mother. Subsequently, however, as Shiwa, he becomes the rescuing all-powerful figure onto whom the child projects his omnipotence, which he then reintrojects as the gift of immortality. The now invulnerable son's fury at mother and his wish for revenge find expression at first in Sadewa's killing of Rangda, mitigated, however, because he commits this act at her request.

The vicissitudes of changes in Sadewa's attitude toward the killing of Rangda can be understood only when one realizes that the plot condenses various versions of the same act, thus reflecting the changing dynamic balance of psychic forces. In the tale different fantasy elements are combined and allowance is made for the conflicting attitudes of the child. Thus:

- The mother is killed but the murder is undone by her redemption and immortality in paradise.
- No guilt need belong to the child for it is mother who asks to be killed as an act of atonement for her wrongdoing toward the child.
- The child's unforgiving, vindictive, and destructive anger, disguised in the killing of Rangda at her own behest, is apparent in the savage interaction with Kalika, who is killed twice and denied salvation.
- Kalika's final transformation into Rangda, who cannot be defeated, represents the child's awareness, in fantasy, of the "bad" mother who is an ever-present threat.

The myth describes the intense, affect-laden reality and imagined internalized interactions with the mother of early childhood as these are experienced, projected, and introjected. The dancers who turn their daggers against themselves because they are unable to vanquish Rangda, the "bad" mother, depict one possible resolution of such mother–child strife. They represent the child whose fury has merged with the experienced maternal rage and who, having succumbed in the futile struggle with mother, also identified with the self-destructive elements in her (Rangda pleading to be killed). Thus the dancers dramatically portray the ultimate consequence of an identification with the destructive aspect of the aggressor (A. Freud 1936): self-destruction.

I suggest that the turning of aggression against the self (as victim) is based on identification not only with the aggressive but also with the self-destructive elements in the aggressor (mother). Such an identification may also imply an unconscious merger with the aggressor (mother). When this occurs, the internalized aggression of the object becomes the tie to the object.

The Rotten Core: Clinical Examples

Every discussion of a specific aspect of pathology constitutes a delimitation that results in an artifact since it is an exploration of but one strand from the interwoven fabric comprising the harmonious and discordant elements of the human psyche. Mindful of the shortcoming of this method, I shall nonetheless use it to highlight a specific form of self-pathology, central and gravely disturbing in some personalities.

The women to be described presented a puzzling picture. Each sought treatment after one or two previous therapeutic experiences; each complained of great suffering even though she appeared to be leading an apparently adaptive social and professional life, even enjoying an at least partially gratifying love relationship. As far as I could ascertain, there was no uniformity in the etiology that initially brought these patients into treatment. On the basis of my work with these women, I did surmise that their previous therapeutic experience was partially successful. It did not enable them, however, to resolve the underlying cause of their recurrent, deep depressions, nor did it enable them to overcome their feelings of discontent with themselves.

In the course of treatment with me, though pained by anxiety, depression, and some physical symptoms, each of these patients insisted that the real cause of her suffering stemmed from "some-

thing rotten within her" that constituted her innermost self and
filled her with a pervasive sense of doom. One patient said: "It is
the sensation of something bad within that makes me feel bad."
Each patient was convinced that nothing she could do or become
would change this fundamental fact. Each one insisted that the
"inner rottenness" was her essence and made it impossible for her
to like and accept herself.

These patients felt as if they had two selves, and thus experienced a sense of duality. In contrast, outsiders perceived only their
well-functioning, capable self. The patients sometimes responded
to such an appraisal with a modicum of pleasure, and sometimes
with a feeling of being a "fake." Though they enjoyed their achievements, they frequently looked upon them as a "way to survive."
In general, achievements, accomplishments, and love were only a
solace. They mitigated the anguish but did not change its fundamental nature. Good feelings and praise expressed by love objects
were appreciated, sometimes even sought actively. They filled
these patients with surprise, made them sad and ready to cry. The
patients explained these reactions as due to their awareness that
good feelings expressed by others neither depicted nor related to
their "real self," that is, to their "inner rottenness."

The analyses of these patients' "outer self," which they considered a sham, did not reveal any significant pathology. Were it not
for their reported suffering, it would appear that one was dealing
with individuals functioning autonomously in a chosen sphere of
ego interests, interacting quite adequately with others, and ob-
taining narcissistic gratification from goals syntonic with their
conscious wishful self-image. Ego strength seemed sufficient for
the achievement of well-sublimated aims pursued energetically.
These patients even appeared to experience pleasure from their
achievements. Such gratification, however, was short-lived. Without any apparent cause these women would become depressed
again and again, filled with suffering, and complain, ascribing their
pain to a "feeling of badness." The patients insisted that the feel-

ing of inner rottenness interfered with their having a sense of well-being. Hypochondriacal symptoms occurred. This type of pathology may manifest itself with different degrees of severity. I have observed it in quite a number of patients of both sexes. Analytic reconstructions indicate that "rotten core" pathology develops when a mother becomes severely depressed during the child's toddlerhood, and also, when she has a sadistic character structure. Subsequently a specific pattern of interaction between mother and child ensues.

In the last ten years chance had it that I analyzed four patients whose mothers suffered from a severe reactive depression while their daughters were in the rapprochement subphase. Family anecdotes acquainted my patients with this historical material, which they recounted as a bit of life history, in a manner that indicated that it was totally split off from their conscious emotions and psychic reactions. I stress this point to emphasize that the patients initially had no conscious awareness of their reactions to mother's depression, nor of its effect on them. In the later phases of treatment, however, the consequences of childhood interactions with a depressed and/or aggressively hostile mother became apparent from the analyses of dreams, fantasies, and specific transference manifestations. Analytic work also revealed that the selection of specific types of object relations was unconsciously motivated by this mother–child paradigm.

The sense of inner rottenness was the focal aspect of these patients' pathology. The analyses of this malformation led to an understanding of the processes by which it developed and its consequences for the psychic life of these women. The clinical case illustrations that follow are extreme examples that depict the dynamic interactions stemming from maternal libidinal unavailability caused by severe depression, and sometimes hostile aggression. I will indicate how such mother–child interactions led to the development of rotten core self-pathology.

Though in the cases presented the mothers of my patients suffered predominantly from a reactive depression, I do not mean to imply that rotten core pathology develops only when this is the case. My cases indicate that the sense of inner rottenness varied in severity depending on the extent of mother's libidinal unavailability.

The following vignettes will serve to illustrate some specific genetic factors and developmental malformations that resulted in the formation of rotten core pathology.

Case 1

Nina, a very successful kindergarten teacher, married and with many friends, could neither accept nor emotionally integrate the love and esteem in which she was held. She would frequently say: "I am 'hateable' because mother hated me. Since it was mother who had these feelings, they must be correct. I always feel I somehow fool all who love me. Only mother knew the truth."

When Nina was 18 months old, her grandmother, a daily visitor in the parental household, died suddenly of a stroke. Mother, as Nina learned from family anecdotes, became deeply depressed following this event.

Nina pictured her mother as angry and morbid, a compulsive cleaner and housekeeper. Mother accused the family of "making her into a workhorse and slave." Nina was a special target of mother's endless accusations. She felt that mother favored her younger sister and treated her like a stepchild. She could not become reconciled to mother's lack of loving feelings toward her. She recalled long hours spent in her room tearfully reassuring and consoling herself that, nonetheless, mother really did love her, that if only she, Nina, *really was good*, mother would show her love.

Nina was fortunate to have had, and been able to make use of, the love she experienced from her maternal grandfather, aunts, and uncles. As she became older, she contrasted their attitudes and lives with the "hell" she experienced at home. It is thus not surprising that in her early teens Nina decided that "mother was crazy." She stood alone in this belief, however, since mother's behavior at home, and especially her abuse of Nina, were "a secret." Mother capably pretended to the world that "all was well," and that she was loving and reasonable. She used the dresses she sewed for Nina—which indeed were extremely well made—as proof of her devotion. Nina realized that no one but she recognized mother's false facade. Occasionally, especially when mother was a little kinder, even Nina wavered in her conviction.

Nina, however, did not apply the accusation of being crazy only to mother. There were times when she felt she also was "crazy inside," and like mother "hid behind the facade of an outer, normal shell." In these instances it appeared almost as if a confusion of self and object representation took place. She kept saying, "I feel like a freak. I raised myself to look normal but inside I am really crazy. Others tell me I handle things well but this is not how I experience it. I feel I know nothing." These convictions about herself were so powerful that Nina refused to have children. She feared that in her relationship with her child she would reenact the hateful interaction experienced by her with mother. She feared she would curse her child to reexperience her own fate.

"I cannot believe I am okay," Nina said, "because I was not okay with mother. I am very angry but I learned to cover it up. I sometimes have a feeling of not being there while I smile and talk and everything goes on. That is how I survived my childhood, by not being there so that what mother did and said would not hurt. I feel everything is wrong with me, though everyone praises me. Now all of them say I do such a wonderful job, but mother humiliated, ridiculed, and destroyed me. I feel sometimes the 'I' of me no longer exists. I feel, most of the time, that the praise I now receive does not relate to me. I can't relate to it and enjoy it. I devalue it."

The patient had broken off contact with mother in her midtwenties and had not seen her for many years when she started her analysis.

Case 2

Professionally successful, married, and the mother of four, Irene was an anthropologist associated with a leading university. Though she seemed to enjoy life, she complained about a sense of doom and a belief that she was damned to eternal hell. She acknowledged these ideas as irrational but could not free herself of their effect. Irene looked on her personal and professional achievements as not related to her real self. Her depression was well hidden from the outside world but she was fully aware of it. Irene remembered she had a sense of "being bad" from about age 5. That was when she began to pray for death at 100. The fantasy of the ensuing long life span seemed to reassure her. She said: "A hundred years seemed like an eternity of keeping the fires of hell away." As a child Irene felt guilty, though she did not know her crime. She grew up to be self-righteous, with an almost compulsive need to rescue those in distress.

Mother was a beautiful, self-absorbed, empty woman. Irene remembers her as an avid practitioner of preventive voodoo, engaged in rituals to "undo the evil eye." She recalls mother scrupulously collecting her nail parings and cut-off hair, packing them into little bundles, and making sure they were completely burned. This procedure was necessary—so Irene was told—to prevent evildoers from getting hold of "parts of her" and causing her harm. Irene, in spite of her seemingly secure environment, grew up always having a sense of foreboding. Her attempts, in later life, to refute mother's warnings of "an evil all around her" did not free her of an inner sense that it was always present.

Irene recalled many days of her childhood when mother was silent, distant, and ignored her. On those days Irene felt that mother's behavior was her fault, proof of her wrongdoing. There were other days when mother would clutch her and hold her tight. Such behavior made Irene want to get away from mother. Yet when she succeeded, and freed herself from mother, a sensation that something terrible was going to happen would intensify and overcome Irene. She would feel evil. Panicked, she would run back to mother only to find her once again distant and silent.

Irene knew since late adolescence that mother miscarried five times during the eleven years following her birth. The first of these miscarriages occurred when Irene was about 22 months old. However, only during treatment did the significance of these facts became clear. The nature of the transference, free associations, the analysis of dreams and memories made the specific mother–child interaction more understandable. It became clear, via reconstruction, how these traumatic events in mother's life, totally incomprehensible to Irene as a child, contributed to her sense of foreboding and doom. Following each miscarriage and intensifying as the years passed, mother expressed her ambivalence toward Irene by possessively holding onto her, the only living child, and at other times by ignoring her for long periods of time. Mother seemingly became more and more depressed and could not stop mourning her lost babies. This supposition appears confirmed by the fact that Irene recalled that her feelings of foreboding and her sense of being evil intensified as she grew older.

Irene described her self-feelings when she came for treatment as follows:

> A time came when nothing good about me felt real. All I knew was the pain of never feeling well. When I made good, kind, and friendly gestures to which others responded with grateful, loving acceptance, it did not make me feel good. I knew that I was only propitiating and warding off their evil intents. I did not extend the good gesture out of love but rather out of fear of their evil, to placate them, to buy their good intent, perhaps even love. Thus the success of my gesture did not ameliorate my sense of inner evil. The knowing, doing, succeeding belongs to the outer part of me. It does not change the rotten core inside. I felt and feared as a child that my rotten core caused others evil. I no longer believe that. Rather, it seems to be sapping my life.

Familiar with analytic theory, the patient added: "My mother's evil, which she projected into the world and then tried to undo with her voodoo rituals, got into me. It is and was her hatred."

Case 3

Vera's[1] father had developed Hodgkin's disease when she was almost 2. Though her mother, a respected homeopathic practitioner, was acclaimed to have special healing powers, father refused her help. Mother's anxious depression apparently started at that time.

Mother wanted to make sure that Vera, at least, was protected. To forestall all possible dangers to her daughter, mother purged Vera once a week with a mixture of herbal laxatives to get rid of all the "bad stuff" in her. Before these sessions began, a struggle would ensue. Vera would try to run away, a vain attempt since mother always triumphed. Finally, exhausted by the ordeal, Vera would crawl onto mother's lap. She would feel mother's body enfolding her, "like a spider's web: safe and suffocating." She would fall asleep.

These experiences contributed to the conviction Vera developed that there was something rotten within her, that the purging must have been to "cleanse me from within." Vera said: "I am stuck with it, and there is nothing that can touch it, this feeling of 'I am rotten.' No matter what happens on the outside, I still feel this way inside. It is like a *malleus maleficarum*, black and in flame. I should go to a sorcerer so he could exorcise it and expurgate it. That is what mother tried to do with the purgatives she gave me. It did not work, it is still in me."

---

1. This analysand is discussed in greater detail in Chapter 2.

Case 4

May, a graduate student with an important administrative job, was in her mid-twenties when she started treatment. She had a long history of therapeutic interventions with at least four therapists starting when she was in her early teens. May had always felt angry, disadvantaged, depressed and isolated, "rotten." She felt something was "wrong" with her. Though the top student in her class, admired, self-supporting, May felt isolated and dissatisfied.

The beginning phase of treatment was filled with expressions of hatred toward mother, who was perceived as unresponsive and accusatory. May spoke of her as "a mother of boys who could only relate and respond to boys," as a mother "who not only did not affirm my femininity, but who consistently tried to deny it by forcing me since early childhood to 'always wear pants.'" Father was seen as a "savior." She loved, adored, and felt attached to him; yet even his positive attitude did not make her "feel good." May complained that neither her grades nor her teachers' positive attitudes, nor her colleagues' attempts at friendship affected her "feeling rotten." She would add, "It was always like that . . . I did good work, I'd be praised, some kids would want to make friends with me, but I'd feel rotten, I mean, I'd feel that somehow I was rotten."

When May was 19 months old, mother gave birth to a still-born child. This was the most significant event in May's childhood. Mother thereafter became severely depressed and could no longer care for her family. It must have been a difficult time since the whole family moved to the maternal grandparents' home, and grandmother, May's beloved Nana, took care of them. Following a ten-month stay, the family returned to their own home. It was painful for May to lose the everyday warm contact with Nana.

As a young child May supposedly sat for hours by herself, playing and observing. Her most typical response was "do it by self," meaning "by myself."

During the phase of treatment in which she began to examine her provocative behavior toward mother, May said: "When mother got angry she used to call me a rotten kid. I felt like I had a fault, a hardness, a meanness—that I was a misshapen miscarriage." While this type of analytic work was going on, I was late for a session, to which I came directly from the funeral of a close friend. I remained absorbed with my feelings and thoughts and thus did not feel attuned to May. She spoke for a while and then fell silent. Preoccupied with my thoughts, I was also silent. Finally May said: "I had an image of the painting by Munch, the one with the mother staring into space and the dead baby in her lap. I had no lap to climb into . . . I tugged at my mother's skirt but she did not respond. No matter how much I tugged, she just looked into space, oblivious of me. She did not feel me."

I responded by confirming the correctness of her perception and explained that I had been preoccupied with my friend's death. In spite of that, however, I had not wanted to cancel her session. May said she understood my grief and asked whether I would like her to leave. She said, "Oh, that will be okay with me." I responded, "Quite to the contrary. I came in spite of the death . . . I felt your tugging at my skirt—you have a lap to climb into." She was silent, and after awhile began to weep for a long time. The intrapsychic significance of the stillbirth and the consequences of this event became apparent when May said: "Mother loved the dead baby brother . . . that is why she kept him on her lap, him and not me." After a little while, still sobbing, "Is that what being rotten is? Believing I killed the baby, believing she hated me because of that . . . feeling she was right to say I am a rotten kid. Is that why I cannot get rid of the feeling I have a rotten core?"

May's inner world was filled by the pain of what she experienced as mother's rejection. To account for mother's attitude, May *came to believe* that it was due to her murderous wishes, for which mother hated her.

Discussion

The term *rotten core* evolved to denote my patients' awareness of an aspect of their psyche that is simultaneously a part of, yet is also alien to, their sense of self. Grossman and Simon (1969) discuss the causes that lead to the description of inner experiences in anthropomorphic terms. The rotten core should be understood along these lines of reasoning as a metaphor depicting a specific inner feeling, "a sense of rottenness," experienced by my patients throughout their lives.

I have used this term in two ways: to provide a phenomenological description of a certain group of observable psychic data and also to categorize them. In this latter sense the term is employed as a hypothetical construct on a level of abstraction corresponding to, but not identical with, such concepts as the bad or good introject and the self-image. Consistent with the structural delineation of the psychic apparatus, the rotten core, along with other self-images, can be conceived as one of the components of the self-representation.

Balint's description of the basic fault, as well as Winnicott's observations regarding the true and false self, are mentioned briefly since, phenomenologically, patients suffering from each of these deviations appear to have certain similarities with patients manifesting rotten core pathology.

Commenting on the basic fault, Balint (1968) states: "The patient says that he feels there is a fault within him, a fault that must be put right.... It is ... something wrong with the mind, a kind of deficiency ..." (p. 21). "A basic fault can perhaps be merely healed provided the deficient ingredients can be found; and even then it may amount only to a healing with defect, like a simple, painless scar" (p. 22). According to Balint, the origin of the basic fault lies in the "lack of fit" (p. 22) between the biopsychological infant needs and the physical, psychological, and affectionate care he receives.

[handwritten margin note: False Self]

According to Winnicott (1956, 1960), the origin of the split into true and false self takes place in early infancy. Differences in the degree of this type of pathology are determined by the stage of development at which the greatest pressure for conformity occurred. Winnicott claims that the true self, which arises from the vital, creative, subjectively genuine aspects of the individual rooted in the biological givens, becomes stilted, distorted, or completely obliterated, depending on the extent to which the infant is deprived of a "holding" environment provided by "good enough" mothering, which is necessary for unencumbered growth. Thus the false self develops in proportion to the absence of such mothering and results from premature accommodations to the demands of external reality. It is serviceable in terms of adjustment but internally unsuccessful since it is primarily reactive, the outgrowth of object pressure (usually maternal) and therefore defensive.

The pathology of the self from which my patients suffered resulted from a specific form of identification with the aggressor, which occurred at a crucial time in the development of the self. The description of rotten core pathology is an attempt to conceptualize the formation and consequences of a specific split in the self-representation that gave my patients the subjective awareness of a duality of their selves. They described an outer self, the shell or persona they frequently regarded as "phoney," and a real self, the rotten core. Though the split of the self-representation predominated as the central problem, derivatives of conflicts from various developmental stages were present and combined into different characterological pictures for each patient. However, typical for all these patients was a superego with many primitive sadistic elements, experienced by them as a harsh conscience, and an ego ideal containing nonmetabolized grandiose and overidealized elements. A well-developed and wide conflict-free sphere accounted for excellent functioning in many areas of secondary autonomy. Ego functioning was related to a strongly developed, conscious, wishful self-image (Milrod 1977).

The pathological mother–child interaction affected the nature and quality of the object representation. It partly reinforced the infantile tendency to split the maternal imago, and it led to a corresponding splitting of the self-image. The persistence of the splitting interfered with the consolidating process of the synthetic function of the ego. As a consequence of these two factors, the achievement of self-constancy and libidinal object constancy remained tenuous. Regressive pulls easily eroded these tenuous attainments whenever a libidinal object assumed an unconscious, pathognomonic maternal significance. When this occurred—for instance, when a lover expressed criticism—the ensuing ambivalence triggered splitting with consequent patterns of idealization and devaluation. These patients on the one hand longed to merge with the idealized object, and on the other acted self-righteously toward the devalued one. Both these feelings were frequently directed, at different times, toward the same object. These patients also had a tendency to choose objects onto whom they could project their unconscious devalued self (Lax 1975) as well as objects toward whom they could act out an idealized maternal role. The patients' pathology, to which there probably were precursors stemming from earlier phases of development, crystallized as a reaction to a specific constellation of internalized object relations (Kernberg 1966, 1976), namely, as a response to mother's libidinal unavailability and its consequences. The patients discussed in this chapter were at that time in the rapprochement subphase. This, as is well known from Mahler's studies, is a relatively difficult period in the life of the young child (Mahler et al. 1975). The "practicing" subphase (Mahler 1968, 1971, 1974), characterized by feelings of exuberance and power that found expression in the "love affair with the world," has come to an end. The child's emotional equilibrium is usually upset by the developmental sequelae. Among those, toilet training usually brings about tensions that may stimulate aggressive impulses. Omnipotent fantasies, related to anal negativism (whether retentive or projective), are sometimes held onto defensively. In more complicated cases anal submission may lead to various forms of masochism. "Shadowing" and "darting-away" behavior patterns are indicative of the conflict between the wish for reunion with mother and the fear of engulfment by her. This is the time when the child's growing awareness of separateness stimulates an increased need for mother's love and a wish to share with her. As is well known, the intensity of the toddler's "wooing" behavior toward mother can be used as an indicator of the magnitude of the rapprochement crisis. Only mother's loving acceptance of the child, of its ambivalence and ambitendency, as well as mother's support and encouragement, provides the necessary ambience for the further growth of autonomy (Mahler 1971). The synchrony of these factors is necessary for the attainment of normal resolution of the rapprochement crisis.

Analytic work with my patients indicated that their mothers were unable to respond with appropriate understanding, acceptance, and empathy to their child's typical, phase-specific conflicts and longings. Such maternal behavior no doubt evoked in the child feelings of anger and perhaps even rage. In such cases it is likely that mother unconsciously was experienced as bad and rotten. The child's conscious self-accusation of badness and rottenness is likely to reflect a reversal of these unconscious feelings. The patients' dreams and transference patterns provided evidence suggesting that mother's psychic equilibrium at that time was seriously disrupted by the trauma she experienced. This manifested itself in different ways.

Irene's mother was inconsistent in her behavior to the child and unpredictable in her reactions toward her daughter's spurts of independence. Mother sometimes reacted angrily, and at other times possessively held on to Irene. The child experienced mother's "clutching" as an invasion of her body autonomy and an interference with "darting-away" behavior. It is likely that mother's clutching expressed her need to hold on to her only living child, a reassurance stilling unconscious fears. Such maternal behavior, however, seems to have intensified Irene's age-specific negativism and led to increased power struggles and outbursts of rage. It also undermined Irene's healthy, narcissistic investment in her striving for independence. Mother's anger and clutching responses to Irene's striving for independence made the child feel that there was something wrong with her impulse, that it was a transgression against mother, and Irene therefore felt guilty about it. Eventually these interactions with mother became internalized and unconscious.

Following grandmother's death, the quality of mother's relationship to Nina changed. The child was now seen much more frequently as either good or bad, possibly indicating a breakdown in mother's libidinal object constancy. Thereafter, mother's hostile aggression toward Nina came to the fore, manifested in criticism and disparagement. The internalization of mother's attitudes, which formed a malignant introject, led to Nina's sense of "rottenness" and devaluation.

May's case, in which depression made mother emotionally unavailable to the child, depicts the most significant factor in the child–mother interaction leading to the development of rotten core pathology. Mother's emotional withdrawal becomes interpreted by the toddler as an expression of justified anger. Such persistent interactions evoke in the child a "hostile dependency" culminating in a sense of guilt that may result in the development of a "basic depressive mood" (Mahler 1966).

Since a young child is unable to comprehend the psychic or reality causes of mother's depression, it regards its own aggressive as well as libidinal strivings as the basis for mother's moods. A child may thus come to regard mother's emotional unavailability as a punishment for transgressions it construes to explain her attitude. Mother's emotional unavailability interferes also with the optimal normal progression of the separation–individuation processes. This is especially true if the child, due to identification with mother, begins to regard its impulses toward autonomy with the disapproval experienced from mother or ascribed to her.

Mahler (1971) points out that a stormy separation–individuation process results in the development of:

> *an unassimilated foreign body, a "bad" introject* in the intrapsychic emotional economy. In the effort to eject this "bad" introject, derivatives of the aggressive drive come into play and there seems to develop an increased proclivity *to identify with,* or *to confuse, the self-representation with the "bad" introject. If this situation prevails during the rapprochement subphase, then aggression may be unleashed in such a way as to inundate or sweep away the "good" object, and with it the "good" self-representation.* [Italics added, p. 412]

Following such a conflagration, a defensive regression may occur to the stage when object and self are less clearly differentiated, and are split into a "good" and "bad" self-object.

I suggest that the prevalence of such a conflictual intrapsychic state may result in the formation of the rotten core, which on the most primitive level represents the fusion of the "bad" (angry-rejecting) maternal introject with the "bad" (rejected) aspects of the self. Subsequently, experienced maternal anger fused with the child's projected anger becomes turned against the self. Under the impact of intensified separation anxiety, a regression may occur, and annihilation anxiety (Winnicott 1962) may become reactivated. Such a condition leads to further defensive splitting in an attempt to preserve the "good" object and the corresponding "good" self (Giovacchini 1972, Kernberg 1966, Mahler 1971). As a consequence, not only the object representation but also the self-representation remains (or becomes) divided. The rotten core represents that part of the self that was "hateable" to mother and the introjected part of mother "hateable" to the child. Continued identification with the aggressor (A. Freud 1936), that is, the internalized rejecting, hostile maternal attitudes, contributes to the establishment of the rotten core as a permanent substructure. Two aspects of this process can be recognized, each reinforcing the existing split in the self-representation.

First, identification with the maternal attitude toward the child fosters in the child an identical attitude toward itself. Thus maternal hostile aggression becomes self-aggression, and the self splits, turning against a part of itself now a victimized object. Aspects unacceptable to the aggressor-mother also become rejected by the child, merging with the primitive rotten core toward which the combined mother–child hatred has been directed.

The second aspect of the process of identification with the aggressor arises from the wish to obtain mother's love and to participate in her power. Identifications so motivated augment early introjections and the merger with the "good" mother and her beloved aspects. They contribute to the formation of the "good" self and its loved aspects.

These two aspects of the self, the rotten core and the "good" self, are formed during the developmental stage when polarization and splitting still prevail (Kernberg 1966, 1971, Mahler 1971). A preponderance of hostility in the vicissitudes of mother–child interaction at that time interferes with subsequent merging of these psychic substructures into a consolidated and integrated self-representation.

Internalization of mother's hostile aggression, self-destructive tendencies, depression, hopelessness, and helplessness, represents an additional aspect of these children's identification with the aggressor—mother. It is as if mother's psychic state persisted in her daughter, forming an introject that constantly interfered with the girl's sense of well-being. The dynamic continuation of these processes was indicated in the treatment situation by the conviction these patients held that change was not possible. The patients frequently felt desperate and expressed suicidal wishes.

The adaptive functioning of these patients and their capacity to make use of their resources led me to the assumption that the earliest stages of the mother–infant/toddler interaction was good enough to result in the formation of a "good" introject. The latter provided the basis for the unconscious identification with loved, admired, and even envied aspects of the maternal imago. Subsequently, selective identifications consonant with the conscious wishful self-image eventuated in satisfactory autonomous ego functioning in circumscribed areas. Mahler's (1966) finding, that autonomous ego functioning can remain unimpaired in children in spite of intense psychic conflicts, supports my observations and conclusions.

The self to which these patients referred as the "persona" or "outer shell" combined all the "good" identifications and internalizations. However, an apparent insufficiency of neutralized libido and aggression interfered with the development of an optimal narcissistic cathexis of this self. Thus adequate self-esteem was lacking. Harmonious interaction among ego, superego, and ego ideal remained impeded. The self-representation remained split because it contained the nonmetabolized rotten core.

I recognized early in my work with this type of patient the cleavage in their self-representation. I remained puzzled, however, by the apparent complete lack of malleability of the rotten core. Its poisonous effect continued in spite of the narcissistically gratifying attainments of the "outer self." Some answers to this enigma were provided by the analyses of the transference and also by the patients' continued and current relationships to their mothers. Thus, in spite of ungratifying and frustrating interactions, these patients persisted in their tenacious demandingness, holding on, and clinging. Likewise, behavior in the transference was demanding, pleading, and provocative.

Analysis of these patterns of relating revealed these patients' inordinate fear of separation and aloneness, which to them meant abandonment. Experiencing the rotten core mitigated these fears by maintaining the internalized object relationship with the malignant introject. Thus the pathological, destructive object constancy alleviated separation anxiety. The tenacious clinging to the relationship with mother was also fueled by an unconscious fantasy in which mother was idealized as the good fairy able to gratify the child in every conceivable way, probably representing the good mother of the symbiotic dual unity (Mahler 1971). The intensity of longing for this fairy-mother grew, depending on the extent of the mother's libidinal unavailability in the child's reality and the painful frustration this evoked. This fantasy persisted into adulthood. Analysis indicated that the patients justified mother's behavior by holding onto an unconscious conviction that her behavior was due to their own inability to evoke mother's goodness. Transgressions in fantasy and reality were used to "explain" mother's anger, aggression, and hatred. These patients felt mother hated them because they were "really rotten." The uncovering and analysis of the fairy-mother fantasy also elucidated the reasons for childhood behavior: it served to change what seemed like mother's incomprehensible anger into an understandable reaction.

Bound up with the rotten core, emanating from the "bad" introject and reinforced by subsequent identifications with the aggressor, the self-turned, hateful anger remained unrelieved in these patients in spite of the gratifications stemming from the well-functioning "outer self." Their continuous "pain of living" (a patient's phrase), stemming from the identification with the self-destructive elements in the aggressor, frequently led to intense suicidal wishes. However, the unconscious fantasy belief that sufficient suffering would bring atonement, and with it the rescue by the fairy-mother, kept these patients in their pervasive self-torture and prevented them from actually committing suicide. Nonetheless, the wish for relief brought by death was great. Expressed in the idiom of the Balinese myth, Rangda, who could not be vanquished, made those fighting her turn their daggers against themselves. In the case of my patients it meant continuous, painful self-injury.

I have not discussed the role of the father since he did not seem to have a direct role in the formation of the rotten core. He was, however, very significant for my patients in their childhood, and as a model for identification (see Chapter 8). Frequently the relationship with father was prematurely intense, complicating the subsequent oedipal involvement. Incestuous wishes added to these girls' feelings of guilt, and were used as further "excuses" for mother's "justified" anger.

5 Girls' Primary and Secondary Genital Feelings and Anxieties

Part I: Girls' Fear of Genital Mutilation and of Being Closed Up

There are two types of genital anxieties that a little girl may develop as a consequence of her erotic feelings. These occur during different developmental subphases. The first relates to the girl's fear that her genitals will be mutilated. The second develops toward the end of the negative oedipal subphase when the girl recognizes the significance of the penis she lacks. There is a temporal sequence in the development of these fears, but once both come into play, their vicissitudes commingle, and the dominant focus depends on various factors impinging on the girl's life. For a girl it is essentially her response to her own anatomy, and not her reaction to the male anatomy, that decisively effects the vicissitudes of her psychosexuality.

The Formation and Significance of the Body Image

Although Freud's concept of the body ego (1923a) has been seriously considered by his followers, psychoanalysts did not apply it to both sexes until the 1960s. Thus they did not acknowledge

that the unique anatomic characteristics of each sex must regis-
ter in the ego with their specificity from the beginning of formation. A careful reading of Freud's papers in which femininity is
discussed (1905, 1925, 1931, 1933, 1937) indicates that he did not
acknowledge that the uniquely female genitals of the little girl
must have a different impact on her body ego than the boy's have
on his body ego. Freud maintained, in spite of evidence to the
contrary (e.g., Horney 1924, Jones 1927, 1935, Klein 1932, Muller
1932), that both sexes are unaware of the existence of the vagina.
He did not acknowledge that the sensations a little girl experiences from all parts of her genitals must become part of her body
ego, even if they are repressed, denied, and/or distorted. The psychic representation of the girl's genitals will also be affected by
her physical and mental maturation as well as the specific vicissitudes of her experiences. Freud did not apply his own theory to
this aspect of a girl's development. This was probably due to the
unavoidable limitations imposed by the phallocentric Zeitgeist
that influenced him (Gay 1988, Young-Bruehl 1988, 1991).

Aspects of Primary Genital Feelings and Anxieties

Freud's view that the little girl's psychosexual development is an
inferior variant of the boy's development, and that femininity
begins with the momentous, narcissistic trauma of the girl's discovery of anatomic differences, has been questioned, challenged,
and disproved by many, among them Applegarth (1976), Barglow
and Schaefer (1976), Chasseguet-Smirgel (1976), Chehrazi (1986),
Fast (1978, 1979, 1984, 1990), Kleeman (1976), Mayer (1985,
1991a), Renik (1992), and Stoller (1964, 1968a), and so on. The
list is long and impressive.

Stoller (1968a,b, 1976) postulates a core female gender identity
that exists well before the discovery of anatomic differences and
the "phallic" phase. He indicates that sex assignment occurs at

birth and that parental attitudes are crucial for the establishment of the child's core gender identity. Early endogenous sensations emanating from the genitals and increasing with the maturation of the infant combine with exogenous stimulations stemming from parenting body care. The genital sensations resulting from these sensuous experiences cue the body ego of the infant of each sex differently. According to Stoller (1976), the early experiences of infant girls, which, due to anatomy, are different from those of boys, result in a primary, unquestioned acceptance by girls of their femaleness. This is supported by a research report (Mayer 1991b) in which 22-month-old girls given a choice between dolls with male or female genitals invariably chose the female doll as representing themselves and indicated that this was the doll they "liked better."

The infant may experience as erotic stimulation mother's ministrations during the daily routines of washing, dressing, diapering, and holding (Bonaparte 1948, Freud 1933). The touch of the mother's hands on its skin, especially the genitals, which are attended to more frequently, is usually experienced by the child as pleasurable. Under optimal circumstances these repetitive mother–infant events become a love game, during which the infant feels admired, mirrored, and cherished. In time they begin to represent maternal love tokens. They may be experienced as maternal seductions when the child starts fantasizing. This was postulated by Freud (1905) and Brunswick (1940), and is now generally accepted. Some researchers have found that vaginal lubrication in female infants corresponds in frequency to spontaneous erection in male babies (Kleeman 1976, Masters and Johnson 1966). One may speculate that these manifestations of sexual arousal are in part responses to mother's ministrations.

With increased motor coordination and the beginning of body exploration, the child experiences the pleasure of self-touching. During these explorations the genitals are discovered, and the child learns that it can give itself the kind of pleasure that it had passively experienced during mother's caregiving.

The toddler girl, during such self-explorations, discovers the different parts of her genitals: the clitoris, the labia, perineum, and eventually the vaginal entrance and introitus. When there is no interference by adults, these are pleasurable experiences that give the little girl a sense of mastery. She learns that she, herself, can give herself pleasure. This stimulates the development of independence. When the little girl finds that her fingers can push around and into the lower part of her vagina, she knows and begins to fantasize about the special place she has "inside." She experiences a sense of "possession." Erikson (1968) speaks of an "inner potential." Erikson (1950) and Roiphe and Galenson (1981) report on the preference for enclosed-space structures in the spontaneous block play of 14- to 16-month-old girls. It can be surmised that such block play expresses symbolically not only the little girl's psychic awareness of the structure of her genitals, but also indicates the progressive specificity in the formation of the body image.

The little girl's self-exploration, the excitement of discovering and self-pleasuring, her narcissistic investment in her own source of pleasure is possible only when the mother is accepting of her female child and delights in her. Under such optimal circumstances the little girl, with her mother's help, learns to name her genitals. This awareness increases her pleasure in herself. The mother's correct labeling of her daughter's genitals is an affirmation of what the little girl has and treasures (Lerner 1976, Mayer 1985, 1991a).

The little girl, like the little boy, starts out with the egocentric assumption: "Everyone must be just like me" (Freud 1905, Mayer 1985). For the little girl, as contrasted with the little boy, this notion is enhanced by her awareness that she and mother are alike. This knowledge is of momentous significance. Because of the "we" of mother and daughter, the little girl can fuse her infantile grandiosity with the omnipotent grandeur she ascribes to her mother. The sense of sameness with the powerful, loved (and also hated) mother precedes and supersedes later selective identifications. It is the source of pride in self and the root of the girl's healthy narcissism. It becomes the nucleus of healthy, nonsubmissive object relations. Knowing herself to be the "same as mother" mitigates the girl's feelings of her own limitations and frustrations, since she can bask in her mother's glory. The mother invites identification with herself to the extent to which she enjoys a healthy self-acceptance that in turn enables her to delight in her daughter. Such an optimal outcome is rather infrequent. As is well known, women and girl babies are devalued in many societies. This is typified by female infanticide practiced in China [*New York Times* 1992], the selling of girls into brothels, the burning of brides in India, and so on. According to a survey of expectant parents, 95 percent expressed a wish for a boy child [Frenkiel 1993].)

For the healthy girl toddler during the practicing subphase, she and mother are focal. The toddler's exploration is turned toward the outside world as well as the self. There is a spurt of independence and separation, with an insistence on "do it myself," but when the child becomes frightened by feeling alone and finding herself small and sometimes helpless, she returns to her mother for "refueling" (Mahler et al. 1975). Such refueling not only reinforces the little girl's sense of sameness with mother, it also increases her sense of strength because she identifies with mother's strength.

The growing independence from mother manifests itself in increased genital exploration and active volitional masturbation. During masturbation, which involves the whole genital area, lubrication occurs. The little girl now becomes more aware of a smell of her own and of her own pleasurable inner space. Richards (1992) indicated the role that voluntary perineal muscular contractions play in contributing to increased awareness and definition of inner genital structures and inner and outer genital sensations in the developing girl. Eventually the girl becomes aware that she can tighten and loosen the vulva and perineum. This awareness contributes to her feeling of mastery and control. (For discussions of masturbation in girls, see Bonaparte [1948], Brunswick [1940], Clower [1975, 1976], Greenacre [1950a], Kleeman [1971, 1975], and Spitz [1949, 1952, 1962].)

Even under optimal circumstances, however, a little girl develops a fear that something may occur to interfere with the pleasure she derives from playing with and stimulating her genitals. This may be due in part to conscious and unconscious memories of unpleasurable genital sensations resulting from parental cleansing practices, such as burning from soap or other disinfectants, or "rough handling," or from minor genital irritations. The little girl's fears may also be due to seeing a boy's genitals, which lack a vulva with an opening, and to her fantasizing that this is due to a boy's being "closed up" (Mayer 1985). Likewise, fears may result from guilt stimulated by incestuous fantasies. In addition, the limitations a parent may set on masturbation can become a source of acute fear. It must be acknowledged that in the prevailing atmosphere a little girl, probably more so than a little boy, is still discouraged, and sometimes even intimidated by verbal threats and physical force, to desist from masturbation.

The little girl's primary genital anxiety[1] is the fear of something "bad" happening to her genitals. This is frequently expressed by a fear of losing part of her genitals, being "closed up" and "sealed over." The little girl dreads losing access to all parts of her genitals, which she enjoys and wants to continue enjoying freely (Glover and Mendell 1982, Jacobson 1937, Mayer 1985, Wilkinson 1991). This is understandable since the little girl's enjoyment of her sexuality depends on her free access to an intact vulva, with its opening between the labia as well as its vaginal opening.

---

1. (Mayer [1985] refers to the girl's fears that her own genitals may be damaged as "true castration anxiety." I use the phrase "primary genital anxiety" for semantic reasons, since neither the fantasied mutilations nor those inflicted upon girls in reality constitute a castration. Mayer made an important contribution by drawing attention to this neglected topic of psychoanalysis, namely, the differentiation between fear of damage to one's own genitals and the fantasied fear of loss of a penis.)

Clinical Examples

A 3-year-old patient who had great masturbation conflicts expressed in a dream her fear and horror at what would happen if she could not "play with herself." In the dream her thighs were sewn together. When she told the dream, she whispered, "I couldn't touch anything. I was so scared." She spent a number of sessions playing with a doll whose thighs she tied together, and who sat and cried because that made her so unhappy. At the end of each session the patient sometimes "set the doll free" and sometimes left her tied up.

The following dream was reported by a patient who was a student in a course on contemporary views regarding female psychosexual development. "I was masturbating and getting excited and suddenly I was changed into a mermaid—there was no opening whatsoever, there was no way I could touch myself—I felt terrified." The patient was silent for a while and then marked, "I guess it was to teach me a lesson. I mean to acknowledge . . . I felt it was so much nonsense . . . all this talk about women 'being open,' having an 'inner space.' Imagine being like a mermaid, all closed up. . . . "

The following vignette, reported by a colleague, indicates how a healthy 3-year-old attempts to resolve her concerns about the nature and integrity of her genitals.

Franny lately has been most enamored with the Little Mermaid, wearing a Little Mermaid nightgown, loving the video story, pretending she is Ariel, and so forth. We were riding in the car one day and Franny said she had to peepee. We asked if she could wait a little while to get to a convenient stopping point. As she waited with mild impatience, she made up a song about peepee, enjoying being silly: "Animals peepee, cars peepee, trucks peepee." So I asked her, "How does Ariel [the Mermaid] peepee?" Franny's cheerful answer was: "She first turns into a person, then she sits down on the toilet and just does a peepee." She added a further explanation: "And her tail goes up over her chest."

In contrast to the patient who dreamed she was changed into a mermaid and "closed up," Franny only played at being a mermaid.

She had the healthy conviction of being a person, that is, having genitals and excretory organs.

An outstandingly beautiful and totally frigid patient in her late twenties spent many hours recalling the ritualized punishment inflicted on her in childhood for having repeatedly been caught masturbating before going to sleep. She was about 10 when it happened. At bedtime, under supervision, after she washed she had to kneel and confess her depravity in having masturbated. She then had to beg God to keep her from sinning again and pray for forgiveness. To "help her," so she was told, each evening the girl was slapped on her genitals with a wet towel, then a kind of chastity belt made of bandages was put on her. She had to sleep on her back, spread-eagle, her feet and hands loosely tied to the bedposts. Both parents and a governess participated in these nightly rituals. The patient reported that she initially struggled "to get free," but finally submitted. Somehow her sexual feelings disappeared. She became listless and docile. Her parents considered this behavior appropriate for a "good girl." Ostensibly, docility brought this patient into treatment: her husband wanted her "cured of frigidity." The patient, who recalled having had sexual feelings as a child, said: "They closed me up and it worked." The patient was referring to the "chastity belt" put on her each evening.

In Western society, even to this day, two myths prevail about little girls' psychosexuality. The popular view has it that little girls are "sugar and spice and everything nice," that is, pure, sweet, and asexual. *Sleeping Beauty* depicted this fantasy of the chaste girl who "sleeps" until a man awakens her sexuality. On the other hand, Freud (1933), maintained that through the "phallic" phase "a little girl is a little man" (p. 118) in her psychosexual development, a doctrine espoused by his followers until recently. Thus, though psychoanalysis endowed the little girl with sexuality, it was not with feminine sexuality. According to Freud, little girls masturbated, but less often than boys, and they did so by exclusively stimulating the clitoris. However, Freud maintained, when girls discover the inferiority of the clitoris to the penis, they suffer a narcissistic trauma of such magnitude that it resulted, in most instances, in repression of their masturbation and active sexuality. Clower's (1975, 1976) findings, which indicate that girls continue to masturbate through latency and adolescence, disprove Freud's contention.

Freud's postulations about the sexuality of little girls were rejected by Victorian and twentieth century society not for lack of accuracy, but rather to maintain the age-old mythic ideal of the virtuous little girl, pure and docile, who was an asexual little angel. In order for society to maintain this ideal, masturbation by girls was strongly disapproved frequently severely punished, its very existence cloaked in secrecy.

I shall present data on female genital mutilations in Western and other societies, as well as some comments by Freud, to depict the cultural, unspoken motivations underlying attitudes toward female sexuality and the means used to curtail it. The clergy and the medical profession, especially during the Victorian era, regarded masturbation and manifestations of female sexuality as a medical problem. This problem was often "treated" and "corrected" in little girls, adolescents, and even grown women by amputation or cautery of the clitoris, or by "miniature chastity belts" achieved by "sewing the labia together to get the clitoris out of reach" (Gornick and Moran 1972). The history of clitoridectomies performed in the United States, England, and Western Europe in past centuries and the early part of this century has been discussed by Spitz (1952), Barker-Benfield (1975), and Scull and Faureau (1986). In the United States the last recorded clitoridectomy for curing masturbation was performed on a 5-year-old girl in 1948 (Ehrenreich and English 1978). As late as 1985 female clitoridectomies have been reported in England and France (E. Shaw 1985).

Clitoridectomies were introduced in England in the 1850s by Isaac Baker Brown, a gynecologist-surgeon, as a cure for masturbation, which was thought to bring about insanity, hysteria, and epilepsy. The operation was performed on thousands of girls and women. Medical documents give clear evidence that clitoridectomies were advocated explicitly to reduce female sexual impulses and masturbation, both of which were viewed as dangerous, unwanted, and unfeminine (Sherfey 1996). Regarding clitoridectomies, Showalter (1985), in *The Female Malady*, states that "the mutilation, sedation, and psychological intimidation . . . seem to have been an efficient if brutal form of reprogramming . . . of girls and women" (p. 68).

The *British Medical Journal* (1867) reports the following procedure of the genital operation performed under chloroform anesthesia to prevent masturbation.

> Two instruments were used: the pair of hooked forceps which Mr. Brown always uses in a clitoridectomy, and a cautery iron. . . . The clitoris was seized by the forceps in the usual manner. The thin edge of the red hot iron was then passed around its base until the organ was severed from its attachments, being partly cut or sawn, and partly torn away. After the clitoris was removed, the nymphae were got rid of, the operation was brought to a close by taking the back of the iron and sawing the surfaces of the labia and the other parts of the vulva which had escaped the cautery, and the instrument was rubbed down backwards and forwards till the parts were more effectually destroyed than when Mr. Brown uses the scissors to effect the same result. [pp. 407–408]

Whereas clitoridectomies in the Western world were performed selectively, at the behest of fathers and/or husbands, ritual genital mutilations on all girls were performed for millennia and are still practiced in Africa, Australia, South America, and the Arab world (Williams 1990). These mutilations are of various kinds: *circumcision* (sunna), in which the labia minora and the tip or part of the clitoris are removed; *excision* or clitoridectomy, in which the labia and the entire clitoris are removed; *infibulation*, in which, after complete excision, both sides of the vulva are sewn together (Barry 1984). Thus the vagina is completely sealed. Only a small opening is left for urine and/or menstrual flow. Access to the vagina can be regained only by tearing the vulva apart with the husband's penis, more often his flint or knife. When infibulation is practiced, the vulva is sewn up after each childbirth.

These practices, according to the 1993 Hosken Report, affect 90 million women (see also *New York Times* 1990). Female genital mutilations, in spite of their traumatic, destructive, crippling consequences for female sexuality and psychic well-being (Konner 1990, Williams 1990), have mostly been kept secret by anthropologists and the Western medical profession. Among psychoanalysts, Spitz (1952) and Bonaparte (1948) are the only ones known to me to have reported on these practices before the 1960s, and Kulish (1991) reports on them currently. Bonaparte considered female genital mutilations, and clitoridectomies in particular, as ways employed to feminize the female. Her thinking was influenced by Freud's "transfer theory" of female sexuality. Bonaparte (1948) stated: "The excision of the clitoris, which many tribes practice, seemed to Freud a way of seeking to further "feminize" the female by removing this cardinal vestige of her masculinity. Such operations, as he once said to me, must be intended to complete the 'biological castration' of the female which Nature, in the eyes of these tribes, has not sufficiently effected" (p. 153).

Róheim (1945) presents clinical material indicating that adult Western males react to the clitoris with castration anxiety. According to anthropologists and psychoanalysts (e.g., Assaad 1980, Bachofen 1861, Barry 1984, Bettelheim 1954, Bonaparte 1948, Lightfoot-Klein 1989, Shaw 1985), the predominant reason for the mutilation of the external female genitals is the intention to curb or abolish female sexual desire and sexuality, which is viewed by males (and women who identify with them) as unbound, uncontrollable, and dangerous. In addition, the older woman's unconscious or preconscious envy of the young, maturing girl may be a factor in the perpetuation of female genital mutilation. Clitoridectomies assuage male castration anxieties and the fear of so-called "female masculine aggression." As can be seen, for the Western as well as the so-called "primitive" world, the conscious and unconscious motivation for the mutilations of female genitals are the same: the fear of female sexuality. Though these views are dictated primarily by patriarchal concerns, they find an echo in

Deutsch's (1944, 1945) and Bonaparte's (1948) descriptions and proscriptions for *proper* female sexual behavior.

The "threatening atmosphere" with which the little girl's sexuality was—and frequently still is—greeted reinforces the internalization of forbidding parental attitudes. It leads to unconscious and conscious fantasies that find expression in girls' fears of being "closed up," "sealed over," or deprived of parts of their genitals. Though probably associated with different unconscious fantasies, girls' fears have the same psychic roots as boys' castration anxiety, namely, actual terror (Rangell 1991) that their genitals might be mutilated or destroyed. Seeing the genitals of the opposite sex may, for girls and boys, serve to confirm unconsciously and/or consciously the potential validity of their fears. Although children's terror may be reinforced by repeated parental threats, it may also be fueled by children's guilt over unconscious wishes to rob the parent of each sex of her or his valuable sexual organs, and by sadistic fantasies of their destruction. There is, however, a significant difference between the boy's reality and the girl's. Though children of both sexes continue to be threatened, the castration of boys belongs to the remote past and has always been limited in number. In contradistinction, genital mutilation of all girls is a current actuality in many parts of the world, and genital mutilations on a limited scale have been practiced on girls in the Western world until quite recently. It is likely that such practices may still continue.

Psychoanalytic thought has for many years addressed itself to the boy's complex castration anxieties, developing theoretical explanations and curative technical procedures. This has not occurred with regard to the girl's primary genital anxiety, namely, her fear about the safety of her own genitals, and the consequences of such anxiety. I suspect this "neglect" was in part due to the phallocentric concepts of Freud's psychoanalytic theory, to his misunderstanding of early female psychosexual development, and to the impact of the generalized disavowal of feminine sexuality in little girls. The current study of feminine psychosexuality began and was stimulated by the recognition of primary femininity and the acknowledgment of infantile feminine sexuality, which involves the whole external genital area (Blum 1976, Mayer 1985, 1991a, Renik 1992, Schuker and Levinson 1991, Stoller 1968a, b, 1976, 1986).

Primary genital anxiety in girls derives from current overt or veiled threats directed toward girls' sexuality or measures taken to prevent its manifestations, especially masturbation. These threats become internalized. The intrapsychic prohibitions are reinforced by tales and cultural mores concerning the enactments of genital mutilations, which are consciously and unconsciously transmitted from generation to generation (Blum 1988). We must acknowledge that major segments of society worldwide still do not recognize and accept the existence of sexuality in infants, toddlers, and young girls. Thus infantile accidental self-exploration, which in time leads to the intentional exploration of all genitals and brings about orgastic masturbation in 3-year-old girls (Kleeman 1975, 1976), is usually denied and frequently actively interfered with and forbidden. These societal and parental attitudes, often forcefully imposed by actions, lead to the toddler girl's primary genital anxiety.

The little girl, like the little boy, has a narcissistic investment in "her source of self-pleasure." Consequently, the danger of losing it at the behest of her love object, and the internalization of this threat, leads to serious intrapsychic conflicts. Some of the grave pathological consequences that may occur are hysteria (Rangell 1991), frigidity, and in some cases, the deadening of the self.

Clinical Examples

The following dream[2] fragment and associations depict dread of genital mutilation related to conflict and fear of punishment for masturbation. The patient, Ann, is in the third year of her analysis; she is in her early twenties.

---

2. I wish to thank Rosemarie Gaeta, CSW, for sharing this material with me.

The dream: "My friend, Jan, is showing me with great excitement a pair of shoes which she bought. The shoes are fancy, elaborate, Indian-like. They are cut off, the toe is cut off and it is square. They are an exceptional pair of shoes: at the cut-off toe they have a simulated Hope diamond." Ann said, "I knew it could not be the real Hope diamond because the shoes were bought on a sale. Nevertheless, it still was wonderful."

Associations: "Jan did not get the diamond as a love gift—she got it on a sale." Ann implies it therefore has a diminished value. Ann cannot make up her mind about whether she values or devalues this Hope diamond. She is conflicted. . . . The Hope diamond is also associated with hope, but what is the hope? Ann implies the hope is not a real hope. Ann refers to the shoes as "circumcised," and then denies it. She says:

"Remember, there is no tip on the shoe, the shoe is circumcised—the source of pleasure is taken away. If the clitoris is removed and the labia are closed up, then there certainly is not going to be any pleasure. When I masturbated, the labia became enlarged. This was bad since it was a visible proof of masturbation. The doctors could see it—I feel ashamed of my labia, ashamed of my body, ashamed of masturbation. The doctors, by seeing the longer labia, would know I masturbated. Maybe I will have an operation on my genitals, a type of circumcision to make me into a girl—corrective surgery, a punishment for masturbation. I have had an anxiety that something will happen to my genitals as a punishment. My fantasy came true, I had to have a hymenectomy. There was something wrong with my genitals, with my vagina, it was closed up, a kind of chastity belt." (Actually, this surgical intervention was performed when the patient was 20, because she could not have coitus.)

Beth, a patient in her thirties, does not have an orgasm during coitus but has orgasms while masturbating with the following fantasy.

They are preparing the girl for the master by getting her to be extremely aroused sexually. While she is so excited, they put a chastity belt on her and tie her spread-eagle to the bed. The girl is almost frantic with excitement but can do nothing to get relief. They and the master enjoy watching her sexual torment.

Analysis revealed threats during childhood about the evils of masturbation. Beth recalls irrigations of the genital area with some mildly burning fluid. These were done by her father. She submitted to these procedures with embarrassment but did not struggle. She says, "It was unpleasant-pleasant but father did it . . . he said to cure me . . . I did not know of what. . . . " It occurred, she thinks, between the ages of 6 and 8. After dinner she had to undress and get into a "sitz bath" with her legs spread apart . . . father inspected and irrigated the genital area and the vagina. In the masturbation fantasy Beth is deprived and tormented. Yet she gets from others the sexual excitement she craves. She thus bears no responsibility. The chastity belt assures her innocence.

Linda, a married, childless woman in her forties has had fantasies since childhood that her genitals are deformed. While visiting, Linda noticed that the 12-year-old daughter of her friend had bloodstained panties. Linda looked at the panties with fascination and horror. She fantasized that her friend mutilated the daughter's genitals. Linda felt agitated and extremely anxious. She had to cut the visit short.

Associating to this experience, Linda described her own mother as "prim and ladylike." Mother used to admonish Linda by saying, "If you touch yourself down there, your fingers will fall off." Linda never touched or looked "down there." She masturbated by rubbing a pillow against the whole genital area. She was always conflicted about "doing it," and afraid she would be discovered. Analysis indicated that Linda's fantasies that her genitals are deformed appears to have been a displacement stemming from her mother's threat that her fingers would fall off, deforming her hands and thus revealing her transgression.

Bonaparte (1948), discussing actual ritual genital mutilation of females, stated that in Western societies, on the whole, "anatomic integrity of females is maintained, *but in the psychic domain our civilization practices mutilations*" (italics added, p. 160).

Part II: Roots of Girls' Penis Envy in the Negative Oedipal Phase

For the little girl, the period of life from approximately 18 months until about 3 years is of utmost significance. It is unique and different from the same time span for the boy. The little girl at this time experiences the confluence of her erotic feelings toward mother, which are pervasive during the negative oedipal subphase; the storms of the rapprochement crisis; and the recognition, due to cognitive and emotional maturation, of the significance of the anatomic differences between the sexes.

During the negative oedipal subphase, under optimal circumstances, when self-pleasuring is not interfered with, the masturbation fantasies of the little girl have mother as her erotic object. These fantasies can have active and passive aims, the girl taking various roles in her imagined erotic interactions with mother. (Brunswick 1940, Laufer 1986). During this period the girl's sense of sameness with mother leads her to ascribe to mother a genital like her own and the sexual excitement with which she is familiar. This period of intense erotic feelings for mother usually coincides with the typical rapprochement crises. The latter are characterized by great angers caused by conflicts aroused by the simultaneous strivings for attachment and spurts of autonomy (Mahler et al. 1975).

An experience becomes meaningful when one is able to absorb it by connecting and integrating it with one's conscious reality and one's unconscious psychic world. Thus the anatomic differences between herself and the boy become a psychic reality for the little girl when she is developmentally ready to perceive and acknowledge the significance of these differences. She then recognizes by analogy based on her experience with protruding objects during masturbation, that "father/boy has 'that' [penis] which can be put in, and which will fit into the hole [vagina] that mother and she have (quote of a 3 1/2-year-old patient). Since this recognition occurs during the girl's phase of erotic strivings toward mother, the negative oedipal subphase, the girl feels envious, deprived, and very sad because "he has and can give to mother" what she lacks (same patient's quote). This is also the time the little girl no longer can avoid recognizing the uniqueness of the father–mother relationship. She can no longer deny, and is therefore forced to acknowledge consciously, what she may have known unconsciously, namely, that the boy has the potentiality she lacks for the type of relationship with mother she would also like to have. The desire for a penis derives from these psychic experiences, which lead to penis envy. At this stage penis envy is based on the love feelings of the little girl for her mother.

The so-called depression observed in a little girl subsequent to her discovery that she lacks a penis (Galenson and Roiphe 1976, Mahler 1966) appears to be related primarily to the girl's awareness of what not having a penis means in terms of her relationship with mother. It evokes in the little girl the unconscious and possibly preconscious fantasy and feeling that she cannot have and give her erotically loved mother the genital satisfaction a boy could. This may also evoke the girl's fears, conscious and/or unconscious, of losing mother's love to those who can satisfy her, namely, those who have penises. The girl now ascribes the possibility of such a danger to her lack of a penis. Thus the desire for a penis and consequent penis envy seem primarily related to a fear of losing the love of the loved mother.

Under optimal circumstances the girl does not feel incomplete or damaged. She values her genitals since she derives pleasure from them and especially since she knows she is "made" like mother, whom she admires and whom she has endowed with potency and power. At this juncture in her development, however, the girl's psychic focus is on what she lacks. She now knows that she does not have "everything" (Fast 1990), and especially that she does not have "what it takes" to gratify mother sexually as father does and the boy could.

Following her recognition of the consequences of genital difference, the girl experiences her relationship with mother as having changed. She attributes this change to her lack of a penis. This assumption usually evokes a sense of narcissistic injury and feelings of inferiority. The girl's unconscious and conscious fantasies at this time, though replete with a multitude of variations, have as their predominant theme "explanations" as to why, how, and when she was deprived of a penis. These fantasies are defensive as well as adaptive measures to cope with the intrapsychic sense of catastrophe brought about by the simultaneously experienced narcissistic injury and the imagined loss of her love object. The fantasy of penis loss is usually placed in the past (Mayer 1995, Renik 1992).

At the waning of the negative oedipal subphase, changes in the psychic reality of the little girl impact upon her dynamic intrapsychic constellation, bringing forth a profound sense of sadness. This feeling state may also include elements of mourning.

Even under optimal circumstances the sense of "we" the little girl felt in her relationship with mother now gives way to an overwhelming recognition of "they," "the couple," "he and she," with the little girl feeling left out. No wonder she seems "downcast," very "low key," sometimes irritable, unable to find a place for herself, and frequently "invading" the parental bedroom. The girl's feeling state at this time, however, does not represent a true depression, unless the assumption or observation is made that the hostile and aggressive feelings the girl experiences toward the father/boy have been repressed and turned against the self.

Secondary genital feelings and anxieties relate to an unconscious fantasy and/or belief, held by the girl, that she was deprived of a penis. Penis envy arises and derives from the girl's painful knowledge that she does not have what it takes to gratify mother genitally. Consequently, the girl fears the loss of her mother's love, and possibly even of mother, her primary love object. These feelings are expressed in fears of abandonment. It thus appears that penis envy at this stage is motivated by the conscious and unconscious fear of losing the love of the loved mother.

Clinical Examples

The following are process notes taken during the middle phase of Janet's analysis. She was expressing penis envy feelings, seemingly stimulated by her perception that she was unfairly treated at work. This was not the first time that such feelings appeared.

J: I thought father wanted a boy. I would have wanted to be *the* boy father wanted. He never said he wanted a boy. I can't say my parents indicated this in any way, not even when Jackie was born. The baby was supposed to be named Jack after some dead relative if it was a boy, so they named her Jackie. I did not want to be a girl because I did not like to wear dresses. I liked playing boys' games. I felt mother let father down by not having a boy.

RL: This seems to suggest that you felt and believed mother was responsible for making boys or girls. As if it was in mother's power to do so.

J: *Janet was silent for a while, then:*) Perhaps I was angry that mother did not give me a penis. (*Silent for a long while and then continues*) This idea does not feel right . . . it's like fantasy. When I was a little child mother held me close and I had sexual feelings for her. I now say sexual. I don't know . . . then it was exciting and close and I wanted . . . it would be wonderful . . . to sort of get into her, like being one . . . Mother did not approve of all this . . . and so she cut off the penis. . . . These were erotic desires for mother. . . . I loved her more than anyone. (*Silent, and after a long while, as if she was coming out of a dream*) Oh, this talk is nonsense. It must sound crazy. Whoever heard of such things. Girls are girls and that's how they are made.

Liz is a 20-year-old girl with a beautiful face and lovely raven-black curly hair. She is about fifty pounds overweight, has a barrel-like body, and dresses in unbecoming, colorless slacks and shirts. She only recently gave up wearing a cap with a large visor, which hid her hair and covered her face. She is in the fifth month of her analysis.

Liz is an unhappy girl torn by her intense love for each of her divorced parents. She lacks a firm sense of self and has a confused sense of gender identity. Liz hides her sexual desires behind walls of fat, saying: "I do not know what my sexual preference is. I know that if I were to make a decision now it would be a political decision, to be a lesbian. I don't want to do that. But I am so disgusted with my body I cannot see myself at ease in bed with a man. He'd be disgusted with me too."

Liz, at 9, was seriously traumatized by her parents' divorce. She felt, and still feels, that the departure of her father was a betrayal of her trust. Father not only left home, he also moved to a different country, communicating infrequently with the family. Though she still can't explain it, Liz blames herself for the divorce and feels responsible for it.

Subsequent to Liz's feeling abandoned by father, a libidinal regression from the positive to the negative oedipal position appears to have taken place. Liz turned to mother for the support and love she so badly needed. Mother, however, leaned on Liz to bolster her own failing self-esteem and to fill the emotional vacuum created by the loss of her husband. Simultaneously with these events, Liz, in spite of her psychic pain, experienced a spurt in her intellectual growth. She became quite precocious and excelled in schoolwork. At this time Liz began to overeat.

Liz reported the following dream during a session that started with a long silence, followed by a lot of hesitation and great embarrassment:

I am in bed with mother. I am on top of her, my mother . . . and I make those movements, you know, like the boy/man, and I am terribly sexually excited. . . . I don't know whether it is really so, or whether I am asleep. I think I wake up and fall asleep, and have an orgasm, and wake up and find I am masturbating. I always masturbate like a boy. I rub against a pillow and make movements like a boy. I don't like masturbating like a girl. I mean I do not like to touch my genitals. I like masturbating lying on my tummy with a pillow between my legs rubbing against it.

Liz's masturbation fantasies have many elements frequent in adolescents. They are filled with violence. The girl "is a slave used and abused, and thus has no responsibility for the sexual relationship."

Liz, in a quasi-sophisticated way, says:

> I somehow know these fantasies must be related to my father. I loved him very much. I still do. I remember as a young girl, maybe 5, sitting on his lap and rubbing against him. I always was very sexual and I had feelings in my vagina. . . . When I rubbed against him, I now know, I must have masturbated. I would ask him if he knew what I was doing. Then I would run away. He always kissed me on my mouth. Then there was a time, I guess I was 8, and I did not like it anymore when he kissed me on my mouth. It felt bad. He was very angry that I did not want him to kiss me that way and said: "You no longer are my little girl." I thought that was why he went away.
>
> I am mixed up. I do not know whether I feel like a girl or like a boy. I always wanted to be a boy. When I was little I loved to get into bed with my mother and hug and kiss with her a lot . . . and even now, when I return home, I want to do it. Mother says I am too big for that.

In contrast with the above cases, the following material comes from lesbian patients who have entered analysis for reasons other than the wish to change their sexual orientation. These cases highlight the muted dynamic shifts that take place in the course of normal psychosexual development during the negative oedipal phase.

M[3], now in her early thirties, recalls having idealized mother and having good feelings about herself until the birth of a brother who became mother's favorite. M. was about 4 or 5 at the time. She remembers feeling envious and wanting to be a boy because mother preferred a boy, not because she, M., devalued girls/women. M. felt that her valuation of women was attested by her choice of her love object: mother/woman.

M. became a lesbian as an adult. For her to be heterosexual had the following unconscious significance: it meant, first and foremost,

3. I wish to thank Dr. Phyllis Hopkins for sharing this material with me.

giving up mother as her erotic love object. It also implied identifying with mother in the choice of a man (brother/father) as a preferred erotic love object. Such a change signified to M. a devaluation of women to which she consciously refused to subscribe. M. as a child experienced mother's preference for brother as a narcissistic blow. In spite of herself, however, and unknowingly, M. unconsciously did identify with what she fantasied and perceived as mother's preference for males. She was a "tomboy," and thus a son to her father in the role she played as his companion. M. eventually chose a career considered "masculine" in which she was extremely successful.

K., a woman in her thirties, sought treatment because she suffered from an extreme writing inhibition. Telling her story, K. recalled her envy of brother, who became the "head of the house" when father abandoned the family. She was 7 and brother was 15. After father deserted them, mother not only favored brother as she always had, but she now also consulted with him in making decisions. K. felt envious, jealous, and unwanted. She felt there was no place for her, and she felt worthless. She continued, however, to idealize mother, whose devotion to the children bordered on self-sacrifice. Brother at 18 left the family to join the Merchant Marine. Shortly thereafter his contact with mother and her stopped. K. used her ingenuity to dispel mother's sadness, which she shared. Mother and daughter now slept in one bed. Mother intensified her work to provide K. with the best possible education. K. started wearing brother's discarded clothes.

When analysis began, K. looked and dressed like a young sailor. She was not consciously aware of her masculine identification and the conflicts this engendered. She consciously felt anger at men, who, she believed, betrayed mother and her. K. maintained men were untrustworthy. She highly esteemed her mother and identified with her values. K. spoke with great pain about her mother's continued hope that brother would return. She, K., felt he was a scoundrel, like all men. Prompted by an unconscious identification with mother's wishes, K. assumed a protective role toward mother, which K. and mother considered "masculine."

After a brief heterosexual relationship with a married man who exploited her, K. chose women as her love objects. In these relationships K.'s role alternated: she was both the child and the mother. K.

regretted not having a penis, which she believes would have given more pleasure to her lover.

Even under optimal circumstances, the girl's sense of denigration stems from her self-comparison with the boy, "who has what it takes." It is the girl's sometimes conscious and sometimes unconscious fantasy conviction that not having a penis brings about maternal devaluation. The girl, unable to distinguish clearly between fantasy and reality, attributes the origin and cause of her sense of debasement to mother's preference for the man/boy (father–brother) who has the penis. Hurt and angry, the girl eventually projects onto mother the feelings she had attributed to mother. After this psychic process occurs, the girl considers the penisless mother as she thought mother considered her, that is, as "inferior to the father," who has the penis that can satisfy either of them. The fantasy of being spurned by mother fuels the girl's angry dejected feelings toward herself and mother. During this period such feelings frequently find expression in violent temper tantrums. The little girl, flooded by these fantasies and emotions may turn to the father, seeking consolation and satisfaction.

The so-called "turning away from mother" (Freud 1931, 1933) is a defensive attempt by the girl to change a passive experience, namely, the fantasy of mother leaving her for father/brother, into an active seeking of the object that could satisfy her, just as he satisfies mother. This is the impetus that promotes the girl's changed relationship to father: the onset of the positive oedipal phase. The erotic feelings and longings of which mother heretofore has been the object are transferred by the girl to the father, who now becomes her love object. The little girl fantasizes and wants father to give to her what he gives to mother, the satisfaction possible only by the use of his penis. The little girl who had wanted to bear mother's child and give mother a child (Brunswick 1940, Freud 1933), and who regarded mother as the sole creator, now knows that the baby comes from what mother and father "do together." She, too, wants to do "that" with father, and she now wants a baby with him and by him.

Secondary genital feelings and anxieties encompass feelings of dejection because of the fantasied loss of maternal love, penis envy, and devaluation. These are the specific psychic experiences of little girls, culminating when the "negative oedipal" constellation comes to an end. They are evoked when the erotic longings and fantasies that the little girl has directed toward her mother are confronted by the reality of mother's unattainability as an erotic object. The little girl attributes this fact to her lack of a penis.

The girl experiences the psychic conflagration of her erotic feelings toward mother while enmeshed in the conflictual rapprochement subphase, which adds intensity to the mother–daughter loving and hostile interactions. The merging tendencies of the girl, which were reinforced by the sense of "sameness with mother" and by having had mother as her erotic object, are curtailed when the girl painfully discovers she "doesn't have what it takes" to gratify mother. The fantasied rejection by mother, which pains and angers the girl and makes her turn to father as her new erotic object, can also, under optimal circumstances, promote a spurt in the girls' growth toward separation, individuation, and autonomy. Such a positive outcome, however, is possible only when the girl's primary sense of intactness and pride as a female are sufficiently strong to overcome secondary genital feelings and anxieties brought about by penis envy.

Father's loving and positive acknowledgement of the girl's femaleness, and therefore desirability as a female, is essential in this process. Father's affirmation of the girl's femininity and his manifest valuation of the mother are necessary to enable the girl, once again, to identify with the mother and with her womanly qualities. Father's valuation of the girl's femininity contributes to her healthy narcissism, depleted by feelings of penis envy. Likewise, crucial at this time is mother's affirmation and encouragement of the girl's femininity, and mother's loving acceptance of the girl in spite of the latter's hostility and ambivalence.

These dynamic constellations characterize the girl's psychic world as she enters the father-related positive oedipal phase. Her primary and secondary genital feelings and anxieties will commingle. The vicissitudes of the transition leading to change of love object, and those occurring during the positive oedipal conflagration, will determine the ascendancy of either complex of feelings and/or the defensive use of each. Thus, depending upon the girl's outer reality and her psychic experiences, the interplay and vicissitudes of primary and secondary genital feelings and anxieties during the positive oedipal phase will determine whether the outcome will be a healthy or pathological one, possibly even the specific type of pathology. Analytic work indicates that a certain type of female homosexuality may be related to anxieties and/or regression to the negative oedipal phase.

Addendum

Freud's theory of female psychosexual development, and especially his pronouncements regarding penis envy, no longer meet with general acceptance even among his followers. For views of the early dissenters, Abraham, Jones, Horney, Jacobson, and Brunswick, see Chapter 1.

Current views emphasize various motivations of penis envy, which come to the fore as a result of deepened analyses. As a consequence of these findings, analysts no longer maintain that penis envy is the bedrock a woman's analysis can reach. To the contrary, analytic exploration of the conflicts and of the dynamics expressed via penis envy leads to psychic integration and a deepened and more complete sense of femininity.

Review of the Literature

Thompson (1942) maintained that for our society the penis symbolizes and represents the privileged gender. She stated: "Characteristics and inferiority feelings which Freud considered to be specifically female and biologically determined can be explained as developments arising in and growing out of Western women's historic situation of underprivilege, restriction of development, insincere attitude toward the sexual nature, and social and economic dependency" (p. 64). Thompson found evidence of woman's underprivileged position prevalent in all societies, in the roots of languages, laws, customs, and religion. She considered societal and cultural factors as the cause of the devaluation of women. According to Thompson, penis envy stems from a woman's feeling of being demeaned. Consequently, women's desires and wishes to have what it takes to change from a position of inferiority to one of superiority are understandable.

Melanie Klein (1957) pointed out on the basis of her analysis of female patients that penis envy can be traced back to envy of the mother's breast.

Kohut (1959) maintained that femaleness cannot be explained simply as a retreat from disappointed maleness. He (1971) viewed penis envy the same way he viewed other manifest symptoms of narcissistic disturbance. Thus, according to Kohut, symptoms of penis envy once understood as a reaction to inferiority feelings can be seen as having the common features characteristic of narcissistic problems. Kohut also assumed that penis envy results, as does narcissistic pathology in general, from the faulty interplay during the crucial interactions in the relationship between the child and its environment, primarily its parents.

According to Moulton (1979), penis envy is a passing phase in the normal process of development of girls who basically value and take pleasure in their femininity. However, when a girl's family constellation has pathological features, penis envy can be reinforced defensively as a concealment for deeper dependency needs or fears of becoming a woman.

Chasseguet-Smirgel (1970) maintains that:

> Like the boy, the little girl, too, has been narcissistically wounded by the mother's omnipotence—maybe even more than he, for

the mother does not cathect her daughter in the same way that she cathects her son. But the girl cannot free herself from this (mother's) omnipotence as she has nothing with which to oppose the mother, no narcissistic virtue the mother does not also possess. She will not be able to "show her," her independence. [I think this expression relates to phallic exhibitionism.] So she will envy the boy his penis and say he can "do everything." I see penis envy *not* as a "virility claim" to something one wants for its own sake, but as a revolt against the person who caused the narcissistic wound: the omnipotent mother." [p. 115]

According to Chasseguet-Smirgel, penis envy does not express the girl's wish to become a man, it expresses the girl's wish to detach herself from the mother and to become a complete, autonomous woman.

Torok (1970) elucidates how penis envy is used to cover up sexual desire abrogated to assuage mother's anger for the incestuous wish to have pleasure with father's penis.

Lerner (1976) suggests that penis envy reflects a girl's unfulfilled wish to have mother's permission to be sexually active and responsive.

Grossman and Stewart (1976) indicate that penis envy can be used as a metaphor reflecting conflicts around identity, narcissistic sensitivity, and problems with aggression.

Edgcumbe and colleagues (1976) point out that the girl's penis envy is specific to phallic-drive concerns. It should therefore not be confused with envy related to other experiences of deprivations.

Karme (1981), in her richly detailed clinical case report of penis envy, illustrates its multiple unconscious meanings and defensive functions, which become evident during the course of an analysis. Thus, for Karme's patient, penis envy blocked the wish for sexual expression by inhibiting her sexual responses and the pride in her femininity. Separation conflicts were central and had to be resolved on a preoedipal level before they could be resolved on an oedipal level. Homosexual wishes manifested themselves in the eroticized transference. The patient felt displaced by the birth of a brother at age 2 and fantasized attacking his penis, which she considered to be his special connection with mother. It is important to note that the patient regarded the penis as a weapon of competition for mother's love.

Silverman (1987) stresses the relational aspects that lead to penis envy as well as jealousy of younger male siblings who disrupt the girl's bonding with mother.

According to Wilkinson (1991), the girl believes "that the phallus is a detachable and transferable object" which she "subjectively perceives as a metaphoric condensation, as well as a metonymic displacement" utilized in defining her femininity (p. 335).

Torsti (1994), in a critical examination of classical Freudian views of feminine psychosexuality, underlines the significance of the girl's vaginal sexuality for her feminine development. This early sense of the genitals informs and guides the structuralization of the feminine self. It contributes to the formation of the female body image during the phase when the conceptualization of the clitoris and the introitus is central. The girl's sense of inner genitality, which in large measure depends on the internalization of a successful mother–daughter relationship leads to a maternal identification and thus to the girl's feminine sexuality. Penis envy, according to Torsti, is most intense during the oedipal phase in which incestuous impulses are directed to both parents simultaneously.

The synopsis of the various views presented above indicates that listening to women's analytic material while being aware of possible theoretical bias, and analyzing one's countertransference, led to the discovery of a great variety of unconscious conflicts and motivations accounting for penis envy. These findings resulted in an understanding that penis envy stems from the internalization of many different sociocultural stereotypes and has many instinctual unconscious determinants. Thus, specific combinations of a variety of unconscious motivations may account for the developmental vicissitudes of penis envy in a particular girl/woman. The working through of the unique complex motivations of penis envy in a given analytic case brings about more successful clinical outcomes than Freud's pessimism envisioned.

Contemporary Freudian analysis of women indicates that penis envy interferes with the development of healthy femininity and self-esteem. The unraveling and understanding of the unique and personal unconscious meanings of the specific intrapsychic determinants of penis envy, as revealed by an analysis, benefit and enhance a woman's femininity and enable it to flourish (Karme 1981, Torok 1970). Penis envy is not, as Freud maintained (1925, 1931, 1933), a primary stimulus for the development of femininity, nor is it the bedrock a woman's analysis can reach (Freud 1937). Thus, the analysis of penis envy in a girl/woman brings about a healthy libidinal cathexis of her genitals, an affirmation of her femininity, and *an erotic desire for* the penis rather than penis envy.

6 "A Child Is Being Beaten": Mother's Role in the Formation of a Woman's Superego

Freud's understanding of "beating fantasies" (1919), widely used to elucidate the motivations underlying this phenomenon and its psychic transformations, has been critically examined in the psychoanalytic literature relatively infrequently. This is surprising since beating fantasies are most likely universally present in the life of every person (Joseph 1965).

This chapter is confined to a discussion of beating fantasies in girls and women. Consequently, the review of the literature will contain a presentation of Freud's ideas and those of other writers as they pertain to observations of beating fantasies in girls and women only.

Review of the Literature

As is now well known, Freud's (1919) findings presented in "A Child Is Being Beaten" are based on the analysis of adults, and probably primarily on the analysis of his daughter, Anna (Gay

1988, Young-Bruehl 1988). Freud maintained that, in girls
and women, the fantasy, though always pleasurable and sexually exciting, is also connected with feelings of shame and guilt.
It appears in preschool years, not later than at the age of 5 or
6 years.

Freud described three phases. In the first, the conscious content is "a child is being beaten." The second phase is regarded by
Freud as the "most momentous of all. . . . But . . . it has *never* had
a real existence [and] is *never* remembered. . . . It is a *construction
of analysis*" (italics added, p. 185). According to Freud, due to guilt
connected with incestuous genital wishes toward the father, the
girl not only represses these wishes, but a libidinal regression to
the anal phase also takes place. Consequently, coitus is expressed
by the fantasy: "I am being beaten by my father" (pp. 188–189).
Thus the girl submits masochistically to the sadistic attack by the
father. The third phase resembles the first, but is a substitute
for the second: "My father is beating the child, he loves only me"
(p. 190). The beating fantasy represents both regressively debased
genital love for the father and, simultaneously, punishment for
the incestuous wishes. Freud considers the fantasy of being beaten
and the libidinal excitation that finds its outlet in a masturbatory
act "the essence of masochism" (p. 189).

Maria Bergmann (1982) states that the role of the mother in
the beating fantasy must be added. Her analytic findings indicate
that the girl can experience pleasure only after she rids herself of
guilt feelings toward mother. The greater the hostility in the
mother/father relationship, the more relentless and severe will
be the beating fantasies.

Novick and Novick (1973, 1987) base their conclusions on extensive child observations, the indexed cases at the Anna Freud
Centre, and child-analytic findings. They maintain that beating
wishes in the anal phase and beating games in the phallic phase
are universal. Beating fantasies, however, do not appear until
latency, are relatively infrequent, and can be transitory or fixed.
The Novicks concur with Freud that beating fantasies represent

both positive oedipal strivings and punishment for incestuous wishes. "The importance of the beating wish in the oedipal conflicts of the individual girl determines whether a masturbatory fantasy involving beating will be formed in latency" (1973, p. 239). However, contrary to Freud's findings, the victim of the fantasy is consciously personified by the child herself. This, as will be seen subsequently, is also true for my cases. The Novicks state that for girls the fantasy signifies the persistence of intense libidinal wishes for the father. The appearance of this fantasy in latency is frequently a transitional phenomenon, provided normal maturation can proceed. The Novicks conclude that though "the beating fantasy is not formed until the phallic-oedipal phase is reached, the primary determinants of the beating wish, which is discharged in the fantasy, are preoedipal" (p. 241). The authors stress the importance of the mother, which comes to the fore when the analysis of these fantasies proceeds past the point at which the child is being beaten. Such analytic work reveals the early masochistic tie to the mother.

Myers (1980) presents an extensive discussion of the psychodynamics of a beating fantasy in a woman patient seen in analytic psychotherapy for a period of fifteen years. This patient, as her insight increased, knew that the surrogate fathers of her beating fantasies really represented her own father. She at first mitigated her sense of guilt over incestuous wishes toward her father by developing a fantasy that her maternal grandfather was her "real" father (p. 638), thus changing her father into an adoptive one. More significant, however, was the finding that the beating fantasy connected with incestuous wishes toward father served as a defensive screen against even more unacceptable wishes, namely, to be beaten by mother (p. 639). Dr. Myers does not indicate the motives or the nature of these unconscious wishes. This patient's strenuous attempts to deny her incestuous feelings toward father support the supposition that her fantasies of mother as the beater may express her unconscious guilt and need for punishment.

In discussing Myers's paper, Galenson (1980) enumerates various pregenital factors that contribute to the formation of beating fantasies in which mother is the beater. Galenson concludes that "the fantasy of being beaten by the mother is far more common and perhaps even a universal development in girls during the anal phase of psychosexual development" (p. 652).

Asch (1980) states that Freud's theories regarding beating fantasies require revision. The fantasies may involve both parents, with the confusion of sexual identity as an additional element. Asch adds, "I suspect that in those patients for whom beating is a persistent masturbatory fantasy, the father is a screen for the preoedipal object, the phallic mother. The ambivalent wishes to remain a symbiotic part of the preoedipal mother may create the difficulties in the vicissitudes of 'normal' beating fantasies" (p. 654).

Ferber (1975) maintains that in beating fantasies, which in conscious or unconscious form persist into adulthood, the pregenital factors are of particular importance. He stresses the role of trauma in the first three years of life. Though Ferber concurs with Freud that the "passive sexual attitude in both men and women . . . is an important and central feature of the beating fantasies," he adds, "nonetheless, the relation to the preoedipal mother is of equal significance" (p. 221).

Bonaparte (1949), reflecting on Freud's three phases of the beating fantasy and his dictum that this fantasy does not pertain to the girl's relationship with her mother, comments, putting her own statement in brackets: "My own opinion is that the active phallic mother at the very beginning and at the very end, in the first and the third phase may, *even as regards the girl*, sometimes replace the father, who, as we now know, regularly superimposes himself upon the mother in the course of the child's libidinal development" (italics added, p. 88). I assume that Bonaparte here has in mind the punishing role of the mother as beater, since this is the role assigned by Freud to father in the first and third phases of the fantasy. It seems to me that Bonaparte, by putting the above remarks in brackets, suggests an apparent timidity in contradicting Freud.

Contrary to Freud (1919), who states, "but it is *not* with the girl's relation to her mother that the beating fantasy is connected" (p. 186), the analysts cited above stress the role the multifaceted mother–girl interaction plays in the development and significance of the beating fantasy. My findings indicate that mother's role is crucial.

I shall discuss beating fantasies of five female patients seen in four-times-per-week analysis for approximately seven to nine years. No parameters were used. These patients came from middle-class homes, held advanced degrees, and led professional lives. All of them had love relations with men that were complex and fraught with conflict. These women suffered from character neuroses with predominantly obsessive, masochistic, and depressive trends. Their beating fantasies followed a different pattern from the three phases described by Freud. During the middle phase of their analysis these patients began reporting the memory of the following persistent childhood fantasy: "A favorite, loved child is being beaten . . . he [usually a teacher] does not want to do it but he must because she deserves it." Though the associations varied in detail, they contained the following elements:

The child, always a girl, provoked the beating by her naughty behavior.

The man, teacher, but sometimes relative, had to beat the child: *it was mandatory.* He was reluctant because of the conflict within him: he loved the girl and had to hurt her.

The child was beaten on the buttocks—usually the child was put "over the knee"; frequently the buttocks were exposed.

My patients experienced a tremendous amount of shame when telling this fantasy, which always accompanied masturbation. The shame was connected to the fantasy and not to the act of masturbation, to which these patients admitted quite freely.

Sadomasochistic elements were quite pronounced in the object relations of all these patients. Their current masturbation fantasies had equivalent elements corresponding to the childhood fantasies, though the specific content varied. A great deal of shame was also connected with the recounting of these current fantasies. They felt embarrassed because of the humiliating aspects of "being beaten," and ashamed when they recognized their identification with the sadism of the aggressor. Though these patients abhorred both these aspects of their imaginary life, they appeared "addicted" to these fantasies and frequently enjoyed masturbation more than coitus. Various masturbation techniques were employed: a pillow or blanket against which they rubbed actively— frequently imagining vaginal intercourse; some masturbated manually, only stimulating the clitoris; some started by stimulating the clitoris and then put their fingers or an object into the vagina. The lifelong presence of these fantasies and of their current fantasy equivalents suggests that these patients have at least partially remained psychosexually fixated at the stage of the beating fantasies or regressed to it.

My patients, via associations, recognized with relative ease the displacement from father onto teacher and from self onto the "beaten child." They were "struck," however, by the mandatory nature of the punishment: "Why *must* the child be beaten?" Analytic work led to the discovery that one of the important factors accounting for the identification with the aggressor stemmed from a sense of conviction that indeed the child "had been naughty, the child did it, what the child did was very forbidden, and it thus deserved to be punished."

A phase of analysis followed during which these patients became more and more resistive and accusatory. I was seen as a rigid, old-fashioned Freudian who insisted on exploring sexual fantasies, quite doctrinaire. The transference now became hostile and accusatory; the analyst was perceived as dangerous, hurtful, and punitive. With these patients, further elucidation of the beating fantasies occurred when oedipal material began to surface in dreams and memories. At this time the manifest dream content dealt with some crime that had been committed, with something that had been stolen. The police were after the criminal. The patients dreamed of being attacked by monsters. All the dreams took place during the dark of night. The patients frequently awoke in a state of fear. Some dreams involved quarrels with mother from which the patients occasionally awoke screaming "no, no, no," and feeling very agitated. Though these kinds of dreams became typical during this phase, associations to them were not easily forthcoming. The patients, after narrating the dreams, would lapse into long silences during which they occasionally smiled, rubbed their eyes, and made almost imperceptible hip movements. When asked about feelings and/or thoughts, the patients insisted they had none. To facilitate associations, I reminded them of their childhood beating fantasies and wondered if these were in any way connected with their dreams and current fantasies. The patients were "struck" by this suggestion. Eventually, memories of pleasure in "doing things with daddy and wanting mommy out" became a predominant, reminiscent theme of associations. It subsequently, therefore, became possible to interpret the incestuous elements of the dreams with increasing clarity.

The patients now experienced persistent growing anxiety. I was perceived as lacking empathy and as being cold. Following continued interpretations of incestuous oedipal themes in which erotic and loving feelings toward father were prevalent, one of my patients accused me of giving her a "tongue lashing," and added, after a long silence: "That's what my mother did—I had fun with dad and she was 'out of it,' and she couldn't stand it and was jealous, and so she would find fault with me and scold me without mercy. She gave me a real verbal beating. . . . "

The following examples of dreams and fantasies illustrate the essential aspects of these patients' wishes, conflicts, and attempted resolutions.

Patient A. was a 30-year-old chemical engineer. She always became entangled in triangular love relationships in which, in her words, she "played second fiddle." Following an illicit sexual-erotic encounter, A. reported waking from a dream she did not remember with the following feelings: "It is exciting to be spanked, hit on the ass, being hit on the back with a cane. I imagine that with Tom. In the fantasy the man is malevolent and dangerous. So exciting . . . I associate this to being spanked by my father—it did not hurt—yet I feel I am being disdained, whipped like a dog. *I feel I deserve to be hit.* I don't want to be hit so if I am hit, I'm not worth much." After a while the patient added, "It was different with mother. She slapped me on the face. I don't know why. When I was in my early teens and wearing a very nice dress with a low-cut neckline, mother screamed that I 'dress like a whore.' I don't know why she was so angry with me. She slapped me a lot. I hated it and I hated her. Sometimes I did not speak to her for weeks." After a long silence the patient continued: "It is difficult to speak about sex—I want to be sexually excited for a long time and sexually controlled. Being controlled reminds me of father—he took care of me and made everything 'right' when I was a little girl. Father held me in bed and enveloped me and it felt . . . [patient is silent for a while] but then mother came and made me get out . . . she would . . . she was jealous of me . . . father liked me in bed with him . . . to play . . . there was something titillating about mother seeing me there. . . ." The patient's voice trailed off.

Patient B., an art historian, was an only child. She was very close to her father, whom she admired and idealized, and defensively scornful of her mother. B. regarded her parents' marriage as a "loving union" and looked upon her own marriage as "one of convenience." Sexually almost frigid and nonorgasmic, B. reported the following masturbation fantasy: "Women trainers by using force and beatings made young girls submit sexually to much older men. The girls did not want to do it—they were forced." The patient was silent for a while, then said, "I really don't know when the content of my fantasies changed, why this fantasy has become predominant." B. was referring to the change in the theme of her fantasies, namely, from being beaten by a man for seemingly "no reason" to beatings by "women trainers" who forced girls to submit sexually to much older men.

Patient C. was a schoolteacher about 50, divorced prior to the beginning of treatment and hoping to find a husband. This patient spent innumerable hours on a monotonous repetition of complaints about father's dislike and criticism of her and his preference for her sister, who, in the patient's words, "was everything to him." The oedipal themes of her complaints and her displacement from mother to sister were interpreted numerous times and were consistently and persistently denied by the patient. Eventually, however, with much agitation and hesitation, the patient said she had "something terrible to tell me" about which she felt extremely guilty. C. "confessed" that to achieve an orgasm while masturbating she was "forced" to resort to a fantasy in which an older woman beat a young girl. C. had these fantasies for many years, even while she was married. Eventually, with much shame and guilt, she admitted that in the fantasies that sexually excited her the most, she was "beating young girls on their naked behinds." C. cried and insisted that these fantasies "made no sense," and that she was perplexed by them. During a session in which C. was especially self-castigating, convinced that her analyst despised her, she suddenly blurted out, "Unless it is I who am being beaten by an older woman . . . it couldn't be my mother . . . what have I done to deserve a beating?"

Patient D., 28, a lawyer, outstandingly beautiful, sought after by men, and nonorgasmic, described that in her most sexually exciting masturbation fantasy "a young woman is being 'beautified' by an older woman, hit in the process because she struggles, and, much against her will, is being tied down and prepared for defloration by an older man, the master."

My patients with beating fantasies began to report changes in the content of their masturbation fantasies when the intensity of their positive oedipal feelings began to surface. At that time women assumed a more prominent role in the fantasies. They became trainers and punishers. The content of these fantasies always consisted of a preparation for the sexual act to follow in which the patients were helpless slaves, sexually used and abused. The unconscious significance of the "women trainers," as analysis revealed, was to absolve the patient from "responsibility" for the sexual act with "the much older men" who unconsciously represented father. Thus, though the fantasies in essence were identical with the childhood fantasies, an important element was added. The child/woman was not the culprit. She was "forced to do it," and specifically so, by a woman, usually described as "older," who most likely represented mother in the patient's unconscious. These types of fantasies became repetitive over many months.

Associations to themes that combined the latent meaning of childhood beating fantasies with the latent meaning of current beating fantasies revealed to the patients the following unconscious material: the "beloved child" represented the self. The "crime" for which they deserved punishment was not masturbation, but the forbidden wish. The disguised fantasied wish-fulfillment led to gratifying masturbation. In the childhood fantasy the beating of the loved child did indeed have, in regressed form, the significance of the forbidden incestuous sexual act that was wish-fulfilling.

Though the general outline of this material corresponds to Freud's construction of phase two, there are important differences. I did not reconstruct the presence of the incestuous wish. My patients achieved the insight that enabled them to become consciously aware of the meaning of the "forbidden wish." Most significantly, however, my patients recognized and acknowledged that their fantasy of the child's "naughty behavior" related to their own seductiveness. They associated to the phrase from the childhood fantasy, "he must, because she deserved it," by recalling their childhood conviction that they indeed could seduce father and that he would succumb.

One patient recalled that from about age 3 to 5 father and she would spend an hour daily during which he played the piano and she "danced for him." She recalled, while associating, that during adolescence she had fantasies of seducing her boyfriend by dancing for him. These thoughts led to recollections of dancing girls in harems and a memory of a conversation overheard between father and mother in which father referred to himself as a sultan and to mother as his favorite wife. The patient was shocked, becoming aware of her feelings and their scope. She said, "He played for me because he wanted me to dance for him. I am sure he enjoyed it . . . it lasted so many years. I was his favorite in the harem. . . . " Until she experienced the emotional impact of these recollections, this patient had denied the presence of any incestuous feelings toward her father. She insisted that an uncle was the object of her oedipal longings.

All my patients with beating fantasies felt what Freud (1919) explicitly stated: " . . . the affections of the little girl are fixed on her father, who has probably done *all he could* to win her love, and in this way has sown the seeds of an attitude of hatred and rivalry toward her mother" (italics added, p. 186).

For my patients the significance of the punishment aspect inherent in the beating element of their fantasies surfaced from the analysis of associations that combined both childhood and current versions. These patients became puzzled and perturbed by the seemingly unexpected change from the consciously remembered punishing teacher/father figure of their fantasies and dreams to its opposite, namely, the appearance of a controlling/punishing older woman. Associations to this figure brought forth childhood memories of mother and of the patients' feelings of rivalry with her and of envy. Mother seemed to have everything they wanted because she had the power to take father for herself and away from them. The patients recalled their feelings of anger, hatred, and their fear of mother. As the uncovering process of the beating fantasies progressed and the patients consciously experienced a sense of guilt related to their incestuous strivings, all of them acknowledged having the feeling that, because of their seductive behavior toward father, they provoked and deserved punishment. Further analyses led to the insight that the beating by the "woman" in the fantasy signified punishment by mother not only for the forbidden wishes, but, as one patient said: "for doing *all* to have these fulfilled." She was referring to the preening, cajoling, and erotically provocative behavior of the little girl who declares her love for daddy and wants him to sleep with her.

Mother was perceived as the judge, prosecutor, and punisher. These patients' sense of guilt was stimulated by two sources: on the one hand by the incestuous wishes and impulses they sought to gratify and on the other by envious and murderous feelings toward mother. Projection of their rage accounted for the unconscious image of mother as ready to punish and even kill them. One of my patients recalled that as a child she was convinced for several months that mother would poison her. During this time the patient refused to eat unless she ate with father the same food he ate. Underlying this conscious fantasy were unconscious incestuous wishes of having father exclusively for herself, being impregnated by him, defeating mother.

Analytic work with these patients indicates that the intensity of the girl's oedipal rivalry with mother and her conviction of being the oedipal victor is proportionate to the intensity of her guilt feelings, fantasies of punishment, and dread of mother.

The beating fantasy is a multidetermined, multilayered fantasy of forbidden gratification and mandatory, deserved punishment. It thus represents a compromise formation. The beating element of the fantasy probably also serves to procure a priori atonement. As is the case in some forms of masochism, the girl, having "suffered the beating," may now enjoy the unconscious wishfulfilling aspect of the fantasy. This occurs via gratifying masturbation.

The condensed version of my patients' beating fantasies has two aspects: the girl, "at a price," is unconsciously gratified since her father, in regressed form, via the beating, commits the incestuous act. The second aspect of the fantasy relates to mother, who, as the unconscious meaning indicates, is the real punisher, administering the "actual" beating for the girl's transgression.

I suggest, based on these elucidations of the beating fantasies, that the unconscious perception of mother as punisher and of father as "sinful gratifier" is a crucial aspect in the girl's development during the oedipal phase. The incorporation of these parental images with their emotional valence has a profound effect on the subsequent structure of the superego. It also results in a specific masochistic patterning in these patients. On the one hand, the superego of these patients is characterized by great harshness, stemming from the introjection of mother's image as judge-avenger; on the other hand, the superego has a specific corrupt-ibility, stemming from the introjection of father's image as the violator of the incestuous prohibition. This complex of inter-nalizations may manifest itself clinically in patients who by suf-fering in advance act as if they have gained permission to sub-sequently commit acts unconsciously perceived as forbidden. Frequently such patients become involved in triangular relation-ships with older, married men. Unconsciously, their suffering, like an advance payment, gives them license to enact the childhood wish by taking the man, for themselves, from his wife. Frequently it appears, at least for a while, as if the superego could be hood-winked by such suffering into not noticing the nature of the act.

Discussion

I will not elaborate on the limitations of Freud's findings regard-ing beating fantasies in girls and women, which stem from the father–daughter relationship of Anna's analysis with Freud and from the resultant unresolved countertransference–transference relationship, which must have influenced and curtailed Freud's conclusions. Current analytic work will continue to fill these gaps and provide the additional insights, which will result in more fruit-ful work with female patients and greater accuracy in the under-standing of women's psychosexual development.

The vicissitudes of the positive oedipal configuration, as is well known, depend in large measure on preoedipal factors. These comprise the multitude of mother–daughter fusing, merging, dependent, conflictual, and nonconflictual, loving/hating, rival-rous interactions—the role of father in relation to mother, daughter, and to their interactions, and the daughter's loving/hostile, defensive identification with mother. The entirety of these object relations and their emotional valences also determines the nature of the negative oedipal configuration. The latter is experienced not only as dangerous because of the incestuous erotic component, it is also anxiety-producing if infantile wishes for fusion and merger are strong and thus endanger the girl's budding autonomy. All these aspects reflect on and affect the perception of mother during the positive oedipal phase.

In my patients' version of the beating fantasy, mother was experienced as judge, prosecutor, and executioner, who did not condone the fantasied incestuous tryst with father. These women patients feared mother's power and the extent of her punishment. Their fantasies revealed that fears of mutilation of their genitals (Lax 1994) occurred in conjunction with guilt over forbidden sexual desires—specifically, as dreaded punishment for the forbidden father-directed incestuous oedipal wishes. The fantasied role girls assign to mother as the punisher in the oedipal drama is equivalent to the fantasied role boys ascribe to father as castrator. For both sexes genital anxiety spurs the internalization of parental prohibitions, the repression of oedipal wishes, and the subsequent structuralization of the superego. Mother establishes the "oedipal law" for the girl analogously to father's doing the same for the boy.

It is beyond the scope of this chapter to explore the historical and sociological factors that contributed to the paucity of discussion in psychoanalytic literature of mother's role as "lawgiver" and "enforcer" during the enactment of her daughter's oedipal drama, and consequently to the view that women's superegos are deficient and inferior to men's (Freud 1933).

I shall restrict my discussion to the vicissitudes the girl encounters during the positive oedipal phase. Let us recall Freud's (1919) statement: "Father has done *all* he can to win her [daughter's] love" (p. 186). Thus the girl's libidinal desires are fixed on father

with his encouragement, and mother is perceived, Freud acknowledges, as the hated rival who interferes with the fulfillment of the
girl's desires. Father's tacit encouragement, which the girl unconsciously interprets as father's compliance with her incestuous
wishes, leads to her unconscious self-experience as the successful
seductress. However, simultaneous with this sense of success is
the foreboding awareness of mother's injunction against the incestuous wish and its fulfillment. Though the girl, because of
father's encouragement, feels victorious in breaking the taboo, she
also dreads the retribution that must follow.

This conflict is the basis for the girl's fantasy of mandatory
punishment. The girl feels guilty even though—and because—
father, in fantasy, has complied in the forbidden act. Father is thus
perceived as succumbing to the daughter's seduction. However,
he may also be experienced as the corruptor, since he not only did
not resist, he in fact "did all" (Freud 1919, p. 186) to win the girl's
love. In the "average expectable environment" (Hartmann 1958)
the girl's usual interactions with father during the positive oedipal phase, and the phase-specific libidinally fueled elaborations of
these interactions in fantasy, culminate in incestuous desires that
the girl *knows* are prohibited by mother. It is thus the mother, not
the father, who establishes the "oedipal law" for the girl, and its
moral foundation.

The girl's identification with mother during the positive oedipal phase has two roots: her guilt and expected retribution contribute to her identification with mother's real and imagined
aggressive aspects; her wish to "win father and/or a man like father" accounts for the girl's identification with mother's feminine
aspects when mother is perceived as "the victorious woman."

The identification with the "judge, prosecutor, aggressor/muti-
lator mother" will at first become the "thou shalt and shalt not"
aspect of the superego. The identification with mother's successful womanliness may merge with the idealized mother image of
the preoedipal phase and become incorporated in the feminine ego-

ideal aspects of the superego. Based on the injunction against incest, these internalized identifications form the core of the female
superego. Such a resolution is optimal, though perhaps infrequent.

In girls, as is well known, the special quality of the daughter–
father relationship, with its seductive, sexualized overtones, frequently continues well into latency and sometimes adolescence.
Repression usually is incomplete, contributing to pathological
resolutions. In such cases the beating fantasy, in different guises,
continues as the primary masturbation fantasy. Because of its dual
unconscious meaning, it simultaneously punishes and gratifies,
thus seemingly contributing to a precarious intrapsychic balance.

The role played by the fear of punishment fantasied to be meted
out by the aggressor/mother is proportionate to the extent to
which the girl imagines herself the oedipal victor and experiences
father as a participant in her unconscious incestuous wishes and
fantasies. In these cases the internalized, punishing mother element forms the moral nucleus of the girl's superego, whereas the
father's complicity contributes a certain component of corrupt-
ibility. This accounts for superego splits that may also affect the
synthesizing capacity of the ego.

When the oedipal law is consciously or unconsciously undermined by father's behavior, which contributes to and colludes with
the girl's fantasies, various types of pathology may develop. Frequently the presence of unconscious guilt leads to inhibition or
suppression of sexuality and to various degrees of frigidity. Such
an oedipal constellation appears also as the dynamic matrix for a
certain type of female masochism in which unconscious guilt interferes with the girl/woman's attainment of success in her love life
and/or profession. It may also lead to various forms of abstinence
and so-called altruistic surrender (A. Freud 1936) in which the
woman abdicates her erotic goals.

Masculinization based on a defensive identification with father
leads to other forms of pathological resolution, including some
forms of homosexuality. It could perhaps be argued that mother's
role as beater may connote, in regressed form, erotic incestuous

feelings for her that are characteristic of the negative oedipal constellation. Such a supposition cannot be excluded.

In the context of the intense positive oedipal feelings that characterized this stage of my patients' analytic process, it was clear that they experienced mother as judge and punisher who forbade the transgression of the incestuous father taboo.

7 An Imaginary Brother: Conflicting Pathways to Womanhood Contribute to Splits in the Ego Ideal

Freud (1933) stated that, "Throughout history people have knocked their heads against the riddle of the nature of femininity" (p. 113), and he, likewise, grappled with this problem. He stressed that women's nature is "determined by their sexual function" (p. 135), even though he recognized that social factors make a significant contribution. He used the suppression of aggression that leads to "truly feminine" masochism (p. 116) as an example. By postulating bisexuality Freud acknowledged the presence of masculine and feminine instinctual components in each human being and he described their psychic manifestations. Freud attributed the disturbances in female development to "residual phenomena of the early masculine period" that could lead "in the course of some women's lives [to] . . . repeated alternation between periods in which masculinity or femininity gains the upper hand" (p. 131).

In current psychoanalytic thinking the instinctual contributions are considered secondary to the role played by parental models and childrearing techniques in establishing so-called femininity and/or masculinity. Grounded in the affective child–parent interaction, the special and significant relationship with each parent results in unique imitations, introjections, and identifications. In the course of development the products of these internalizations lead to the formation of psychic structures. Intersystemic and intrasystemic conflict may result when parental objects are polarized and the child's identification with each of them remains unintegrated.

This chapter is limited to the presentation of relevant case material and analytic findings that illustrate the patient's conflicts between narcissistic and libidinal strivings in making object choices, and indicate the identifications that played a significant role in the formation of her wished-for self image (Jacobson 1954, 1964) and ego ideal. I discuss the role of genetic and familial contributions to the formation of intrapsychic factors that interfered with a harmonious resolution of the conflicts between narcissistic ego interests and libidinal aims. The analysis of this patient, a woman in her late forties, highlights the role of conflicting identifications that produce discontinuities in the content and functioning of psychic structures. The differentiation, establishment, and role of the unconscious ego ideal, and the development of a conscious wished-for self image, ego values, and autonomy, are also discussed.

Fran came to treatment as two relationships were ending: a conventional marriage of over twenty years' duration and a love relationship that had started in her late teens and continued intermittently and in various forms throughout her life. Fran was distraught, felt defeated, was sad and depressed. Her professional life and goals appeared to have lost their significance, as had occurred on previous occasions when her love life was disrupted. Although she felt she "had nothing to live for," she ruled out suicide because of concern for her children.

She felt quite apathetic, but continued to work and pursue her usual activities. She relied on friends for support. Fran said she wanted the analysis "to solve the puzzle of my life." Fran's attitude indicated she unconsciously hoped I could magically restore the narcissistic and libidinal losses she had suffered. She spoke of "putting herself in my hands." She wished to be "taken care of and tended to in her misery." She said, "If I were free to do what I want, I'd go to bed, put the cover over my head, just sink into nothingness, and stay there forever."

Relevant Background

Fran's birth brought disappointment to both parents, who wished for a boy. The mother, a beautiful, narcissistic woman, responded to Fran as if she were "a blemish." She gave the care of the infant to nurses and restricted her own participation to unavoidable, rigidly scheduled nursing routines. These followed the same pattern irrespective of the infant's state of discomfort. Nurses and governesses took care of Fran until her early teens.

The father, an autocrat and tyrant, headed a powerful industrial conglomerate. He saw women as sex objects only, and wanted sons to enlarge his success and assure its future. Known for his choleric temper, he was also a compassionate man, capable of concern. He was the one who played with Fran and cared for her while she was in distress during a long and serious illness in the first two years of life. He had come to accept his daughter, blaming his wife for the lack of a son.[1] He gave Fran a boy's nickname. Family anecdotes describe Fran as a beautiful child, extremely curious, and very active.

An only child, Fran grew up with the shadow of mother's frequent and sometimes prolonged illnesses. Mother's attitudes and feelings toward her daughter were unpredictable. Fran never knew what to expect since mother's moods determined the nature of their relationship. At times mother showered her with kisses, hugs, and held on to her; at other times mother was distant and ignored

---

1. See Chapter 8 for the general pattern of this type of family object relations.

her, not speaking to Fran for several days. Though Fran hated the excessive fondling, she suffered greatly when her mother withdrew. She experienced a sense of unease and feelings of guilt that were associated with mother. She did not know what she might have done to have made her mother so silently angry and so withdrawn. Fran also blamed herself for her mother's sadness. Though she tried, Fran could never succeed in cheering mother when she saw her weeping. This made her feel helpless and unlovable.

Fran's relationship with her father varied. He was maternally caring during her childhood whenever Fran was in distress or ill. He demanded, however, that Fran excel at all times, in all activities important to him, whether sports or studies. A relatively uneducated man, father imbued Fran with his deep admiration for learning. In contradistinction to mother, father supported Fran's quest for independence, her tomboyishness, and her involvement in boys' games and activities. As compared with women and girls generally, Fran had special privileges usually reserved for boys. Her mother and the extended families disapproved.

Till the age of 10 Fran was tormented by a persistent fearful fantasy that, unwanted, uncherished, and unloved, she would be abandoned by her parents. She experienced a continuous pressure to do everything "better than others" or else "everything in her life would be lost." She believed her existence depended on "measuring up to this standard."

Fran was counterphobic as a child. Those around her, however, saw her as plucky, enterprising, and able to take care of herself. She had many playmates but had recurring difficulties getting along with them because of her domineering manner and a wish to have things her way. A very good student, Fran was favored by some teachers. She tutored those in need and held a leadership role in a youth organization. In her late teens Fran became active in an underground political organization. She championed unpopular social causes benefiting "the poor and dispossessed," challenging the prevailing social order. Her rigid adherence to certain political programs betrayed the unconscious reactive motives for this behavior.

At 17 Fran met a boy several years older. After a brief period during which she experienced extreme feelings of envy regarding him, fought and quarreled with him, Fran became aware that she had "fallen in love." The feeling was reciprocated. Paul now became Fran's main preoccupation. Her thoughts and fantasies centered on him, and she spent every free moment with him. During this first period together (about one and a half years), Fran idealized and adored Paul. She became immersed in his activities and interests. From being quite independent and frequently negativistic, she became dependent, clinging, and seemingly always in agreement with Paul. Her parents, especially her father, were amazed and disapproving, since she withdrew both emotionally and socially from her family, concentrating totally on Paul. Her moods depended on him completely. If their relationship was going well and Paul was loving, Fran was happy. She otherwise became quite depressed, her self-esteem depleted, feeling "life was not worth living." During this first period, irrespective of Paul's involvement in activities that upset her, Fran felt no anger toward him. She likewise consciously felt no envy or sense of competition, taking pride when Paul was honored and praised. Analysis revealed the significance and role that vicarious identification played in this process. At the time, being Paul's girlfriend, which attested to his love, appeared sufficient to satisfy Fran's needs.

However, imperceptible changes occurred during the second year. The intellectual gap between Fran and Paul began to shrink. Whereas she previously listened to his discourses admiringly, she now became more critical. Retrospectively, winning her first debate with Paul appeared like a turning point for both. Fran felt a peculiar sense of inner triumph. She became more watchful and more critical. Coincidentally, Paul began to have somewhat less time for her and started to notice other girls. Fran became jealous. They started quarreling. No longer feeling certain and secure in the relationship, Fran began to fear that Paul would leave her. This anticipation in fantasy colored Fran's perception of reality. She felt hurt and angry by Paul's attention to other girls. Her depressive moods increased, and she lost her cheerfulness. Derivatives of unconscious childhood fears were now expressed in a pessimistic attitude. Paul accused Fran of having "an instinct for unhappiness," disregarding the contribution made by his Don Juanism. Fran compared his behavior to that of her father, whose attention (but not attentiveness) was always completely centered on her mother.

Fran began to feel unloved. She now experienced her relationship with Paul as torturous and in moments of despondency would break it up, only to resume it again because she "could not live without him." She was unable, although she tried, to tolerate what she experienced as a lack of exclusivity.

Fran's approach toward sex was a mixture of Victorian and ultramodern attitudes. Her response to Paul's advances, though passive, was extremely seductive. She enjoyed Paul's caresses, especially his adoration and exultation in her beauty. They had intercourse for the first time during one of their rapturous reunions in the third year of their relationship.

Although Fran considered herself "modern," this experience had an overwhelming psychological impact. She felt she had "given herself" to Paul, and that their act bound and bonded them forever. She felt exalted, engulfed, and cherished. She had no sense of being violated or soiled. On the contrary, her feeling of closeness with Paul gave her a sense of union for which she had longed. Neither of them felt guilty about having premarital sex since their marriage had become a foregone conclusion. They spent a week intensely together. Paul thereafter left town in connection with his work. Fran spent the next month feeling anxious and very alone. The lack of contact with Paul gave her a sense of abandonment. When Fran finally did hear from him, he confessed to an affair, yet insisted he really loved Fran and was "returning." Fran felt betrayed, her trust in their togetherness shattered; she considered their union a fantasy and illusion.

Fran once again broke off with Paul, determined to pursue her own life and interests. However, when confronted by Paul, she submitted, agreed to resume their relationship, and to give up her pursuits. The next two years consisted of breakups and reunions. Fran did not regain her trust that life with Paul was possible, yet she could not stop trying. She became bitter and felt guilty about her anger. She no longer enjoyed or wanted to share Paul's interests. She became competitive and envious of his successes and felt "life was much easier for him because he was a man." Fran masochistically blamed herself for making their time together fraught with conflict, yet she could neither forget nor forgive his betrayals. Fran felt her attitude contributed to Paul's seeking the companionship of other women. For Paul, political activities, which he claimed accounted for his friendships with various women, were of primary importance. Fran experienced his behavior as both narcissistically wounding and as a libidinal loss. She became increasingly self-critical, depressed, almost despondent. When Paul suggested the postponement of their engagement because of some political meeting that took him out of town, Fran, in a fit of rage and despair, once again broke off the relationship.

Anger, it would seem, enabled Fran this time to make the decision to depart for a remote country in pursuit of her professional interests. The act of leaving helped her recover some of her self-esteem because it made her feel less dependent on Paul's decisions and therefore less helpless. She berated herself for having been at his beck and call for such a long time and jeered at herself for having no backbone. These self-criticisms were based on attitudes stemming from the period preceding her submission to Paul. They were attempts, unconsciously motivated, to utilize self-inflicted narcissistic pain as a means of shielding herself from the anguish of object loss.

In the months that followed her departure, Fran pursued her own intellectual interests, altruistic endeavors, and political crusades. These activities were motivated by her former values and goals. They were also unconscious attempts at self-healing.

In the years to come, Fran oscillated with varying intensity between the pursuit of her ego aims, in which she was successful, and Paul, whom she continued to love. Their reunions, rapturous and temporarily successful, never lasted long. Past conflicts reactivated always led to a breakup. Fran felt she could not free herself of her attachment to Paul, yet could not remain in a relationship with him.

It is unclear what eventually mobilized sufficient anger in Fran to enable her to leave Paul and to pursue her ego aims. She frequently regretted this decision. Even though her life after the final breakup appeared quite successful, Fran did not feel really satisfied with herself or happy, nor did she really love again. She remained enthusiastic but was never cheerful. Her attitude was basically masochistic and pessimistic. As will be seen from the analytic material, Fran's conflicted parental identifications determined her faulty libidinal object choices.

Eventually Fran married "on the rebound." She and her husband were in a similar profession, sharing the same political outlook. She had four children. The marriage was without passion, conventional, at the time suitable for both of them. They were "good friends." It ended after 20 years when Fran discovered her husband had a mistress.

Material from the Analysis

During her analysis Fran told me about her fantasy of Older Brother. She had not mentioned it to anyone, even though she never thought of it as a secret to be hidden. Fran maintained she had always had this fantasy. She became aware during analysis that her involvement with it and conscious memory of it varied at different times. Older Brother was two or three years her senior, tall, and, in contrast to her, had fair hair and blue eyes. She thought of him as handsome, very strong, very kind, fearless, and very clever. As she described him, Fran realized that his attributes changed as she matured and that she re-created him in terms of her changing values and interests. He was *her* brother, embodying all *her* aspirations and all *her* hopes. She said, "I had to create a brother. In my world boys 'were like that,' girls were not. I could try but he was it. I had a feeling that he was like that because he was born a boy, he was perfection. I was sure that if I really had a brother, that is how he would have been. Girls—girls in my world could try—but being girls, they could never 'make it.' I was afraid of many things—darkness, heights, strange people. I hid my fears because of my brother. I felt, if he could be fearless, I could at least pretend. It was this way with many attributes I supposedly had. For instance, he was really kind. I would get angry. I was repulsed by ugly or by maimed people. However, I made myself be nice and able to go up to them and give them charity. In my early teens I volunteered to nurse the very ill at the municipal hospital. I hated being near the patients, it made me so nauseated."

Fran recalled solitary walks during which she imagined Older Brother in different life situations. He was always heroic: the protector, defender, and champion of the underdog. From being a daredevil he became a fighter for righteous causes, able to stand up to bullies, hypocrites, and pretenders. Fran felt encouraged by imaginary conversations with Older Brother. She saw herself as following in his footsteps, urged on by him.

Brother did not have a name. Fran always referred to him, both in her mind and to me, as "my older brother," with an emphasis on "my" and "older." Theirs was an ideal relationship—without anger, jealousy, or envy. It had for Fran a most significant sense of inner reality: she identified with Older Brother and wanted to become and be like him. Older Brother was clearly a narcissistic creation, an embodiment of Fran's ideals, of the values contained in her ego ideal. Older Brother also represented her ego goals: he was a fantasy personification of her wished-for self-image. When libidinal strivings did not interfere, Fran's wished-for self-image was almost identical with her self-representation.

During her analysis Fran recognized with amazement that Older Brother had receded during her relationship with Paul. She had not lost her memory of Older Brother; rather, her preoccupation with the fantasy ended when Paul became the center of her emotional existence. During the initial phase of their relationship Fran reacted to Paul as if he were "Older Brother come alive." He seemed to represent the most coveted aspects of herself. Freud (1933) refers to such choices as "made in accordance with the *narcissistic ideal of the man whom the girl had wished to become*" (italics added, p. 132). Lovers, as is well known, always identify with each other, and the lover is frequently imbued with various idealized qualities. The unconscious fantasy of merger with the ideal lover enhances gratification obtained from vicarious identifications and thereby reduces ambivalence. At that time Fran regarded Paul as the embodiment of all her ideals. It was equally or perhaps even more important, however, that Paul also satisfied Fran's romantic fantasies and needs. He thus was both a narcissistic and a libidinal object choice.

Fran's personality, when she fell in love, seemed to have changed abruptly. Strikingly, from being an active, striving, achieving person in competition with boys and envious of them, Fran became extremely submissive. It seemed as if her ego interests ceased to exist. This change could partly be explained by her unconscious identification with Paul, which vicariously satisfied her narcissistic aims (Reich 1953). Analysis revealed, however, that the narcissistic gratification derived from Paul's loving admiration of her beauty was of even greater significance. It enabled Fran for the first time not only to feel beautiful but also to accept and own the feeling. In the past, told she was beautiful by relatives or friends, Fran would shrug and respond, "Mother is beautiful," and whisper to herself, "Beauty is empty, I want to be a Mensch." This rationalization helped Fran cope with father's disregard of her girlhood and femininity, which evoked unconscious feelings of inferiority and envy of mother.

The internalization of Paul's adoration made Fran feel for the first time acknowledged as a woman. This experience was of momentous significance for her psychic equilibrium. It became the transitional bridge that led to the activation of her unconscious identification with mother, conceived and acknowledged by Fran as father's only erotic love object. Fran transferred onto Paul derivatives of her repressed oedipal feelings and enacted in their relationship her perception of mother's role.

The following material from the analysis elucidates some of Fran's perception of the family scene.

The mother–father interaction contributed to Fran's conviction about women's inferior role and status. She believed that her father loved mother as a beautiful sex object needed by him to fulfill his desires and as a narcissistic object he could show off to. Mother also provided the perfect and perfectly run home he required. Fran ascribed father's frequent brutal quarrels with mother—his screaming at her and leaving her in tears—to his disappointment and anger because of mother's failure to provide him with a son and more children. In her analysis Fran was able, for the first time, to recognize and consciously acknowledge the extent of her father's sadism. The sessions preceding this break-through were stormy and torturous. She became extremely anxious, her state bordering on panic. Fran accused me of being unfeeling and mean and of wanting to destroy her "one anchorage in life: father." Her resistance to analyzing father's image was extreme. Fran said, "He was my savior, whatever his shortcomings. I would have become crazy if not for him, dangling continuously on my mother's inconsistent moods, unable to evoke her smile, and helplessly feeling rejected. Father was a hard taskmaster, but it was possible to please him. For mother I was a defective being like she was. This was the reason mother could not accept me. I had a sense of security with father. I felt he loved me, but I knew I had to 'measure up.' Father was never mean to me.

He was the only one who took care of me. Perhaps my hatred of mother blinded me to the pain he inflicted."

Fran's unconscious awareness of father's sadism was indicated in her elaborate masturbation fantasies in which the woman was devalued, disregarded, physically abused, and used as a vessel for procreation. The man in all these fantasies appeared brutal, unfeeling, concerned only with his own wishes and pleasures. In the course of her analysis Fran shamefully realized that she was identified with both protagonists of these repetitive fantasies. Fran's stance, until she met Paul, expressed her reaction and opposition to this type of male–female relationship. She did not want to be a woman like her mother, nor did she want to be a man like her father. She was critical of both. But Fran admired her father, who was strident, achieving, and stood up for himself, and she despised and devalued her mother, who, she felt, submitted without a struggle. From Fran's associations to her masturbation fantasies it became apparent that she suspected her mother of "submitting willingly." She felt disgusted with mother's subservience to father. Fran concluded that mother felt defective as a woman since she could not produce "sons," and only "produced" a girl, defective like she was.

As a child Fran remembered mother's frequent illnesses and her lethargy. Aspects of the unconscious significance of her reaction to mother's illnesses came to the fore from fantasies following my sudden and unexpected cancellation of a week of sessions. Fran was convinced during this interval that only her sessions were canceled. She also worried that something terrible had happened to me and I would not recover for a long, long time. In her unconscious fantasies, angry, hostile, and loving elements were present. The analysis of these fantasies linked them with feelings about and toward mother's illnesses, her rage at mother's unavailability, her guilt about her murderous impulses, and her longing for the good mother.

Fran's interaction with her father, who encouraged her tomboyishness and treated her like a chum, cast a shadow upon the vicissitudes of the oedipal phase, its resolution, and the further course of object relations. Throughout her analysis Fran could not recall any amorous fantasies or wishes directed toward her father, although she remembered having such fantasies in relation to a family friend and an uncle. The structure and content of her masturbation fantasies, however, suggest that father was the unconscious object, perceived as sadistic and ungratifying. Most prominent from about age 4 was Fran's fantasy of a male teacher beating the beloved child, a girl who "deserved it." During the beating the girl lost control and peed. With great embarrassment Fran associated to an incident when she provoked her father, who indeed hit her, and this resulted in loss of urinary control. Fran hesitatingly admitted being for years confused about sexual excitement and urinary pressure. She was never "quite sure." Analytic material indicated that Fran experienced father's hitting her as sexually exciting.

In the course of the analysis, the presence of two internalizations leading to the formation of two disparate self-images became clear. Predominant until she met Paul was the Older Brother ideal that led to the formation of Fran's conscious wished-for self-image. The values and ideals with which she endowed Older Brother were eventually incorporated into her ego ideal. Living up to them enhanced Fran's self-esteem. Totally unconscious and revealed only by the analysis was Fran's identification with her mother, leading to the formation of her feminine ideal, which, however, was not incorporated in the wished-for self-image. Consciously the masochistic submissive nature of such a feminine ideal was appalling to Fran.

Fran's relationship with Paul was multidetermined since he was both a narcissistic and a libidinal object, initially providing both types of gratification. While this state lasted, Fran was ideally happy, satisfied to live in Paul's shadow and bask in his glory. This type of object relationship eventuated in her tenuous psychic balance, which was upset by Paul's philandering. She experienced this behavior as a continuous assault on her self-esteem as a woman. Consequently, Fran's sense of being affirmed in her femininity became illusory and was lost. Analytic material suggested that Fran believed her mother's submissive suffering was "the price" for father's fidelity. Unconsciously, Fran felt that her self-abrogation had not succeeded in achieving this aim. During this period Fran no longer identified with Paul, and therefore derived no vicarious gratification from his achievements. She was more and more frequently painfully aware of the extent to which she had renounced her ego strivings and goals, and she felt envious of Paul, who continued to achieve his goals. Her relationship with Paul now evoked a conflict between her conscious wished-for self-image and her unconscious feminine ideal. During this tempestuous period of breakups and reunions with Paul, Fran felt like a failure both in the area of erotic femininity and in her functioning based on the Older Brother model. She did not measure up to either. The libidinal loss and narcissistic depletion in both areas eventuated in an overwhelming loss of self-esteem. It evoked a sense of helplessness and led to a narcissistic depression (Lax 1989) manifested by emotional withdrawals and suicidal fantasies.

Discussion

Nagera (1969), in his extensive discussion of imaginary companions, points out that they fulfill a variety of functions, depending on the needs of the child. The imaginary companion, according to Nagera, may be an "impersonation of the child's primitive ego ideal, which may contain ideals beyond its reach. This function can be observed in children who feel rejected. By endowing the ego ideal with the attributes the child lacks, the child can vicariously participate in the loving relationship with parents" (p. 196). Frequently the narcissistic function of the imaginary companion is of utmost significance in that it helps the child preserve a sense of omnipotence, an illusion of independence and freedom of choice (Sperling 1954). Bach (1971) adds that imaginary companions often represent some vital aspect of mastery or competence, a core element of the active, spontaneous self.

The intrapsychic fantasy represented by Older Brother became Fran's imaginary companion. It also represented the ideal to which she aspired and whose values became incorporated in her ego ideal. Though initially based on what Fran imagined her parents would have wanted in a son, it became a composite image that changed and grew as she matured. It included demands Fran experienced as expected of her, aspects of heroes, and selective identifications with chosen models. Older Brother likewise contained some characteristics Fran valued in her father (his enthusiasm, capacity for caring), and in important respects was a reaction to the traits she disliked in him (for instance, his tyrannical manner), thus also expressing her critical view of father. The fantasy of Older Brother has characteristics that correspond to Freud's (1914a) description of a narcissistic object since it represented what Fran would have liked to be. Older Brother was an inner aspect of Fran's personality, yet distanced from the ego core, which took on the qualities of an object representation (Meissner 1971), an ideal that served as her model. She strove to become like Older Brother. In this process Fran unconsciously felt she gave her parents the son she thought they had wished for.

Since Fran experienced the devaluation of women as a narcissistic injury, creation of the Older Brother fantasy and the identification with it were attempts at self-healing in a situation in which a girl, "on principle," was not wanted. However, Fran's psychic need to create Older Brother, a male, as a model indicates the extent to which she unconsciously accepted the cultural standard and devalued her femaleness. Analysis revealed that her identification with Older Brother also had a defensive function. It protected her, until she met Paul, from the insidious effect of her unconscious identification with mother, which formed the core of her feminine ego ideal.

When Fran acknowledged her love for Paul, her competitiveness, independence, and even autonomy seemed to have vanished.

She felt she could not be in conflict with him. Analysis revealed the unconscious causes for this startling change. It appears that during the entire relationship with Paul, an unconscious intrasystemic conflict raged in Fran between her formerly dominant wished-for self-image modeled on Older Brother and her previously unconscious feminine ideal modeled on her mother. The latter prevailed and was enacted by Fran during most of her relationship with Paul. The breakups, which she instigated when hurt and angered by him, were an expression of the temporary resurgence of behavior prompted by identification with the Older Brother ideal.

Throughout her analysis Fran frequently spoke about her certainty regarding father's love for mother. The vehemence with which she insisted on this fact struck me as greatly exaggerated, and indicated to me the strength of her childhood oedipal erotic feelings and longings for her father. Fran's conviction of maternal victory helped her repress the narcissistic injury caused by her failure to win father's love and her hurt at the unavailability of father as an erotic object. The sense of narcissistic defeat is very significant in every oedipal conflagration. When convinced of father's fidelity, the little girl consoles herself by insisting that no one but mother is father's sole erotic love object. Mother is thus perceived as the victorious female whose attributes give her the power to win and hold her man. The belief in mother's triumph unconsciously motivated Fran to emulate her. Unconsciously she perceived mother's submissiveness, masochistic surrender, her succumbing to humiliation, painful as they were, as devices enabling her to achieve her goal. To Fran, unconsciously, a man's erotic fidelity and zeal signified his affirmation of the woman and her power to hold him. Consequently, for Fran, absolute exclusivity in a love relationship meant being affirmed as a successful woman. Because of the painful deficiencies in her relationship with father, namely, his lack of positive acknowledgment of her femininity, her need for such affirmation was indeed intense.

In her relationship with Paul she wanted what she believed her mother had attained with her father.

Consciously, however, Fran disparaged mother as a model of womanhood. This became quite evident during sessions in which she bemoaned the fact that women engage in "masochistic orgies" or in so-called "altruistic surrender." She saw women as losers.

Fran's sense of affirmation as a woman and her gratifications based on the maternal identification ended when Paul manifested his need for amorous diversity. She became at that time consciously aware of the conflict in her values and goals. Strivings for autonomy and the need to live in accordance with her wished-for self-image, which were suppressed during the first phase of her relationship with Paul, once again became much more prominent. Yet, masochistically, Fran blamed herself for Paul's behavior. She was torn by the question, "How and what should a woman be?" During her analysis Fran discovered that in her relationship with Paul the submissive, compliant, passive, and available woman, who loves without questioning man's priority, conformed much more strongly to her ideal of a woman than did the emancipated, so-called modern counterpart. According to this feminine ideal based on the identification with her mother, a woman existed solely to fulfill a man's bidding and was loved and depended upon in proportion to the excellence with which she fulfilled this task. Thus the ideal woman was an embodiment of all the requirements of a masculine, fantasied, anaclitic object. Such a woman had no aims or goals of her own. She lived through her man and for him.

Further analysis, in which Fran's relationship to and with her father was explored, revealed also her deep and unconscious identification with his values and attitudes toward women. Based on this identification, to be a woman unconsciously meant to Fran to be the kind of woman father would desire and on whom father would bestow his love. This type of woman was represented by mother, perceived by Fran as the erotic slave-woman. Thus her feminine ideal based on the identification with mother was reinforced further by her identification with what she conceived as father's ideal of femininity. During her love relationship with Paul, Fran became passive and submissive and gave up the conscious goals of her wished-for self-image, becoming, as she finally could say during her analysis, "my father's kind of woman." Libidinal strivings predominated, though the narcissistic identification with Paul was significant.

This psychic resolution, however, was short-lived. Fran's re-action to Paul's infidelities expressed not only the pain of object loss, but also, as analysis revealed, the repressed anger stemming from the frustration of her ego aims. During each of their frequent breakups, Fran, though upset and depressed, acted with increasingly greater autonomy and began to resume her former ego interests. However, her behavior, based on her wished-for self-image, contributed to difficulties during periods of reunion with Paul. Their divergent ego aims clashed and they found it more and more difficult even to conceive of a harmonious life together. Eventually, because she did not feel sufficiently affirmed in her womanliness by Paul, Fran reverted to a more narcissistic position. Thus the patterns modeled on Older Brother once again came to the fore. Fran felt she could no longer fit herself into Paul's schema.

A long analysis of masturbation fantasies in which women with artificial penises assumed the role of men during intercourse, but derived no pleasure from their activity, contributed to the understanding that for Fran the achievement of the goals of her wished-for self-image, though consciously gratifying, unconsciously also signified a partial defeat. This became apparent when analysis revealed that Fran had given up the hope during her childhood of ever being acknowledged by father as a "girl-woman to be." She consciously accepted and appeared to be proud of father's designation: a "girl-like boy," which was a deprivation of her femininity. Disappointed by father in her girlish/womanish strivings, Fran aimed to "measure up" to fulfill the role of "girl-like boy." Thus she at least experienced the pleasure stemming from the gratification of father's demands, which enhanced her narcissism and boosted her self-esteem. The final break up with Paul signified to Fran that she was "not sufficiently desirable as a woman." This deeply injured her budding sense of femininity. Partly motivated by the pain of the failed libidinal involvement, Fran once again reverted to the pursuit of her ego goals. She became a workaholic. Gratification from work helped restore aspects of her wounded narcissism. She felt once again she was a Mensch. However, the sense of pain remained. Unconsciously Fran regarded the achievement of her ego goals as "masculine," a notion she consciously, vehemently denied.

Fran was racked by two disparate needs. Her well-being required the adoration of a loving, loved man. Without such continuous "feeding," she was unable to maintain the sense of being a desirable woman. The lack of such affirmation contributed to feelings of depression since she felt rejected. Fran also needed the fulfillment of ego values and goals that she had expressed via the Older Brother fantasy. These became incorporated in her wished-for self-image. Achievements in these areas gave her gratification, a sense of mastery and well-being leading to excitement, accompanied by narcissistic pleasure that increased her self-esteem.

Fran's identificatory systems were disharmonious (Kernberg 1980a, 1984, Schafer 1983). This resulted in intrasystemic conflict. Her self-representation could not fuse because it contained two self-images with contradictory aims and objects: the unconscious, parentally determined feminine ideal and the wished-for self-image based on her identification with Older Brother. The ego ideal likewise contained two conflicting sets of ideal standards (Hartmann and Loewenstein 1962), one based on the feminine ideal, the other comprising the values and ideals embodied in the Older Brother fantasy. The split within the ego and within the superego interfered with the attainment of self-constancy as well as the attainment of psychic integration. Consequently, Fran lacked sufficient sustaining healthy narcissism.

The case of Fran indicates that the wish to be a boy need not necessarily lead to a simple development of character traits and goals stereotyped as masculine. It also need not lead to the formation of a reactive character type of woman who gives up her strivings and "loves the man who represents her own, externalized, former ego identifications" (Reich 1953, p. 25). Instead, Fran "created" Older Brother, a precipitate of what she sensed and imagined was expected from a boy and from selective paternal identifications. She subsequently externalized this psychic creation and made it into her ideal, with which she reidentified. This secondary internalization led to the absorption of Older Brother into an aspect of the ego ideal and to the development of Fran's wished-for self-image with goals she could easily achieve. The persistence of the Older Brother fantasy suggests that it also had a defensive function. It protected Fran from succumbing to the unconscious maternal feminine ideal that at times led to her pathological self-abrogation. The lack of cohesion and integration that characterized Fran's psyche, torn by conflict, resulted in a life subjectively experienced as lacking in gratifying fulfillment.

8 Masochism in Women: The Role of Internalization and Ego Psychological Considerations

Introduction

Aspects of masochistic behavior in women have been regarded from many different points of view. Bonaparte (1949), Deutsch (1930, 1944), Freud (1924b, 1931, 1933, 1937), Lampl-de Groot (1965), and Reik (1941) among many others have emphasized constitutional, economic, moral, and psychodynamic factors. I shall not review these findings since they are well known and have been investigated extensively.

My discussion of women's masochistic self-defeating behavior will focus on specific kinds of internalization[1] processes and ensuing identifications that typically occur within the framework of certain object-relations constellations. I will indicate how such

---

1. Throughout this chapter the terms *internalization, incorporation, introjections, identification, self image, self representation,* and *object representation* are used according to the definitions in Moore and Fine (1990).

internalizations may lead to the subsequent formation of deviant ego and superego structures. Those aspects of developmental phases that contribute to such pathology will be explored.

My patients suffered from a predominantly obsessive character neurosis with hysteroid, narcissistic, and depressive features. Each of them, upon analytic scrutiny, seemed strangely at odds with herself. Though each appeared to be striving assertively toward the achievement of her goals, each failed repeatedly for reasons beyond her comprehension. These patients identified with progressive causes, appeared to have good, though somewhat competitive, relations with both sexes, were physically attractive, "free" in their love life, and sought self-fulfillment.

Analytic investigation disclosed, however, that their assertive, achieving behavior and their conscious convictions corresponded only to one aspect of their personality. Unconsciously provoked failures both in their professional or in their love life revealed the other aspect of their selves. These patterns of self-defeat, like a leitmotif, ran through these patients' lives, resulting in narcissistic mortifications that eventually led to a lasting depletion of their self-esteem. The narcissistic hurts evoked feelings of depression and worthlessness, unending ruminations, and a growing sense of perplexity when they sought explanations for the "mess" they had made of their lives. Eventually these women sought therapy to discover why things went wrong with their lives that appeared so promising.

The following clinical case vignettes illustrate some manifestations of these patients' pathology.

Case 1

Mrs. Y., a much sought-after lawyer who specialized in family law and civil liberties cases, started treatment after staying for twenty-four years in a marriage that she experienced as demeaning. She had married because of extreme sexual attraction to her husband as well as great respect for his professional standing. Soon after their marriage, however, Mrs. Y. discovered that her husband did not regard her as his peer; instead he expected her to take care of all their domestic, financial, and social responsibilities, which he regarded as "chores." Mrs. Y. complied "for the sake of harmony." Eventually, however, her husband's attitude reactivated repressed childhood conflicts and she began to feel denigrated. She became extremely angry about her "lot in life," but continued to fulfill her marital role, rationalizing she was doing so "for the sake of the children."

Analysis revealed that, unconsciously, Mrs. Y. experienced her marital situation in terms of the childhood paradigm. She had a much older brother who had been held in high esteem by both mother and father. Nothing was ever permitted to interfere with brother's intellectual pursuits. Mother served father and brother "hand and foot," and expected her daughter to do likewise. As a child, Mrs. Y. had felt that her intellectual achievements, which equaled her brother's, were of no real significance to her parents. She felt that brother also treated her as an inferior. Since neither parent took issue with brother's attitude toward her, Mrs. Y. concluded that they concurred. Recognizing that mother's status in the family's pecking order did not equal that of father or brother, Mrs. Y. likewise regarded her mother as inferior. Mother's obvious preference for brother, and her catering to him, confirmed Mrs. Y.'s own feelings of inferiority.

In her unconscious, Mrs. Y.'s husband represented a combined father–brother image. She was hurt and angered by him just as she had been by father and brother in the past. In spite of being successfully assertive in her professional life, she was unable to oppose her husband directly. Analytic work revealed that Mrs. Y. unconsciously equated her husband's love for her with the love bestowed on mother by father and brother. Modeling herself on mother, Mrs. Y. believed that only by submitting to her husband and fulfilling his demands would she be able to gain and keep his love. In her unconscious, father, brother, and husband were merged into the desired, idealized oedipal object whose love she sought unconditionally.

Mrs. Y.'s unconscious identification with mother, perceived as inferior, became clear both from her submissive attitude toward her husband and from her contrasting attitudes toward her own son and daughter. Mrs. Y. repeated in her relationship to her children the pattern her mother established. She catered to her son and exalted him and expected her daughter to do likewise. Without being aware of it, she continued to act out her unconscious identification with the image of the debased and debasing mother.

Case 2

Mrs. G., a successful travel agent, suffered from chronic depression. She considered her husband's repeated and prolonged love affairs, which had begun approximately one year after the birth of their child, the precipitating factor. Prior to that, their marriage could have been considered conventionally happy. After the birth of their child, however, their sexual contact decreased. As Mr. G.'s love affairs took on increased importance, he withdrew all sexual interest from his wife in favor of his mistresses. Mrs. G. responded to this with extreme mortification. As her feeling of being rejected by her husband grew, professional success, rich enduring friendships, and varied extraprofessional interests lost all significance for her. She spent hours imagining her husband's love life. She also brooded about her inability to divorce him. Mr. G. was a rather superficial, callous, and emotionally unavailable person. Mrs. G. knew she did not truly love him. However, in spite of this awareness and in spite of her professional and financial independence, she was unable to leave him. This distressed her greatly and resulted in further loss of self-esteem.

After several years of analysis Mrs. G. was finally able to reveal the following masturbation fantasy, which she had had since adolescence.

A sultan with a great harem had a first wife whom he no longer desired, but by whom he wanted to have children. It was his custom, while he was engaging in sex play with a current favorite, to have the first wife in bed at the same time, tied in such a way as to be available to him for impregnation. The mistress would excite him and he would fondle her and sexually gratify her. Finally, at the very last minute, he would impregnate his wife.

Associations connected this fantasy with her parents and linked it to conflicts of the oedipal phase. Mrs. G. recalled that during adolescence she had overheard mother reading to a friend a fragment of a letter in which father had referred to himself as a sultan and said that "even if he had a hundred wives, she [mother] would always be his first wife." Mother felt complimented and honored by this. The patient, however, had felt humiliated and appalled: she experienced father's remarks as denigrating women and was horrified that any woman could feel honored by them. Mortified, Mrs. G. admitted that her masturbation fantasy started shortly after this incident.

Upon analysis, Mrs. G. realized that she idenetified in her own marital situation with the "first-wife–mother" of the masturbation fantasy. This realization was facilitated by the fact that she had become a mother and that she experienced her sexual deprivation as the result of her husband's involvement with his mistress.

Further analysis revealed, however, that the patient also identified with the mistress of the masturbation fantasy. This identification had several meanings. It signified that the patient accepted mother as father's prime love object, but it also expressed the patient's vengeful fantasy—her wish to deprive mother of the sexual gratification she (mother) received from father. The patient had thus attempted, via the masturbation fantasy, to resolve her conflicted feelings experienced toward mother during the oedipal phase. In fantasy the patient accorded mother the superior position of "first wife-procreation vessel," but simultaneously deprived mother of sexual gratification, which the patient desired for herself.

The point in the fantasy at which the patient orgasmed varied. Sometimes it took place when the wife was impregnated and sometimes when the mistress was excited to the utmost. Further analysis indicated that the patient also identified with the sultan, who misused both women for his pleasure. The fantasy thus served as a compromise solution for the hostile and positive aspects of the oedipal conflict. Elaboration of the meaning of identification with the sultan revealed profound feelings of self-debasement, which seemed to go beyond the parents' jointly held attitude regarding women's "inferior" status.

The detailed analysis of this masturbation fantasy contributed to the understanding of the causes that had led to Mrs. G.'s difficulty in leaving her husband. The unhappy marital situation, in which she was sexually deprived, represented for her unconscious the oedipal triangle in which she had identified primarily with the humiliated yet elevated "first-wife–mother." Mrs. G. had become immobilized in her painful and frustrating marriage because its specific constellation masochistically gratified all the forbidden, repressed oedipal wishes.

Acting out the unconscious identification with the bound "first-wife–mother," the passive receptor for the paternal phallus, Mrs. G. inhibited all her assertiveness and became masochistically tied to her husband, who represented for her unconscious the father-sultan. The vicious cycle of reality frustration and unconscious gratification perpetuated the marriage. It led to increased self-destructive behavior, depression, and eventually seriously affected Mrs. G.'s professional and social life.

Case 3

Ms. Z. was an account executive in her early thirties, successful and respected by her firm. She was known for her assertiveness and capabilities in dealing with business executives, and was usually given difficult accounts to handle. However, in spite of her successes, Ms. Z. had an erratic work history, which seemed puzzling. She would start a job enthusiastically, work for months with great diligence and devotion, and then suddenly, when a promotion was in the offing, begin slackening in her efforts: she would get to work late, do her assignments at the last minute, become unpredictable in her dealings with clients and so on.

Careful scrutiny indicated that this change in her functioning usually coincided with an upheaval in her love life. It would occur when Ms. Z. felt "deeply in love" and wished for her lover to take care of her. At such times Ms. Z. would fantasize that she was becoming pregnant and she would look forward to having a baby. She would declare in moments of sexual ecstasy that her lover could do with her anything he wished—even kill her.

The men Ms. Z. picked as lovers, although highly gifted and of unusual intelligence, were, for a variety of reasons, unable to meet her dependency needs. In spite of this, Ms. Z. would for a long time continue to devote herself to them and to their needs. Ms. Z's analytic sessions, however, were filled with complaints about them. Though she was usually very independent and enjoyed flirting with many men, Ms. Z., when she fell deeply in love, wanted to be asked by her lover to become his wife. She would at such times turn her back on her hitherto cherished independence and agonize over the fact that she was still unmarried. She saw this as a sign of her "worthlessness" and would become excessively self-critical and self-doubting.

During such periods of personal upheaval, Ms. Z. would endanger her position in the firm by various subtle and unconscious provocations. As a consequence, she would either be threatened with dismissal or fired outright. Distraught, she would turn to her lover for support. In her fantasy the lover at this point would propose marriage and assume complete care of her. This fantasy, however, was never fulfilled. Disappointed, disillusioned, and angry, Ms. Z. would eventually turn against the lover, openly find fault with him, and finally break off the relationship. She would then return to work full of enthusiasm, whether to her old job or a new one. Since Ms. Z. was extremely attractive and charmingly seductive, she would very soon find a new lover and the entire cycle would begin anew.

Ms. Z. suffered from an obsessive character neurosis with hysterical, depressive, and narcissistic trends. She had had several abortions following so-called "accidental" pregnancies. The following is a terrifying dream she had while coming out of anesthesia following a D.&C.:

> She was a small part of an elaborate scientific "instrumentation system, consisting of pipes, tubes, and U-shaped vials, all connected and in motion." She was "at the bottom of the U." She could do nothing to stop what was going on; she was immobilized by it. She could not express her needs or desires.

She woke from this dream in a state of panic and remained haunted by it ever since. She spoke in connection with this dream about a married lover whom she had adored and whose "sex object" she had been. Although he called her his "love nymph," he was such a callous lover that her genitals were injured and always sore. She did, however, in no way indicate her pain to him. On the contrary, Ms. Z. "made a pretense of bliss."

After several years in analysis, Ms. Z. recognized that her repeated provocations at work were unconsciously motivated and that a connection existed between the upheavals in her business life and those in her love life.

The patient was greatly embarrassed to admit at that time that she masturbated by rubbing against the corner of the mattress, "in a humped position like a man." She was reluctant to consider the possible implications of this manner of masturbation and seemed intent on dropping the subject altogether. However, as if at random, Ms. Z. began to speak about the certainty with which her parents, while mother was pregnant, anticipated the birth of a boy. She added, sadly: "They even bought cigars and liquor in advance of the *bris*. No one ever drank the liquor or smoked the cigars."

She had slept in the parental bedroom until the age of 12. Her understanding of the sexual interaction between the parents slowly became clear. She felt mother did not want sex and father imposed it. "Mother gave in for the sake of peace, to get rid of his nagging and to have it over with. Mother had no choice; she just had to." The patient reported the following recurring masturbation fantasy: "I am in bondage in a concentration camp, tied up and being whipped. The assailants are nondescript and the cause for the punishment unspecified." In association the patient recalled sex play when she was 8 or 9 years old: "It was a cowboys-and-Indians game. I was the Indian. I would let the cowboys catch me and tie me up. They would then tickle me in the genitals, especially the clitoris. At first I directed them 'how and where.' This was the 'torture.' Then they took over. It was too much. I couldn't move. I would scream. It got worse." The patient maintained that she never "did it" to anyone. After some silence Ms. Z. "confessed" that she wanted "it done" to herself: "it was delicious torture."

Analysis revealed that the patient identified in fantasy with both the tortured and the torturer. Exploration of the masculine manner in which Ms. Z masturbated revealed her enormous envy of the male role. Yet though she envied the male and identified with him, she also identified with the woman. She wanted to be both. Since early childhood Ms. Z. had been made aware of the greater importance of men. She said with a sigh, "In my house the man was boss, the woman catered to his every need, even if she did not like it." Ms. Z always wished she had been a boy. In many ways she acted like one. During latency and early adolescence Ms. Z. hated every developmental change that forced her to recognize her femininity. However, as she matured, she became a beautiful woman, aware of and able to use her beauty.

During her analysis Ms. Z. became aware of her masculine and feminine trends, which varied in their intensity during different periods, but which, nevertheless, were always in conflict with each other. Thus, in addition to her envy of the boy-man she wanted to be, Ms. Z., because of her unconscious oedipal longings, also wanted to be the most beautiful and feminine of all women. Her ideas, however, of what constituted femininity were confused, since they were based, in part at least, on her conception of mother's debased role. Ms. Z., enraged, complained: "Why are women masochists? Why was mother a slave?" (The effect of oedipal jealousy coloring Ms. Z.'s interpretation of mother's reactions were explored and analyzed.)

The masochistic relationship of the slave woman to the sadistic male, depicted by Ms. Z. in her masturbation fantasies, had its intrapsychic parallel in the sadomasochistic interaction between the patient's ego and superego (Schafer 1960).

Case 4

Renee, a scientist in her late twenties, came into treatment because of pervasive feelings of depression that were associated with a sense of humiliation and shame following the dissolution of an unhappy love affair. Though she had many friends and admirers, Renee felt worthless and regarded her rewarding and successful career as "meaningless." She felt at a loss, and wondered whether she should give up her way of life—perhaps even her life.

Renee was the daughter of a prominent businessman turned politician. She remembered always feeling disadvantaged by comparison with her older and younger brothers as well as her father. As a child she envied her brothers for being allowed to walk around naked while she and mother "had to be modest." She wondered what shame she had to hide. Father and brothers could "go places," stay out late, tell dirty jokes, and drink, while she and mother had to be "ladies." Father expected the boys to excel at studies, sports, and work, while she and mother were expected to be "sweet things" who had to sit around "available to do father's bidding."

Mother appeared to share father's attitudes. She permitted father to dominate while she passively went along with each of his demands. Renee described her mother as a beautiful woman, greatly loved by father. According to Renee, mother had been vivacious before her marriage, but for father's sake had given up her uniqueness and her individuality. "Mother complied," Renee complained to me with anger. "Mother was a martyr. She lived only for the family, doing what everyone wanted, but no one did anything for her." Mother's favorite among the children was the youngest brother, whom Renee had mothered a great deal. He remained her favorite brother, and as an adult Renee developed a close companionship with him.

Although father spoiled Renee by fulfilling her wishes, expressing his admiration for her, and choosing her to become his "companion"—which she greatly enjoyed—she never felt that father respected her. She felt that he did not regard her as a potential equal nor did he want her to be one. Father did, however, grant Renee financial privileges he denied his wife—and even some he denied his sons. Renee believed that father wanted her around "only for his pleasure." She regarded this attitude as similar to the one father had toward mother, whom, Renee felt, he "held in bondage." Renee was torn by her feelings toward father, which oscillated between adoration and fury. She resented the different standards father had for her and her brothers and demonstrated her wish to be accepted as an equal to her brothers by striving for achievement and excellence. However, though Renee did succeed in living up to the high standards father held for the boys—and though father occasionally even held her up as a model for the boys—Renee felt father did not praise her for her intellectual achievements as much as he did for "looking pretty and being charming."

After going to college, Renee became fully aware of her disgust with father's "double standard" and her intense anger toward him. She openly rebelled by joining a very "left" and "liberated" group, becoming the top student in her class, and qualifying for a grant that made her financially independent of father. During this period they became estranged from each other and her strong love feelings for father were repressed. Renee became quite successful in both her personal and professional life. She developed a serious love relationship with a colleague who regarded her as his peer and treated her with love, tenderness, and consideration. Their tastes, attitudes, and ways of life were harmonious and their relationship flourished. It would have been perfect but for the fact that Renee felt sexually unfulfilled. Although she did find Peter sexually attractive and even exciting, she responded to his sexual advances as to an "imposition," finding them difficult to tolerate. Renee concocted excuses to avoid them and was almost frigid during intercourse. She was aware of feeling pleased that her brothers liked Peter, and she thought that he reminded her in some ways of her favorite brother.

Several years after Renee and Peter established a joint household, she went to another city to attend a scientific meeting. The outstanding researcher in her field was a charismatic Frenchman who quickly swept her off her feet. Renee not only regarded him as brilliant, she was overwhelmed by his machismo and by his conviction that he could make her sexually happy. They spent several exciting weeks together, during which Renee had orgasmic experiences for the first time in her life. She came to feel completely dependent on Louis for sexual fulfillment. During those weeks Renee's adoration of Louis grew, and he kept assuring her of his love.

Renee returned home to Peter with a sense of disloyalty and guilt. Some time later, however, after Louis contacted her and beseeched her to join him, Renee agreed. She made a full disclosure to Peter and left. Her feelings toward Peter contained both sorrow and affection. She was happy they "parted friends."

Renee stayed with Louis for six months, a time she eventually considered "the unhappiest of my life." Shortly after her arrival, Louis's attitude toward her began to change: he stopped courting her. Having become absorbed in a new scientific project, Louis now expected Renee to take care of all domestic responsibilities and to be "available" to him at his bidding. His interests and pleasures came first. Though Louis's demands gradually enraged Renee, she remained completely submissive. She felt as if she were "in bondage," convinced that only Louis had "the power to give her an orgasm." Renee became aware that her sexual excitement and gratification with Louis were somehow related to her "feeling inferior and degraded."

Ever since she experienced orgasms during intercourse, Renee felt increasingly dependent on Louis. She wanted to hold on to him all the time, becoming anxious whenever he left her. Louis belittled this clinging behavior and was irritated by it. He wanted to be free.

Renee became depressed by her everyday life with Louis, who showed no interest in her activities and had no patience for her "moods." However, in contrast to his attitudes toward Renee, Louis expected her to become involved in *his* projects whenever that suited him, and to show understanding for *his* "humors."

As Renee's despair about the quality of their relationship and interaction grew, Louis became increasingly angry with her, and finally began to avoid her. This brought about Renee's increased despondency. She became pregnant. Her wish to bind Louis to her through the child was the predominant motive. The pregnancy, however, made their estrangement even worse.

After Louis clearly indicated his wish that she leave, Renee was finally able to break away. She toyed with the idea of having the child and raising it alone. However, under the influence of friends, Renee gave up her strong wish to do so. Louis did not help her either financially or emotionally with the abortion. Renee felt totally abandoned.

Renee's reactions to her experience with Louis, to the abortion, and to two subsequent short-lived love affairs motivated her to seek treatment.

Case 5

Dr. K., in her late forties, came for treatment at the urging of the head of her department.

She was depressed, but also very angry at not having been advanced along the academic ladder. She felt she deserved a promotion in view of her research achievements and publications. It soon became clear that Dr. K. had experienced this type of disappointment several times in the past. It had led each time to a change of position, since she claimed she could not tolerate staying in a work situation where she felt unappreciated. Analytic exploration revealed that being bypassed for a promotion signified to Dr. K. a rejection, which filled her with shame. Following such an experience, she felt narcissistically wounded and mortified. She could not bear to face the witnesses of her defeat.

Dr. K.'s work pattern indicated that she began each assignment with a lot of enthusiasm. She was a gifted teacher and administrator who initially got along well with her students and peers. She would quickly become a sought-after supervisor and was very popular with her colleagues. After a period sufficient to consolidate her position and make her eligible for a promotion with the strong backing of her entire department, Dr. K. would start—without any conscious awareness—doing things that eventually led to the defeat of her conscious aims. During such periods her actions provoked antagonism and disregard from colleagues in contrast to their previous attitude of friendliness and respect. Consequently, by the time Dr. K.'s candidacy for promotion came up, the climate of the department was highly unfavorable to her and thus her application was defeated.

Analysis disclosed that Dr. K. unconsciously equated the work situation with her experience of the oedipal situation. The marriage of her parents, which started as a "great love affair," was "on the rocks" by the time she was 4. Father verbally abused mother and quarrels were continuous. Dr. K. did not know the reasons for these quarrels. She suspected, in retrospect, that they were caused by mother's immaturity and her overdependency on her own mother. She believed that father did not respect mother and that he pushed her around. She considered herself "father's girl" and did everything to please him. Father was an athlete. Highlights of her memories center on going, as a little girl, to sporting events in which father participated. She admired him greatly.

The shock came some time between the ages of 4 and 5 when father "without any warning to me [i.e., her] walked out." She could not "fathom it." Mother and she returned to live with grandmother. She was deeply hurt by father's not being in touch with her for several years. It meant to Dr. K. that he really did not care for her or about her, and that he devalued her as much as he did mother. During her analysis Dr. K. recalled what she probably had known since latency, that father stayed away from his family because he was unemployed and ashamed that he could not support them.

In the work situation Dr. K. initially sought the admiration and appreciation of the head of the department, who unconsciously represented her father. She did not, however, want his erotic love. She was extremely competitive for the "No. 2" spot in the department. She had to be the chairman's closest associate and his deputy. However, when Dr. K. succeeded in attaining these aims, complications resulted, evoked by unconscious oedipal longings, and she also sought to become the erotic love object. Her behavior, which became self-destructive, appears to have been based on the childhood model of mother, the "unsuccessful devalued woman" whom Dr. K. unconsciously sought to emulate. When this psychic shift took place, Dr. K.—without any conscious awareness—time and time again would begin to sabotage her very excellent work. The result was disastrous for her career.

Analysis revealed to Dr. K. that she transferred her oedipal wishes to her boss, unconsciously aiming to win father's love from him. She thus enacted by her professional defeats the familial mother–father childhood situation in which mother was the loser.

Relevant Object-Relation Constellations

I will now outline the childhood histories of the patients described above, emphasizing factors that reappeared in each case and that had a pathognomonic significance for the development of their syndrome. I will focus on the importance of internalizations that occurred within the framework of specific libidinal and aggressive object-relation constellations that were crucial for the development of the character neurosis of these patients.

The unconsciously provoked defeats of my patients were related to distortions in the structure of the ego, reflecting structuralized derivatives of primary object relations that in turn influenced the patients' subsequent object relations. Thus ego deviations caused by internalizations during specific developmental phases were the most significant factors determining the pathology.

The patients came from middle-class families characterized by a pronounced patriarchal structure and a definite bias in favor of the male. Each of these patients felt—at least during the early years of their childhood—that the parents loved one another. They stressed, however, the Victorian nature of their parents' relationship. Thus father and mother adhered to definite stereotypical roles in the household: father was admired and deferred to as a generous and good provider on whom mother depended and was expected to dance attendance. He decided all matters of importance. Mother was cherished as the good homemaker and the valued sex object. While father stressed mother's beauty and her domestic skills, he never regarded her as his peer or adviser.

The threats to the narcissistic cathexis of the self, which exist from the moment of birth and stem from the interaction of the child's libidinal and aggressive drives with the demands, frustrations, and gratifications of the real world, were affected in a unique way by the familial constellation into which these patients were born. Thus, although these patients believed their parents had wanted children, they did not feel themselves to be as valued as they might have been, had they been boys. Further, though the birth of a daughter was a disappointment to both parents, it appears to have been more painful for mother than for father (Freud 1933). Thus the patients experienced the phallocentric orientation more strongly in their relationship with mother than with father.

These subjective feelings are corroborated by a report by the *New York Times* (April 5, 1974, p. 47) of a study conducted by the National Fertility Association in 1970 indicating a preference ratio of 189 boys to 100 girls with regard to the sex of the firstborn.

The investigations by Benedek (1959) and by Coleman and colleagues (1953) indicate the significance of the role played by cultural and individual variations in influencing parental attitudes. These authors also illustrate the extent and variety of unconscious meanings that a particular child may have for a parent. For the mothers of my patients the birth of a daughter was an upsetting experience. It is likely that their acceptance of phallocentric values that denigrate women intensified these mothers' unconscious longings to have been a male. This wish might have been gratified via identification with a male child. Thus the birth of a daughter may have reemphasized their unconscious feelings of being deprived and narcissistically diminished.

The mothers of my patients were unable to develop a genuine "maternal preoccupation" (Winnicott 1956) because their infant daughters did not represent the embodiment of their "fantasy child" (see Chapter 3). Thus the infants were cared for but not truly nurtured. They therefore lacked a sense of being cherished, a feeling derived only from mother's narcissistic valuations. The patients consequently felt "needy" throughout their lives. Jacobson (1954) indicates that the affective identification between mother and baby results in the *inducement of mother's affects in the infant.* Thus the conscious and unconscious displeasure on the part of these mothers had been experienced and internalized by their infant girls. Giovacchini (1972) states that such trauma in the symbiotic phase leads to the development in the child of a sense of identity that incorporates mother's devaluing attitudes, which are subsequently directed toward the developing self. As a result, the self is experienced as being unlovable, worthless, and inadequate. Consequently, self-esteem is lacking and vulnerability becomes excessive. During the oral, anal, and phallic phases these early internalized feelings became merged in my patients with the affects related to conflicts specific for these developmental stages. Feelings of denigration stemming from these sources were directed primarily toward the self, but also in part toward the mother who thus became devalued.

These mothers were unable to provide the necessary "refueling" that would have made successful mastery of the rapprochement subphase possible (Mahler 1968). Consequently, complete separation and individuation could not be achieved. Thus, unconscious aspects of early child–mother linkage persisted, affecting these patients' internalization of maternal attitudes and facilitating specific identifications with another.

The patients' recollections indicate that as children they sought out father rather than mother because they experienced him as more accepting. They felt father liked to be with them and play with them. These circumstances, as well as the high esteem in which father was held by the entire household, led to his idealization and lent impetus to the girls' wish to be like he was.

As is generally the case, mother, experienced during the oral and anal phases as unloving and depriving, was also blamed for experienced deprivations during the phallic phase. My patients recalled that following the discovery of genital differences an extremely stormy period of interaction with mother ensued. Since they had felt rejected by mother because they were girls, they had great difficulty accepting their femininity. It was therefore not surprising that analysis revealed long periods during childhood in which these girls denied their lack of a penis, and even longer periods during which, after they finally acknowledged their "defect," they simultaneously expressed desire and hope that a penis would eventually grow. These patients as little girls not only identified with the phallocentric attitudes of their parents, they magnified them. They experienced with pain mother's wish to make of them little mothers and ladies and keep them in their place, and rebelled against it.

Mother's rejecting attitude, experienced and incorporated from the symbiotic stage onward, fueled a vicious cycle in which the girl, feeling rejected by mother because of her supposed "defect," rejected and profoundly depreciated mother for the same reason, finally reintrojecting these feelings and turning them against herself. This experiential complex was influenced in a specific way by the attitudes of both parents toward women, and by father's special attitude toward his daughter. My patients as girls considered themselves exceptions because their fathers had accorded them a special, privileged position by exempting them from the status to which women were generally relegated. Since father's attitude was not based on an erotized relationship with his daughter, the girl child felt accepted in spite of her sex. The fathers, in large measure, gave them the privileges usually granted to boys. At times and to varying degrees, these daughters became the fathers' companions, in contradistinction to the mothers, who simply went along with their husbands. Intrapsychic reactions to the ongoing relationship with father led to an intensification of the girls' identification with his attributes, which they valued.

In the early years of their analyses, expression of the hostile affect toward mother predominated. It was related to the patients' feeling that mother was unresponsive and "unappreciative" and that she lacked understanding. Most important, however, was their complaint that, regardless of what they did, they never were accepted as "good enough" by mother. In the middle years of the analyses feelings of pervasive depression, helplessness, hopelessness, and loss surfaced. The patients held the conviction that mother had really not wanted them and they could do nothing about it.

The relationship with father was experienced as loving, often understanding, supportive, and sometimes even nurturing. Though father was regarded as much more demanding, he was considered to be more accepting. These patients felt they knew where they stood with father: they were accepted, provided that they fulfilled his demands. Consequently they molded their attitudes and behavior to become successful in areas meaningful to father. Since the girls could and did fulfill father's demands easily, their feelings toward him and his expectations became linked with active striving toward mastery and a sense of hope. This gave them a good feeling about themselves. They were saddened, however, by their awareness of not being accepted, even by father—as one patient said, "accepted just for being who you are." Nonetheless, father's conditional acceptance did not evoke in these patients the same feelings of hopelessness and helplessness they linked with a sense of a priori defeat felt in relation to mother. This conviction possibly accounted for the suicidal element in some of the patients.

The devalued view of woman with which these patients grew up, had a profound and devastating effect on the development and shape of their self-image during each psychosexual phase (Sandler and Rosenblatt 1962, Sandler et al. 1963). Since they never felt fully accepted by either parent, their wish to have been born a boy persisted, as did their envy of the boy's status. Consequently, their self-image remained insufficiently cathected with healthy narcissism, and genuine self-acceptance was almost impossible.

Analysis revealed that these patients' images of mother were not monolithic. Thus, during the negative oedipal phase, mother was greatly admired, the object of the girl's erotic impulses (see Chapter 5, Part II) and of her envy. Identification with the successful, powerful, womanly mother contributed an important aspect to the patient's maternal imago, which contrasted with the usually denigrated image. Treatment indicated that both these aspects of mother coalesced in the unconscious.

Each of the patients traversed both oedipal subphases. The male-directed positive oedipal feelings predominated but took a specific form. The patients' erotic feelings, however,—usually directed toward father—were displaced onto a male relative or close family friend. The eroticized relationship with this surrogate was highly charged. It involved a lot of kissing, lap-sitting, and hand holding. Evidence suggests that these relationships were overstimulating and resulted in sexual excitement and sexual frustration. The patients recalled that masturbation fantasies belonging to this time in their lives had as their conscious theme exictement, frustration, and deprivation of urinary discharge. Greenacre (1950a) discusses the frequent confusion between sexual excitement and urinary need.

The oedipal period was relatively long and dissolved slowly. The relationship with father during this time appeared not to have undergone any marked changes. The girls' conscious aspirations were modeled on father, with whom their companionship seemed to have grown even stronger. However, significant changes took place in the girls' inner world. Mother's image consolidated, and she emerged during the oedipal phase and thereafter, triumphantly, as father's undisputed love object, admired and envied by the girl for her beauty, grace, charm, and femininity. Thus the mother imago combined both coveted and devalued aspects. The girl who felt rejected by mother unconsciously felt enraged by father's love for mother because it empowered mother. This was an additional cause for envy.

None of my patients recalled any kind of seductive behavior toward father. They believed they had never competed with mother for father's erotic love since they were convinced such an attempt would have been doomed to failure. They did remember feeling jealous and possessive about the erotic feelings of the object of their displaced oedipal longings. Analytic material indicated that this displacement had defensive functions. It kept unconscious the patients' real rivalry with mother, and protected the "companionship" quality of their relationship with father. Nonetheless, as analysis indicated, the unconscious desire—even though displaced—to be or become father's erotic love object predominated during the oedipal phase. This became clear during the course of treatment. While struggling with intensely self-deprecatory feelings, the patients, with inappropriate shame, "confessed" that as children they had admired mother's beauty, envied it, and wished to become as beautiful when they grew up. Some of them even admitted to a belief that father would then love them better than mother.

Analysis of the feeling of mortification associated with the "confession" of this deeply guarded secret revealed a complex of emotions related to the core of these patients' pathology. It led to the uncovering of an unconscious identification with an exalted and simultaneously denigrated maternal imago conceived as a slave, a sexual object used for pleasure and gratification of desire, debased, mistreated, beautiful, adored, and thus wanted and loved by father. The formation of such a maternal imago probably stemmed in large measure from these patients' envious, hostile, and sadistic impulses toward her. The formation and internalization of this disparaged yet idealized maternal imago, the unconscious identification with it, and the subsequent inclusion of it in these patients' psychic structure had profound consequences. It became the component of these patients' unconscious self-image and wishful self-image (Jacobson 1954, 1964). The unconscious identification with this maternal imago was corroborated by the themes of repetitive sadomasochistic masturbation fantasies that had persisted in these patients' consciousness from early adolescence into adulthood.

Intense narcissistic mortification was associated with the recounting of these masturbation fantasies. This was due in part to the extreme contrast between the avowed ideals and goals to which these patients were consciously committed as adults and the manifest content of the masturbation fantasies that culminated in orgastic gratification. Even though the patients were completely unaware of the latent significance of their masturbation fantasies and of their unconscious identifications, the mere recognition that they were able to engage in and enjoy sadomasochistic fantasies filled them with self-disgust.

During latency and early adolescence the patients were tomboys. They played almost exclusively with boys, engaged and often even excelled in the games and pursuits of boys. These girls wanted to dress like boys. Some of them had a particular boy as a "special" friend. Such a relationship had a predominantly narcissistic character inasmuch as the girl identified with the boy who in part represented her ego ideal (Reich 1953).

The relationship with mother worsened during this period since mother strongly objected to the girl's tomboyishness. Father, however, either encouraged or condoned it. As a consequence, a further detachment from mother followed, associated sometimes with an intensification of the "companionship" with father. Analysis revealed that for the girl, father's acceptance unconsciously signified his approval of her goals and wishes. These girls wanted to be and became strident, active, and independent. In the phallocentric families in which these patients were reared, such wishes were considered masculine. The girls experienced mother's disapproval as an attempt to curtail their strivings. Some felt it stemmed "out of envy." They believed that mother wanted to subjugate them, to make them like she was, to deprive them of their opportunities. The girls raged against mother in horror and disgust. They felt they had to defend themselves. They experienced father as an ally in their struggle.

During adolescence these patients developed a narcissistic pride in their "inner values," their moral integrity, the high level of their standards, and the relentless strength of their ideals. Jacobson (1964) considers such values as constituting the feminine ego ideal. Most of my patients as adolescents wanted to be accepted and admired *only* for their character and achievements, their intellect, and their ethical and moral standards. These young women denied the significance of their attractiveness and charm even though they were frequently complimented on this account. They appeared to be somewhat haughty even though they were in fact gracious. They were unusually efficient and decisive, and seemed very independent. They knew that they appeared "strong and able to others," and this behavior fitted in with their goals. They were also aware, however, of having feelings "way down" of being weak and helpless, having dependency longings and needs. They expressed these feelings to their close friends and lovers.

Since adolescence these patients experienced periods of severe mood swings, despair, depression, and a sense of hopelessness and futility. The great vulnerability of their self-esteem indicated that the libidinal and aggressive cathexis of their self-representation had never been sufficiently neutralized. The disturbances in the regulation of their self-esteem reflected the pathology inherent in their self representation.[2]

Discussion and Theoretical Considerations

The specific etiological factors just described provide the necessary background for an understanding of the vicissitudes that led to the establishment in these patients of conscious and unconscious identification patterns, paternally and maternally derived, that eventuated in the development of a conscious and unconscious wished-for self-image and ego ideal.

Freud explored the phenomenon of splitting from different points of view. He recognized as early as 1923 that incompatible object identifications may lead to a disruption of the ego (1923a). He subsequently (1923b) asserted that splitting of the ego may follow as a consequence of disavowal (1937, 1940a, b). Freud's final conceptualizations regarding the causes and effects of splitting, stress topographic and structural differences that occur in different pathological conditions. Freud implies in his discussion that

---

2. Jacobson (1954) states: "Self-esteem is the ideational and specially emotional expression of self-evaluation and of the corresponding more or less neutralized libidinous and aggressive cathexis of the self representations" (p. 123).

two consequences may arise as a result of splitting. In the neurosis proper, in which the psychopathology is less severe, the disavowed aspect is repressed but continues to have the kind of influence typical for the repressed and that, in Freud's words, leads to "psychical complications." However, when the pathology is more severe, splitting of the ego results in the coexistence of two contrary dispositions throughout life that do not appear to modify each other.

Freud's formulations regarding developmental processes leading to structural ego distortions have been elaborated further by the findings of child psychoanalysis and the contributions of psychoanalytic ego psychology. Kernberg (1966) clarifies what is being split in splitting stating: "Splitting is typically a mechanism of the early ego in which identification systems have not crystallized into higher organizations such as the self or the representational world, but *it can pathologically persist at higher levels of ego organization and characteristically then affects the self, and ego identity in general*" (italics added, p. 249).

Kernberg (1966) elaborates further the nature and role of the split of the psychic component when he conceptualizes a "dynamic unconscious as a system composed of *rejected introjection and identification systems*" (p. 248). He describes the repressed portion of the id as possessing "an internal organization, and specific structures composed of self-image, object image and unacceptable impulse components" (p. 248). When considering lack of impulse control, Kernberg (1967) speaks of the emergence into consciousness of a dissociated identification system that is ego syntonic during the time this impulse behavior lasts and that is characterized by its repetitive nature and the lack of emotional contact between that part of the patient's personality and the rest of the self-experience.

The specific parental object relations experienced by my patients resulted in developmental vicissitudes that led to the formation of a conscious and an unconscious identification system, as defined by Kernberg (1966). The former was paternally and the latter maternally derived. These two identification systems did not become fused and they did not modulate each other. However, their existence and interaction affected the structuralization and the characteristics of these patients' self-image, wished-for self-image, ego ideal, and superego. Thus the divergent attitudes of these girls toward father and mother, combined with the differences in attitude exhibited by each parent toward the child, led to the formation of separate mother and father object representations that did not fuse into a parental representation. Subsequently the maternal and paternal representations were not fused in the superego and the ego ideal, nor were they depersonified. The patients had created on the one hand an idealized, grandiose image of a powerful and loving father and on the other hand an image of a rejecting mother who was a powerful "depriver, beautiful, loved, and yet devalued because she was a woman."

This lack of integration and depersonification led to the development of a specific form of self-representation that characterized these patients. Based on the identification with father and interaction with him, the patients developed a self-image characterized by assertion, striving, and a recognition that active mastery was indeed possible. This self-image was invested primarily with libidinal feelings experienced by the girls in their interaction with father and with neutralized libidinal cathexis withdrawn from the paternal imago. The patients' avowed standard of aspiration was derived from the internalized paternal model. These factors contributed significantly to the structure and content of these patients' *conscious, wishful self-image*, which was paternally derived. (These patients were aware that by the standards of our society many of their personality characteristics were considered masculine. They believed that such an appraisal was biased, reflecting the attitude that active and assertive goal-oriented activity is the prerogative of the male.)

Analysis demonstrated, however, that only one aspect of these patients' self-representation was revealed by their behavior patterned on the paternal identifications. Owing to the specific constellation of object relations existing during their childhood, my patients developed two identification systems simultaneously. The self-image maternally derived was invested primarily with feelings of rejection experienced as coming from mother and secondarily with aggressive feelings first projected onto mother and subsequently reintrojected and directed toward the self. As has been indicated, concurrently with the process of identification with father these patients during the positive oedipal phase also wished, as all little girls do, to become, like mother, father's love object. These oedipal longings spurred their wish to become as they perceived mother to be. The girls' sense of sameness (see Chapter 5) with mother and the residual feelings of oral and anal dependency on her fueled their identification with the introjected, powerful, magnificent, and yet devalued maternal imago that became the basis for the formation of these patients' maternally derived feminine wishful self-image. It was cathected predominantly with self-deprecatory and hostile feelings. (The exaggerated devaluation of mother, no doubt, was also based on the child's wish to take revenge on her for the infantile helpless dependency, which had not been experienced as a loving interaction. Similar views of factors leading to maternal denigration have been suggested by Lerner [1974] and Chasseguet-Smirgel [1976].)

These patients thus had two disparate wishful self-images, each based on different internalizations. These wishful self-images were antithetical to each other and differently cathected. They persisted in the ego as permanent substructures. The maternally derived wishful self-image may have had a degree of consciousness during some part of the oedipal phase but subsequently became totally repressed. It was ego-alien since it conflicted with those aspects of the paternally derived conscious wishful self-image that had become the avowed level of aspiration; assertion, excellence, mastery, a desire for autonomy, and certain ethical principles became these patients' narcissistically significant values. This structure had become during the process of maturation sufficiently depersonified to function partially as an ego ideal. However, the existence and the disruptive effects of the maternally derived unconscious wishful self-image interfered with the development of a complete and harmonious ego ideal necessary for integrated, cohesive character formation. The unconscious wishful self-image continued to manifest itself via seemingly inexplicable masochistic masturbation fantasies as well as by perplexing, self-defeating behavior patterns. Sandler and Rosenblatt (1962) and Sandler and colleagues (1963) have found that the changing character and shape of the self-image is normal during childhood. However, as maturation progresses, a more stable and integrated self-image should evolve. The extent to which such development was absent in these patients represented a specific aspect of their pathology. Their self-representation had a faulty structure because it contained two diverse, yet permanent, self-images—one conscious, the other unconscious—that were split-off, and could therefore neither modify each other nor fuse.

The analysis of the vicissitudes of interaction between the split-off conscious and unconscious wishful self-images was most significant for the understanding of these patients' pathology since affects emanating from the dissociated identification system influenced their behavior. The interaction came to the fore under specific circumstances and was beyond the patients' control. Thus, when erotic impulses prevailed, the split-off maternally derived wishful self-image, cathected mostly with aggression turned against the self, became activated. At such times longings to become like the maternal imago predominated. Since the unconscious of these patients knew only of love for the devalued woman, these patients, swayed by love, acted in accordance with their understanding of the oedipal model. They chose for their love object men who in many ways resembled the unconscious image of their aggrandized phallic father rather than men who had the characteristics of their mature idealized male imago. In these relationships the patients recreated the oedipal scenario, easily provoking the devaluation they unconsciously interpreted as a manifestation of love. Since these choices were unconsciously motivated, they remained perplexing to the patients, who complained that love is irrational. Analysis disclosed, however, that in these relationships, which soon after inception repeatedly became sadomasochistic, the patients unconsciously emulated their image of the loved yet denigrated mother, and their love object unconsciously represented the oedipal father.

These patients' masturbation fantasies were elaborations of oedipal themes contaminated by anal, urethral, and phallic preoccupations about power and love. Though the fantasied abuse of the woman may have also been a gesture of atonement toward the harsh superego for incestuous wishes, the main function of the fantasies was the attainment of the unconscious gratification through total enactment and identification with the parental sexual interaction as perceived by the child. Since these patients' unconscious wishful self-image was embodied in the identification with the fantasied slave woman who represented the introjected devalued mother, their predominant erotic gratification was unconsciously linked with debasement. This theme was compulsively repeated during masturbation in all their masturbation fantasies.

The fantasies, however, gratified other unconscious impulses as well (Waelder 1936). Thus analysis indicated that these patients identified also with the male who enjoyed the woman's debasement. These fantasies frequently contained lesbian impulses and wishes to castrate the male and usurp his power. Such impulses were usually expressed in the latent content of fantasies. Following is an example of such a fantasy: "Women with artificial penises trained young girls to become 'experts' in giving sexual pleasure to their future male masters. These phallic women were cruel and demanding. They were the real rulers of the harem."

When strivings to become like the conscious wishful self-image predominated, these patients were active, assertive achievers, molding their behavior in accordance with their aspirations and attaining their ego-syntonic goals. During such periods the patients experienced, at least temporarily, a sense of accomplishment and an increase in self-esteem, probably related to the presence of more abundant narcissistic supplies. Yet even during such periods of relative well-being, the insidious effect of the unconscious wishful self-image persisted and was experienced as a vague chronic sense of inner dissatisfaction.

Though with less frequency, self-defeating behavior also occurred in these patients' professional lives. It most frequently took the form of "inexplicable" failure in the course of apparently successful attempts to attain a leadership position. Prolonged analysis revealed that these failures were caused by an unconscious conflict brought about by the patient's wish to attain simultaneously the aims of both conscious and unconscious wishful self-images. Typically, the patient in such a state unconsciously feared that professional success would preclude the possibility of being "really loved" by the transferential representative of the oedipal father, whose acceptance and recognition she simultaneously sought by excelling and achieving. Such a psychic conflict resulted in erratic behavior, inconsistency, and mood swings, factors that interfered with the attainment of the goals of the conscious wishful self-image. Intrasystemic conflict (Hartmann 1950) at such times led to almost continuous psychic discord, manifested by these patients' contradictory and self-defeating behavior and by their concomitant sense of helplessness and dejection.

The chronic subliminal depression of these patients intensified at times when their impulses and behavior approximated the characteristics of the unconscious wishful self-image. Such behavior was contrary to their conscious aspirations, aims, and avowed goals. It is likely that during such periods narcissistic libido was withdrawn from their psychic self-representation and an increase in aggressive self-cathexis followed. The patients' feelings of narcissistic mortification increased.

Cohesive character formation, for which a uniform ego ideal is necessary, was precluded by the split in these patients' self-representation. Conflicts and misunderstandings on the oedipal level superimposed upon conflicts about passivity and activity, aggression, submission, and dominance remained unresolved.

Nonintegrated parental introjects—respectively the cores of these patients' conscious and unconscious wishful self-images— persisted in their psychic structures. This contributed to the formation of their noncohesive superego in which primitive, harsh, and sadistic elements predominated. The patients in moments of greatest despair felt they had a "rotten core" (see Chapter 4) that they believed could not be eradicated. The genetic root of these patients' depression lies in their conviction that they never fully satisfied their mothers' fantasy-ideal of the wished for child, and that they thus had never been fully accepted and cherished by mother. Their depression was aggravated further by their awareness that father's acceptance and love was conditional upon their compliance with his demands.

From the life histories of these patients it appeared they were doomed to feel pain no matter what they did. If they succeeded in attaining their avowed goals, they felt unloved as women; if they gratified their libidinal impulses, patterned on the oedipal model, they became involved in object relationships that were essentially sadomasochistic and unsatisfactory. The psychic contradictions inherent in the pathology of these women's ego structures manifested themselves in the oscillations of their behavior and in the oft-repeated patterns of masochistic self-defeat.

9 The Menopausal Phase: Crisis, Danger, Opportunity

A brief history of ways in which menopause was regarded and understood in Western societies is necessary to comprehend the enormity of the changes that have taken place in the last fifty years. Women's life expectancy at the turn of the century was only forty-eight years. Many women died during childbirth or from complications and illnesses that followed thereafter. Thus menopause was a relatively rare phenomenon. Women's sexuality was tied to childbearing, which was both longed for and dreaded. Understanding and use of birth control methods was minimal; thus childbearing frequently was not controlled by women, or volitional. The cyclicity of women's functioning and its cessation appeared mysterious and therefore frightening. It led to the formulation, mostly by men, of many theories that demeaned women, and to therapies damaging to women. There was a widespread

---

Author's Note: This chapter will not consider and compare findings pertaining to women in the Western world with cross-cultural studies.

belief that a woman's life was determined by her uterus, humors, and plethora. Menopause was viewed as a condition in which menstrual blood accumulated in the uterus. (as it did in amenorrhea). It was believed that this blood could enter the brain, causing insanity, various nervous diseases, hot flashes, and so forth. Bleedings were considered the treatment of choice (Formanek 1990).

It was only with the discovery in the 1920s of the active ovarian hormone estrogen that menstruation and menopause became scientifically understood and explained. By the 1930s and 1940s menopause became medicalized as a deficiency disease. Hormone replacement therapy (HRT) ameliorated the most pervasive symptoms that with varying intensity affect about 75 percent of women. The remaining 25 percent have no symptoms (McKinlay and Jefferys 1974, Mulley and Mitchell 1976). As yet it is not understood what factors determine the physiological variability with which a given woman will respond to the hormonal changes of menopause. However, some evidence indicates the presence of a hereditary predisposition.

The medical categorization of the menopause as a deficiency disease is a misnomer. A woman's decreasing estrogen levels, which usually bring about a period of physiological imbalance and change, are a natural process specific for the menopausal phase. The cyclicity of a woman's life, which begins with a period of physiological imbalance and change at puberty, comes to an end with the climacteric, the normal milestone marking the end of her reproductive years.

The significance of this event, whether acknowledged or denied, has a profound impact on the woman's inner world. This is almost inevitable since most societies, though in different ways, perpetuate the ancient cult of the fertile mother-goddess, giver of life and sustenance. Mankind depended and depends on women's fecundity for survival. Thus it not only worshipped the procreative mother, it also, from time immemorial and by every means available, indoctrinated its females to embrace motherhood as their supreme life task, contribution, and duty.

In this chapter I discuss women's experience of the menopausal phase in the light of their conscious and unconscious sense of body integrity, body functioning, self-image, self-esteem, life tasks, and ego interests.

Review of the Literature

The psychoanalytic literature on the menopausal phase is sparse, and most authors, with the exception of Deutsch, Benedek, Lax, and Notman, have focused primarily on the involutional melancholia it may trigger (Fessler 1950, Jacobson 1971).

Benedek (1950), Benedek and Anthony (1970), and Anthony and Benedek (1975), the foremost exponents of the developmental point of view, considered the climacteric within the context of the lifecycle. Benedek (1950) maintained that the manifestations of the climacteric "are dependent upon the previous history of the individual . . . are motivated by trends which . . . may be reactivated by the internal changes associated with that period" (p. 1), and she questioned whether the "normal climacterium represents a progressive psychological adaptation to a regressive biological process" (p. 2). According to Benedek, the manner in which individual women respond to the stress of menopause depends on the vicissitudes of their identification with their mothers, which determines their acceptance of the feminine role. She stresses the connection between the reactions to menstruation and to menopause as well as the significance of pain, which she considers an "integrative part of the psychosexual experience of women" (p. 6). On the basis of a clinical case, Benedek (1950) formulated the concept of a sense of "*internal frustration*," defined as the patient's perception "of her inability to be gratified" (p. 13). Such a condition, according to Benedek, is not due to dammed-up libido, but rather to a *lack of libidinization* (italics added) related to inefficient ovarian production. It is this type of frustration that accounts for the symptoms of premenstrual tension and depression, and is "in the center of the emotional experience of the climacterium" (p. 13).

Benedek implied that the struggle between sexual drives and the ego, which begins at puberty, diminishes or ends with the climacteric. "As the desexualization of the emotional needs proceeds, the balanced personality finds new aims for the psychic energy" (p. 21). This change frees the woman from conflicts centering around sexuality and gives her spare energy, providing a new impetus for socialization and learning. Benedek's ideas about pain being an integrative aspect of women's psychosexuality, and her notion that emotional needs become desexualized during middle age, date her papers. Surveys and research indicate that women's sexual desires continue into old age and that women continue, when possible, to be sexually active. In the Western world, with the relaxations of mores regarding virginity, a woman's struggle between sexual drives and the ego has for the most part abated.

In contrast to Benedek's optimistic point of view, Deutsch (1945) maintains: "The climacterium is under the sign of a narcissistic mortification that is difficult to overcome" (p. 457). She compares many aspects of the preclimacteric and the climacteric proper with prepuberty and adolescence. Deutsch points to the frequent thrust by women into new intellectual or artistic activities that they use to defend against the imminent disappointment and mortification of the climacteric. She also asserts that woman "is not merely a servant of the species, not a machine for bearing children, that she has higher brain centers and a complicated emotional life that is not restricted to motherhood. Thus she may succeed in actively finding a way out of the biologic complications" (p. 459).

These statements were indeed avant garde in 1945, especially since they were made by a devout adherent of Freud's (1925) position that "anatomy is destiny" (p. 178). Nevertheless, Deutsch corroborates and contributes to Freud's position by asserting:

The changes that take place in the body of a climacterical woman have the character not only of the cessation of physiologic production but also of general dissolution. Woman's biologic fate manifests itself in the disappearance of her individual feminine qualities at the same time that her service to the species ceases. As we have said, everything she acquired during puberty is now lost piece by piece; with the lapse of the reproductive service, her beauty vanishes, and usually the warm, vital flow of feminine emotional life as well [p. 461]. Almost every woman in the climacterium goes through a shorter or longer phase of depression. While the active women deny the biologic state of affairs, the depressive ones over-emphasize it. The physiologic decline is felt as the proximity of death, life begins to seem pale and purposeless [p. 473].

Deutsch also believed that narcissistic, feminine-loving women have a milder climacteric than masculine-aggressive ones. She asserted that women "whose life content is mostly beauty and feminine charm remain young and beautiful for a strikingly long time" (p. 474). Such women know how to continue to get gratification from recently developed interests. However, in spite of this observation, Deutsch stated:

In the course of a woman's life, masculinity often plays the part of a rock of salvation. This is also true of the climacterium. An intellectual sublimation through a profession protects her against biologic trauma. This applies to an even greater extent to feminine women who have not staked their feminine qualities on the single card of eroticism and motherliness, but have also invested them in good sublimation [p. 476].

According to Lax (1982) the increased vulnerability occurring during the menopausal phase is related to a sense of loss of physical well-being experienced by the majority of women, combined with the manifold vicissitudes of the middle age passage. This accounts for the frequent presence of an expectable, reversible, nonclinical depression during this time of the lifecycle. Successful mourning for the many different losses a woman experiences at this time is necessary to enable her to make a new, gratifying adaptation during the postmenopausal years.

Malka Notman (1977, 1979, 1995), the National Health Organization, feminist writers, and others (Ehrenreich and English 1973, MacPherson 1981, McCrea 1983, Seaman and Seaman 1977) disagree with the medical contention "that Menopause is a deficiency disease." This is correct. The menopause is *not* a disease. It is a natural event in the woman's lifecycle, a part of the beginning of the aging process. Notman (1979) concurs with the observation that "there may indeed be *some* psychological mourning required before one can move on" (p. 1273). Her survey of research studies until 1979 confirms that "depression has been linked with menopause and that it does constitute an important clinical entity" (1979, p. 1272).

In her 1995 paper Notman observes that the biological event of the menopause is *not* accompanied by definite symptoms or personality changes, but it does occur in the context of the personal developmental processes and family constellations of midlife and is affected by culture and social class. This is a sweeping generalization, partially correct. It fails, however, to take into account the physiological symptoms most women report and the significance of their reaction to them. Though women's reactions at midlife are multidetermined, the physiological changes of the menopausal phase play an important role. Characteristically, at that time, most women experience great sadness for their lost youth irrespective of their denials and cover-up techniques. The analyses of many women indicate that youth and aliveness are unconsciously symbolized for a woman by being able to give life.

A review of the scientific nonpsychoanalytic literature on the menopause (Bardwick 1971, Bart and Grossman 1978, Haspels and Musaph 1979, Kronenberg 1984, McKinlay and Jefferys 1974, Mulley and Mitchell 1976, Perlmutter 1978, Wilson 1966) indicates that research in this area has begun in earnest. The relevance and interaction of biological, psychological, and cultural factors are now recognized, but need further exploration.

An outstanding psychosocial survey by Severne (1979), based on intensive interviews with 922 climacteric Belgian women 46 to 55 years old from four different socioeconomic groupings, presents significant data. It indicates what Deutsch already observed in 1945: that sublimations and professional interests make it much easier for women to deal with menopausal symptoms.

Severne's sample was divided into working women and housewives belonging to the lower and higher socioeconomic groups. The data from this survey indicate the following:

1. Vasomotor symptoms, of which hot flashes are most frequent, increase during the peri- to postmenopausal period. Although these symptoms supposedly are independent of socioeconomic factors, their highest incidence occurred among housewives belonging to the lower socioeconomic group.

2. Working women of the lower socioeconomic group found it very difficult to cope with both a job and the turmoil of the menopausal phase. Thus their "nervosity index," defined as the presence of insomnia, nervousness, irritability, headache, and depressive mood, was the highest and their level of dissatisfaction with their current life situation was the greatest. Compared with these women, housewives belonging to the lower socioeconomic group were somewhat less dissatisfied with their life situation and their nervosity index was somewhat lower.

3. Compared with women of the other three groups, working women of the higher socioeconomic group showed the highest level of satisfaction with their current life situation, and their nervosity index was the lowest. The researchers concluded that work had a rewarding quality for women of the higher socioeconomic subgroup.

4. All of the women participating in this research project reported a decrease in their sense of physical well-being during the perimenopause. This effect, however, was more pro-

nounced for housewives than for working women of the
higher socioeconomic group.

5. The researchers also developed a composite "index for subjective adaptation" (p. 114), which included a woman's subjective evaluation of her attractiveness, accomplishments,
   well-being; pleasure in family and social life; and sense of
   purpose and usefulness. Notwithstanding the presence of a
   generalized decrease in their sense of self-worth and self-
   esteem, working women of the higher socioeconomic class
   were able to maintain a more positive self-image during the
   menopausal phase than did women belonging to the other
   three groups. It is also noteworthy that housewives of the
   upper socioeconomic group had the steepest decrease in their
   sense of self-worth during the perimenopause, with working women in the lower socioeconomic group coming next.

6. The notion that menopause is a pseudo-ailment of the privileged class of women was definitely refuted by the findings
   of this study.

7. The data indicate that rewarding work is a mitigating factor during menopause and a stabilizing factor in postmeno-
   pause. In this connection it is especially significant to note
   the findings of Bart and Grossman (1978), which indicate
   that women for whom childbearing and childrearing are
   main life tasks experience more depression during the menopausal phase than women with other goals and interests.

During the mid-life years, women not only have to deal with
the usual vicissitudes of middle age (Kernberg 1980a) that apply
to both sexes, they also have to cope with the unique psycho-
physical effects of the menopausal phase. At the very least, these
contribute to a specific vulnerability that distinguishes women
from men during this same phase of their lifecycle. This is corroborated by a statistical analysis reported in *The New York Times*
(January 2, 1979) that indicates that the highest incidence of suicide occurs among women between the ages of 45 and 59 and

among men after age 70. This difference suggests that the phase-specific midlife menopausal conflicts many women experience are more severe than the phase-specific conflicts experienced by men during their midlife crisis.

The Effect of Phase-Specific Psychophysiological Changes

In his paper on "Normal and Pathological Narcissism," Kernberg (1975) states:

> General good health reconfirms both the integrity and the libidinal investment of the self. Because the original self representations are strongly influenced by body images and because the earliest intrapsychic instinctual gratification is closely linked to the reestablishment of psychological equilibria, physical health and illness significantly influence the normal and abnormal equilibrium of narcissistic investment. [p. 320]

Erikson (1959), discussing the changes throughout the life cycle, stresses that "each stage becomes a *crisis* because incipient growth and awareness in a significant part-function goes together with a shift in instinctual energy and yet causes specific vulnerability in that part" (pp. 53, 55).

Psychoanalytic developmental theory recognizes that transitions from one stage of the lifecycle to another, coupled with changes in the psychophysiologic equilibrium, may evoke affective distress even in individuals who have a basically healthy psychic structure. The menopausal phase occurring at mid-life is an especially stressful period. How a woman will respond to the end of her procreativity, to the "empty nest" phenomenon, to the waning of her attractiveness, and to the many fears associated with aging will depend in large measure on her psychic structure, determined significantly by her past experiences and pathognomonic predisposition, her intrapsychic conflicts, internalized object relations, the strength of her libidinal investments, the width of her conflict-free ego sphere and the strength of her ego interests, the extent of her healthy narcissism, her current object relations, and her familial social setting. The range of variability is influenced also by the extent to which a woman unconsciously, idiosyncratically, accepted or rejected the role assigned to her by parents, family, and society. A woman's conscious and unconscious reaction to, and the type of her identification with her menopausal mother for whom HRT may or may not have been available, is of significance.

The type and relative severity of physiological symptoms a woman experiences during this time will be an additional factor, determining her reactions. Symptoms vary greatly from woman to woman, which accounts for the variability of response. It is important to consider that during hot flashes the body temperature rises to 103 degrees within a few minutes. In some women this is accompanied by cardiac irregularities. It makes an enormous difference whether a woman has one or two hot flashes in twenty-four hours, or whether she has several *each* hour, day and night, and whether they continue for months or years (Gannon 1990, Nachtigall 1986).

In some women the unpredictable and uncontrollable nature of intense vasomotor symptoms may reactivate infantile fears of loss of control. Reactions of this kind have been present in some of my patients who revealed during analysis that hot flashes and the feeling of "being bathed in sweat" evoked in them not only childhood fears of loss of urinary control, but also humiliating memories of being discovered "with wet pants." In patients who suffered from erythrophobia, hot flashes reactivated unconscious conflicts about exhibitionism and the sense of shame experienced in their youth. The hot flashes once again made them feel exposed and defenseless. Recurring hot flashes and sweats evoke in many women feelings of being overwhelmed since they are unable to control what is happening to them. The dreams of patients at such times reflect their feeling states and are replete with scenes in which they are being victimized. For some women each occurrence of hot flashes becomes a repetitive traumatic incident. Under such circumstances, transient anxiety states may occur. When present, hot flashes, a menopausal psychophysiological symptom, may disrupt and interfere with the preservation of a feeling of body integrity as well as with the body's harmonious functioning. This results in a decreased sense of well-being, greater vulnerability, and a relative withdrawal of libidinal cathexis (Freud 1914a) from the body.

Stereotypes and myths depict the "older woman," the "menopausal woman," the "nag," the woman at "this time of life" in negative and derogatory terms. These societal attitudes are frequently incorporated by women into their unconscious, less frequently consciously acknowledged and dealt with.

Women have various responses to the complex of factors they experience during the menopausal phase. Some respond by new and healthy integrations, others by ways that may lead to pathological development. The stereotypes a woman has internalized throughout her life are powerful in determining the roles and the goals to which she will aspire.

To fully understand and evaluate the nature and scope of the psychic crisis women experience at midlife, one has to take into account and analyze the ways in which the phase-specific physiological changes affect their self-image, their sense of body integrity, their experience of body functioning, and their life tasks and ego interests. During the menopausal phase, disequilibria occur in all these areas of psychic functioning. This simultaneous convergence of psychic stress is of momentous significance and accounts for the complications most women face in their coping attempts. When these exigencies are taken into account, it becomes understandable that a woman's experience of self-constancy is painfully disturbed. Under such circumstances it may be anticipated that a woman with average mental health will initially meet the expectable stresses and vicissitudes of the midlife menopausal phase with an expectable state of distress that may include a depressive reaction and some reversible regressive features, but eventually she will reach a new adaptive resolution.

The following presents the reactions of a patient approaching 50 who had her second child at 45. She spent hours complaining about a plethora of symptoms that indicated her approaching menopause. After she finally saw her gynecologist, she reported the following: "He told me the tests indicate that I am menopausal—I felt he pitied me as if it was a disaster. Maybe I felt it is a disaster but could not face it so I pushed it onto him. You want to know how I *really* feel . . . it's not that I can't have any more babies—I have two, they are wonderful. We couldn't afford more even though I would have liked to try for a girl. As you know, I hoped for a girl. But the real rub is in being *ashamed* because I don't feel bouncy, cheery, and always on the go. *I am ashamed* of my headaches, hot flashes, and I do not sleep well. I am exhausted because I don't have a good night's sleep and it makes me cranky and angry. I feel I have to hide all of these feelings, everything that is happening to me and work hard to keep up. It is so hard to accept knowing it's an end to *how it used to be.* . . . A change of life . . . but perhaps it will all disappear with HRT."

Findings based on the analysis of women during the menopausal phase indicate that attempts at denial of bodily changes and of concomitant affective reactions are most intense during the perimenopause. This is the time when the changes begin to emerge, menstruations are no longer quite regular, and hot flashes begin. Dreams during this period reflect a struggle, symbolized by various forms of attempted flight and escape—and simultaneously a pervasive awareness of a paralysis that makes such attempts impossible. Analytic hours are filled with complaints of bodily discomforts, fatigue, and a disconcerting awareness that somehow everything "takes longer than it used to."

During the perimenopause, which usually occurs between ages 40 and 50, gonadal hormone production declines, and, over the ensuing years, physiological changes continue. As ovarian activity ceases, a hormonal imbalance develops that usually, and concomitantly, results in a systemic disturbance of the equilibrium between the sympathetic and parasympathetic nervous systems. This disequilibrium frequently causes the following symptoms, which can occur in different combinations and with different degrees of severity: (1) uncontrollable vasomotor discharges, which manifest themselves in hot flashes (hot flashes are regarded as *the* physiological symptom directly related to hormonal decline (Greene and Cook 1980, Kaufert and Syrotuik 1981, McKinlay and Jefferys 1974, Mikkelsen and Holte 1982, Wood 1979), sweats, palpitations, and other cardiac discomforts; (2) night sweats and insomnia, which frequently, secondarily, evoke a sense of fatigue that may contribute to generalized irritability; (3) restlessness, often associated with a decreased capacity to concentrate; and (4) vaginal dryness, which may interfere with sexual intercourse and may make the woman feel undesirable. Most women experience these symptoms as alien manifestations, different from "how they used to be," something they watch and observe, an ongoing process they cannot reverse.

Menopausal symptoms greatly reduce a woman's sense of well-being (Severne 1979). This is a typical reaction to any prolonged physiological malfunction that disrupts the feeling of body equilibrium. Additionally, however, analytic investigation indicates that women may also experience menopausal symptoms, especially the hot flashes and sweats, with a painful sense of mortification, since they reveal their condition to the world. Such a reaction is not surprising in our youth-oriented ethos in which aging in itself evokes a sense of shame, and therefore is a process most women want to hide.

The cessation of menstruation, the climacteric, brings to a woman's consciousness what she may have wanted to deny: "It is now, the Change of Life . . . it is here." For many women the changes in their faces and bodies, which accentuate the difference between their youthful body image and the reality of their current body self, are at first experienced with a sense of incredulity. A patient, still a beautiful woman, tearfully told of hours she spent looking at photographs of herself as a young woman, and then at herself in the mirror. She broke into sobs, saying, "I can't believe it. When did I get so old?" Aging is a traumatizing process for women who, for well-known intrapsychic and interpersonal reasons, have a special narcissistic investment in their appearance. Such women, when they eventually recognize the irreversibility and the permanence of the changes, experience a narcissistic loss. Thus the fairytale stepmother, asking "Mirror, mirror, on the wall, who is the fairest of them all?" probably expresses a universal sense of envy, loss, and hostility—experienced sometimes consciously but mostly unconsciously by many menopausal women—toward young women by whom they feel threatened and who now possess what the middle-aged women used to have, and have lost. Frequently such envy damages the mother–daughter relationship. It may also underlie the enmity between mother-in-law and daughter-in-law.

Analytic work with many women indicates that the bodily changes accounting for the disequilibrium of the menopausal phase have a profound effect on their psychic reality even when the physiological symptoms are alleviated by HRT. Women use intensified activity, various forms of cosmetic surgery, and so on to fortify the denial of their intrapsychic responses to the end of menstruation, "the change of life," to the recognition of their changing body, and to the narcissistic hurt resulting from an awareness of a decrease in peak functioning.

Frequently, during analytic hours, concomitantly with the many complaints about menopausal symptoms, narcissistic hurts, and so forth patients also speak about new undertakings in their professional lives, some strenuous sports activities, and the doubling of the time they work out.

It is now fashionable among some feminists and certain groups of "hip" women to maintain that the menopausal woman has to "reinvent herself." Women who adhere to these attitudes deny the psychic significance of the menopausal phase. They strive to behave as if what is occurring within them has no significance. Such women frequently start a new career, even a new life.

Upon analysis, it becomes apparent that such behavior has a defensive function. Thus, when manifest derivatives of the many forms of denial are analyzed, the psychic reverberations become apparent in a sense of loss, sadness, and the recurrence of depressive moods. The reality of limited time, so absent in the adolescence of unending tomorrows, contributes to the sense of aging. This intensifies the mourning for the conscious and unconscious wishful self-image of one's youth, frequently for unattained youthful goals, unfulfilled loves, and the realization that many cherished hopes may never be fulfilled. Acknowledgment of these experienced losses results in a psychic pain only mourning can heal.

Many women, however, cannot tolerate this psychic pain. It evokes in them an unconscious wish to break with the past, to be free of the hold the past has upon them. The denial of the losses and the pain connected with the past helps to give these women an illusion of being set free. A patient who during her midlife menopausal phase was left by her husband, with whom she had shared a 25-year-long marriage, could not bear to analyze her pain and loss. She was filled with despair and rage. She searched for something to do, and eventually decided to utilize her past educational background. She applied and took a position teaching English at a college in Kenya. She explained this action by saying, "It is to leave my past life." Women use many ways to deny the pain connected with a past still longed for, or one that cannot be resurrected or changed. Anger is often used to reinforce repression of disappointment and despair.

The traditional values of a society are reflected in superego and ego ideals and demands that profoundly influence its members. Thus it is not surprising that even in Western culture, in which the emphasis on childbearing has definitely decreased, most women still regard and experience childbearing, childrearing, and homemaking as their significant—and frequently only—life tasks and ego interests. Consequently, for such women fulfilling these roles is consonant with the goals of their wishful self-image. These tasks become significant psychic organizers, providing women with a sense of achievement and a source of gratification.

The climacteric signals to women that their uniquely feminine function, childbearing, has come to an end. For many women, especially those who are not professionals, the end of their fecundity may cause the most serious midlife crisis. Deutsch (1945) describes it as an experience of "partial death." Even when a woman may realistically no longer wish to birth a child, her awareness that she is not able to—the irreversible end of her procreativity—may bring a profound feeling of sadness and regret. The perimenopausal years are also the time when active care of children may be greatly reduced, especially when emancipated and grown children seek final separation and individuation. With the curtailment or termination of mothering tasks a woman may experience a cessation of her achieving self, since she is now deprived of the means by which she used to fulfill the goals of her wishful self-image. Such psychic losses may result in great sadness and possible depression.

Married professional or working women confront a different situation at this life juncture because, throughout their lives, in addition to so-called feminine occupations, they have also pursued specific ego interests. The conflict between social values and ego interests, which in the past may have engendered guilt feelings about not being a full-time mother and wife, abates now, since family demands have greatly decreased. By seeking creative endeavors to fulfill their ego goals and aspirations, working women are able to find compensations for the narcissistic assaults abounding during the menopausal phase. Thus working women who continue to gratify their ego interests derive from the achievement of cultural and intellectual aspirations narcissistic supplies that reinforce their self-esteem. These continued gratifications also facilitate the resolution of envy evoked by the growing competence and creativity of the younger generation.

When possible, mothering needs, irrespective of whether or not a woman actually is a mother, may be gratified by functioning as a role model, mentor, and/or teacher. The fulfillment of such roles gives a woman narcissistic gratification via her identification with the growing autonomy, capacity for achievement, and creative success of young people. However, if the woman is seeking narcissistic self-fulfillment in such a relationship, she may experience separation struggles and conflict. In general, women seem to have a greater capacity for identification than men. This may be due to their predisposition for motherhood, which makes it easier for them to come to terms with the painful middle-age realization that the younger generation now occupies center stage.

In the past ten to fifteen years changing social conditions have made it increasingly possible for single professional, as well as married women in their late forties to adopt babies. This is a new phenomenon that testifies to a woman's powerful wish and need not to be childless.

Single women in their late thirties frequently feel threatened by the biological clock. They experience the approach of menopause much sooner than women who are in a gratifying relationship. When this occurs, their search for a man frequently reaches frantic proportions. They often become entangled with unsuitable married men, who nevertheless fulfill some aspect of their unconscious fantasies. Out-of-wedlock pregnancies, a form of acting out, may occur, causing intense conflict since the woman usually would like to keep the child but also recognizes the accompanying difficulties. If a woman has an abortion under such circumstances, she frequently goes through a severe depression in which the sense of bereavement predominates, while factors related to oedipal guilt are secondary.

Women's increased narcissistic vulnerability due to the ending of their procreativity may also be heightened by the fact that male procreative capacity does not end during their middle-age. This fact accounts for a significant difference between the sexes during this phase of the lifecycle, namely, a man can, or could, start a new family with children, but a woman cannot. This awareness may temporarily lead a woman to experience increased feelings of envy and hostility, even toward the loved man. Repressed or resolved feelings of so-called penis envy may flare up within her again. A woman at this time envies the man's biological makeup that spares him all the painful psychophysiological concomitants of menopause and does not interfere with his capacity to make babies with younger women. Menopausal women tend to deny men's psychic and physiologic midlife crisis and feel deeply ashamed of their own bodily changes and psychic distress. For example, a patient whose marriage worsened during her meno-pause felt exceedingly threatened by any attention her husband showed younger women. During a session, while she was experi-encing painful feelings of inadequacy, she exclaimed: "And he can just pack up and go, and start all over, and start all over as many times as he wishes, like so many of them do . . . and I am stuck with the kids I have and can have no more. It's like I am dried up and another flowering is no longer possible. I am stuck with my life . . . he is not."

During this period lesbian impulses may surface in single women. It appears that such tendencies are often triggered by a conscious or unconscious feeling of being scorned by men. Un-resolved conflicts related to repressed feelings associated with oedipal rejection experienced in childhood come to the fore. It appears that these women go through a partial psychosexual regression as a consequence of having given up hope that a mutually loving relationship with a man is possible. Their early libidinal feelings for mother are reactivated and acted upon. Like-wise revived are their feelings of having been hurt, experienced in childhood as a result of father's rejection. These feelings, al-though they are not consciously available to the patients, can be inferred from their hostile, defensive attitudes toward men, and can be confirmed only by analytic evidence. Contrary to Deutsch's (1945) findings, these women show no evidence of homosexual panic. This is probably partly due to the present-day relaxation of mores.

Depending on the specific aspects of a woman's wishful self-image, her ego interests, and her goals, depressive feelings will be triggered when she realizes she is no longer as effective as she used to be in areas of her primary involvement. For a significant number of women in our culture, such feelings still relate to their sense of declining familial significance and fading appearance. In addition to these concerns, some professional women may find it more difficult than it used to be to concentrate, to absorb and retain new material. However, irrespective of the area in which it occurs, narcissistic injury follows the experience of a sense of decline. Though these feelings are aspects of middle-age vicissitudes, they are intensified by the concomitant occurrence of physiological menopausal changes and sequelae.

Women use many methods to deal with those experiences of the menopausal phase to which they react with a sense of mortification. They may use as a coping mechanism frenetic activity of any kind—sports, lovers, partying, overwork, involvement in "good" causes, and so on. "Pathological health" (Musaph 1979) is a defensive coping mechanism used by women who, because of narcissistic pain, cannot face the psychophysiological symptoms of the perimenopause. Professional women who use overwork to protect themselves from self-confrontation predominate in this group. In all these instances women attempt to deny their feelings of shame and depression associated with change of life. For example, a patient who was acutely sensitive to her psychophysiological menopausal symptoms described "the change," as she called it, in the following way: "It is not only that I do not function as I used to, I do not feel physically as I used to, and when I look in the mirror, I don't look like I used to." Another patient, aware of differences between present and past functioning, and between her present and past sense of well-being, said: "I no longer feel as good as I used to be—I am getting worn out—and the thought creeps into my head: Will I be replaced?"

Discussion

According to E. Bibring (1953) and Zetzel (1970), depression is
an affect integral to psychic life that occurs when a loss is experienced. Such a loss is frequently, although not always, associated
with an awareness of a discrepancy between the wishful self-
image or ego ideal and the limitations of the self (E. Bibring 1953).
During each person's lifecycle, phase-specific, depressive states of
varying intensity and duration occur. These are exemplified by
the mood swings of little girls when they have to acknowledge
that they will never have a penis and by little boys who have to
accept that they will never give birth to babies—the sadness of
rapprochement children who recognize their limitations (Mahler
1966), likewise, the typical adolescent depressions related to
separation and autonomy conflicts, and the frequent transitory depression specific to the vulnerabilities, losses, and changes of the
menopausal phase.

Zetzel (1970) states: "Insofar as clinical depression is confined
to a sense of inadequacy and loss of self-esteem, we are dealing
with a symptom within the range of normal or neurotic experience" (p. 59). Zetzel maintained that the depressive affect present
throughout the lifecycle when a loss is experienced does not
necessarily involve a qualitative regressive alteration of mature
ego functions or the appearance of primitive archaic mechanisms.
Thus, even though the depressive menopausal reaction is associated with a loss of self-esteem, a decreased sense of narcissistic
well-being, and increased vulnerability, it does not result in a loss
of mature ego functions.

Stimulated by phase-specific physiological changes, the intrapsychic tensions of the menopausal woman are very different from
those that characterize a young woman's strivings to achieve as
yet unreached, highly narcissistically cathected ego goals. The
menopausal woman's frequently growing inability to achieve
narcissistically charged aims that she until recently took for
granted is exceedingly painful, even mortifying, a harbinger of

aging. It may be associated with a temporary state of psychic disequilibrium, characterized by anxiety and an increasing feeling of helplessness and/or powerlessness, resulting in a decreased sense of mastery (Benedek 1950). Underlying these feelings is an unconscious, intrasystemic, narcissistic conflict between the wishful self-image and the image of the deflated, failing self to which the menopausal woman's anger becomes directed. A hostile devaluation of the self usually follows, accompanied by a loss of self-esteem, mortification, and shame (Jacobson 1971).

These circumstances result in the development of an expectable depressive menopausal reaction, usually manifested by sadness, a sense of loss, and mourning for the youthful self of one's past. Such a reaction may vary in duration and intensity. Like the changes caused by the physiological processes of adolescence, the changes caused by the physiological processes of the menopausal phase lead to upheavals in all aspects of psychic functioning. All phases of development, as Anna Freud (1976) pointed out, "can be shown to contain disturbing concomitants which are characteristic for them" (p. 402). When psychic reactions to the physiological process of the menopausal phase are regarded from this perspective, the need for time to adapt to the changes and their consequences becomes understandable.

When in relatively good mental and physical health, the menopausal woman is able to use her available resources to work through her subjective losses. She can then reconstitute a meaningful life for herself by facing challenges and making optimal use of all present opportunities for creative and libidinal fulfillment. A successful outcome depends in large measure on the woman's adaptive capacities, her libidinal resources, and her ego interests.

However, within optimal limits, the depression that accompanies the menopausal process is expectable since, as Zetzel (1970) points out:

> However slight its overt expression may be, *the experience of depression is a prerequisite for optimal maturation.* Depressive affect . . .

occurs in response to loss, disappointment, frustration, illness, retirement, and other painful, though inevitable, experiences. [p. 87, italics added]

Thus, with these considerations in mind, the depression occurring during the menopausal phase can be regarded as a phase-specific affect, indicating that the necessary mourning process is occurring. The psychic capacity to contain and tolerate such a depression is a prerequisite for a healthy resolution of the menopausal phase.

At least initially, especially during the perimenopause, women frequently use denial as a defense mechanism. If used excessively, distortions of inner and outer reality may result, interfering with the necessary mourning process.

In rare cases, if a woman has a pathological predisposition, the narcissistic loss of self-esteem engendered during the menopausal phase may trigger a severe regression. When this occurs, a reactive psychotic depression, determined by earlier developmental failures, may ensue. Paranoidal features, angry faultfinding, and/ or extreme self-deprecation usually characterize this type of involutionary psychosis.

When denial does not prevent the woman during the menopausal phase from working through the psychic pain accompanying this process, the depression—a concomitant of the disturbed narcissistic equilibrium and of mourning for one's youthful, wishful self-image—contributes to an adaptive, progressive move toward greater psychic maturity (Zetzel 1970). Mourning, when successful, allows a woman to renounce no longer attainable hopes and goals. This frees the libidinal capacities tied up with her past. Subsequently, with additional energy, an adaptive and creative resolution of the menopausal process becomes possible, since the woman now can restructure aspects of her wishful self-image and ego ideal. When the mourning process is accompanied by a working through that results in greater self-tolerance and self-acceptance, object relations are enriched. A woman can now identify with idealized matriarchal models whose characteristics of generativity, generosity, and compassion become her own goals (Erikson 1979, Kernberg 1980a, Kohut 1966).

The menopausal phase is a time for conscious self-assessment; it contains the challenge of the present and opportunities for the future. A healthy resolution of menopausal conflicts enables a woman to own age. However, the greater a woman's inborn vitality, enthusiasm, and energy in pursuit of her life goals, the longer will the process of aging be delayed. A passionate pursuit of a vital involvement may, for a particular woman, appear to stop the clock even though time is ticking on. The physical status, the psychic past, and the psychic structure are the strongest determinants of the mode with which a woman will cope with aging.

Addendum I

The awareness and sensitivity of the analyst to the experiences of the menopausal woman are important both for a proper therapeutic stance and for future research.

The significance of the countertransference was illustrated by Bemesderfer's (1996) report on how her feelings toward her own beginning menopause influenced her treatment of a patient. During the analysis of a middle-aged woman who was also beginning the menopause, Bemesderfer at first found herself attributing the patient's symptoms to factors *other* than the perimenopause. Self-analysis eventually enabled her to recognize that this reaction was due to a wish to disregard her own symptoms and to deny that they were related to her approaching menopause. Subsequently, the analyst also recognized that she was experiencing competitive feelings toward the patient, which included the wish to handle her own menopause better than the patient was handling hers. Further self-analysis led to the understanding that these feelings were rooted in envy toward her older sister, with whom she had competed during childhood for the attention of their parents. Once the analyst understood her own responses, she acknowledged to the patient her failure to pay sufficient attention to the patient's description of symptoms. A thorough analysis of the complex symptoms and psychic reactions to the menopause began at that point.

This brief vignette illustrates the importance for both female and male analysts—each of whom have their own, different counter-transferential reactions—to be not only knowledgeable but also *open* to the recognition of perimenopausal symptoms.

Addendum II

In the last decade, as contrasted with the secrecy of the past, the menopause became a topic discussed quite widely by the media. A number of scientific and popular books appeared, though the analytic literature is still meager. Simultaneously, a debate about the significance of the menopausal phase began in some feminist circles, and even among some analysts. No one denies the decrease and eventual cessation of menstruation, but a considerable number of lay writers, and even some analysts, deny the psychic impact of the physiological changes on the inner world of the woman.

Part of this movement may be motivated by opposition to HRT. Betty Friedan (1995), verbalizing the position of many, maintains that the menopause is medicalized to make money for the pharmaceutical companies and doctors with disregard to the danger to the woman.

Such a position, though partly correct, does not take into account the positive effect estrogen replacement has on osteoporosis and cardiac symptoms. Significantly, it also disregards research that indicates that estrogen deficiency is directly related to hot flashes and vaginal dryness. These symptoms of the menopausal phase affect the well-being of 75 percent of women with varying degrees of severity. Though estrogen is a hormone and its function was unknown until the 1920s, shamans and herbal practitioners for centuries knew of plants and foods that alleviated menopausal symptoms.

The denial of the impact of the menopausal changes may also stem from a conscious/unconscious wish to deny the differences between men and women at mid-life. Such an illusion has a distorting effect on a woman's efforts to attain a mature adaptation toward aging.

Addendum III

The reaction to changes of the menopausal phase may be strongly influenced by cultural factors. Nancy Datan's (1990) anthropologic research among Moslem Arabs, North Africans, Persians, and Central European orthodox Jews indicates that these women welcomed the menopause because it signaled the end of their childbearing years. This is not surprising since women in these cultures have an enormous number of pregnancies. They are thus exposed to the dangers of childbirth and possible death with each pregnancy, in addition to being more and more exhausted. In these cultures women are almost child breeding machines, incubators for the male sperm, since having many children, especially sons, attests to the masculinity of the male.

Past the menopausal phase women in these cultures are more freely accepted into male society since they no longer endanger the men with unclean menstrual pollutants. Women's increased acceptance may also be related to the fact that men no longer find them attractive; women, therefore, no longer have a dangerous seductive power. Some women at this time of their lives, in some societies, become matriarchs who are listened to and recognized as wise.

10 Growing Older; Getting Old; Psychic Reality in Aging

Whereas the menarche signifies entrance into womanhood—the ripening, the time of lovemaking, babies, and the mystical belief that the chain of tomorrows will bring fulfillment of one's hopes, the menopause signals the beginning of the psychic response to the experience of aging. Following a healthy resolution of climacteric conflicts, a woman is ready to own age. However, the greater a woman's inborn vitality, enthusiasm and energy in pursuit of her life goals, the longer will the process of true aging be delayed. A passionate pursuit of a vital involvement may, for a particular woman, appear to stop the clock even though time is ticking on. The physical status, the psychic past, and the psychic structure are the strongest determinants of the mode with which a woman will cope with aging. Eventually, however, a woman's relative youthfulness becomes but an echo of the vibrant qualities that pulsated in her past.

There is a struggle, specific for each woman yet inescapable, namely, the need to face and eventually be able to accept and cope with the incrementally increasing less potent sense of self. This can be one of the most painful aspects of aging. The realization of a decline in functioning, especially in areas significant for the woman and her self-comparison with the superior prowess of those younger than she, can become a source of mortification and envy, a potential for a constantly festering narcissistic injury.

Women whose narcissistic investment is centered on the allure of their body are painfully envious of the beauty of youth. Such women feel that their own aging body has betrayed them. However, for women who had loving grandparents and parents, whose bodies with wrinkles and frailties they loved, their own aging bodies may bring happy memories of childhood and security. Such women, identifying with these elders who became their models, can continue in spite of the ravages time brings to invest narcissistically in their own bodies and the bodies of their loved companions. Generativity provides for them a lasting link with their nourishing past. One of my older patients told her pregnant daughter: "I am so impatient for your baby to be born. I'll be to it like grandma was to you. Your little one and I shall have so much fun in our times together, like you had with grandma. . . . "

As the years go by, everything seems to be taking more time, requires more effort, and perhaps, though one is loath to admit it, no longer is done as well as it used to be. Clinging to goals and aims of one's youth, which no longer can be realized, indicates that the conflicts that aging brings interfere with the capacity to adapt. When aging is acknowledged, standards of perfection become more flexible, more attuned to the signals the body and the psyche give. Women who cannot accept these changes frequently become more and more dissociated from the psychic and physiological processes which, in spite of being denied, relentlessly take place. Such an estrangement from one's psychic reality may interfere with the capacity for meaningful relationships so essential as aging advances. It may, when it persists, lead to pathological consequences.

Frequently, women who are unable to accept the inherent changes of the aging process also cannot relinquish the unfulfilled hopes and dreams of their youth. Their anguish often brings them to analysis or therapy. These women become quite depressed and blame themselves for what they now consider their past failures. In the treatment of these older women the trauma is constantly relived in memory, and one hears over and over again, "If I had only . . . " "If I had understood . . . " "If I had given in. . . . " It becomes evident upon analysis that their self-fault finding is a way of holding on to the past, of keeping the memory alive by reliving it repeatedly. The pain embedded in not letting go, in the "if only . . . ," is like a mantra forging the chain of attachment to the past, to youth when hope was alive, to past loves and hurtful disappointments. For these women their pain represents aliveness, even though it is ripe with the narcissistic hurt of self-flagellation.

These patients do not mourn their losses, they brood. Their pain is suffused with anger, fed by the unfulfilled hopes and dreams of their youth. Analytic work with these women is successful when a psychic separation from this past can be achieved. This occurs when a woman can connect the disappointments of adulthood with her pivotal childhood experiences. A recognition that adult choices were motivated by an unconscious compulsion to repeat, by a need to master past traumas, facilitates a woman's acceptance that her failures were predetermined. Such insight makes genuine mourning possible. As a consequence, both the libidinal and aggressive cathexis to objects of the past, and to the self in relation to these objects, slowly decreases. To the extent to which a letting go process occurs, and is followed by detachment, self and object can be forgiven. It is as if a cathectic melting took place, dissolving the hold of the "if only" ruminations.

Whereas developmental tasks characterize youth and even adulthood, adaptational coping characterizes successful vital aging. The vicissitudes of specific events during this last phase of the life span may require great flexibility combined with a capacity to cathect new goals.

At whatever the age, and for whatever reasons, retirement, so prevalent in our society—be it from mothering tasks, the work force, or profession—usually evokes an identity crisis. This change in one's lifestyle, unless prepared for in advance, is frequently experienced as a shock. It may be reacted to as a displacement, a loss of status, a loss of a significant place in family and/or community. A pervasive sense of uselessness may follow, leading to a loss of self-esteem, to helplessness that may culminate in rage and a profound depression. A patient summed it up by saying, "There were days when I did not know what to do with myself. The kids were gone. I'd automatically start preparing to go to the office . . . and then I'd remind myself . . . I wasn't working anymore, I'd already had my retirement party. So I'd sit, nothing interested me, I felt I had no place to go, and I realized with pain there no longer was a place for me." For many women retirement may increase the fear of gradual loss of independence, even of autonomy, that could eventuate in a loss of control over one's life. Such anxieties may bring about a state of psychic agitation, magnifying fears of the unknown, loneliness, infirmity, and illness, the helpless dependency on children, and, even worse, on strangers who might at best provide negligent care (K. Menninger 1981).

Evidence indicates that women who have led active gratifying lives, especially if they combined marriage and motherhood with a satisfying work experience, have the ability to cope with retirement in an adaptive way. Having had multifaceted experiences, they have at this time the psychic flexibility that enables them to give up some of their former identity roles and responsibilities, and to enjoy the new freedoms and opportunities retirement can offer.

Analytic work with these women indicates, however, that certain psychic changes are necessary to make such successful coping possible. Whereas maturity in youth is recognized by the attainment of landmarks, maturity in aging requires self-reflection and the courage to face the true score of one's life. It requires in most cases the acceptance that the past cannot be modified. Aging with growth is possible when a divestment of the narcissistic preoccupation with ambitious goals that cannot be reached takes place. A patient in her early seventies, a successful journalist, said:

"I know I am good at what I do but my dream was to write the great American novel. I wanted to express the pent-up dreams, the hurts, the loves, the hopes. . . . In my youth I'd tell myself all the time that for sure I'd start writing next year. Then I turned 50, and I knew it would never happen. I was not only sad, I was mortified. I hope now to write a few short stories. . . . I'd like to let my fantasy roam. . . . "

Successful aging also requires an acceptance of the changes in one's aging body-self, and the ability nonetheless to continue to cathect it narcissistically.

Such psychic changes, combined with a libidinization of possibly new ego interests and aims, are necessary to infuse age-appropriate goals with enthusiasm and curiosity, the true guarantors of lasting youth. Feminine and masculine strivings that frequently resulted in psychic conflict in younger years can now be integrated, enabling the older woman to be both assertive and nurturing. As a result of this integration, women become relatively independent. They enjoy many forms of giving, but do not use their gifts to bind and assert power. They are generative and continuously involved in life, pursuing their choices to the utmost. These women discover pleasures that are possible for them and take time to luxuriate in them. They delight in various areas of aesthetics, make new discoveries, and frequently pursue their own latent talents. These are women who cultivate the art of attaining the maximum possible enjoyment. They know that "tomorrows," which sustained youth, for the elderly are but a hope they trust will be fulfilled. During vital aging, which may last well into the eighties, these woman are self-affirmative yet accepting of the limitations years impose. They acknowledge the realities of their time in life, relish and maximize the opportunities it offers.

For many women aging is most successful when they are involved in youth-oriented activities, teaching, grandparenting, mentoring, and so on. Such activities enable them to shift the focus to the young person. This simultaneously provides an opportunity for the satisfaction of generativity and for a vicarious identification with youth. It reinforces the sense of aliveness by making the woman feel she is still needed and still can give. Some women devote their energies to various forms of community work. Such activities give a woman the opportunity for a passionate involvement in her endeavor, and enable her to focus on the future with a sense of participation.

Interests, goals, generativity, and the capacity for emotional involvement do not obliterate some of the painful experiences of aging. They do, however, strengthen the will to live by constantly maintaining a vital pursuit of future goals. As long as there is something to strive for, there is a sense of inner urging, and hope remains alive.

Even with good physical health, when psychic pain is present, successful aging becomes disrupted. Thus many older women come to analytic treatment because of unresolved conflicts, an existential sense of futility and despair, a feeling of having been betrayed and of having been the betrayer. They hope treatment will enable them to resolve their childhood angers, envy, and hatred, which resulted in a malevolent sense of guilt. These patients seek from treatment the attainment of inner peace, the capacity to clasp one's hand lovingly and reassuringly. They find it difficult to be alone because they lack the soothing presence of a benign internalized object for which they long. Analytic work with these women reveals that their interaction with mother did not result in such a loving internalization. Nor did these patients achieve a loving identification with their mothers. These women frequently find in themselves mother's hated traits to which they react with the critical lack of forgiveness characteristic of mother's attitude, which they have internalized. They consequently cannot forgive her or themselves. They are haunted by the realization that they are like mother, and by memories of destructive acts they committed because they did not want to be like mother. Mother's devaluation of her womanhood, which these women accepted and with which they identified, precluded a successful integration of the feminine and masculine aspects of their psyche.

Consequently, their assertive strivings and generativity remained conflicted. A combination of all these factors resulted in a lack of sufficient healthy narcissism to sustain their aging with continued self-esteem.

As aging progresses, many women find their loving and sexual needs and desires painfully unsatisfied. This increases their narcissistic and libidinal sense of depletion, their angry frustration, and frequent feelings of abandonment. The preponderance of such conflicts interferes with women's wishes, as they age, to become reconciled with themselves, be themselves, and live and die in peace. One patient said, "If I could just have a loved one close to me with arms entwined . . . if I could fantasize it so intensely that I would feel it and be soothed, even though just my arms and hands would be touching me. . . . "

Many elderly patients spoke a great deal about death. They wanted, as a result of their analyses, to become sufficiently self-loving to be able to end their lives when suffering became intolerable. They implied that such suffering could at some time include psychic pain. One patient said: "I'd like to know and believe I could feed myself medication, and that it would be soothing, like a good mother's milk . . . and I would fall asleep feeling her arms lovingly holding me tight."

Flexibility and the capacity to accommodate come into play when something one has dreaded, and therefore did not have the courage to face, actually happens. It may be learning that the little growth indeed is cancerous, that the chest discomfort is a sign of angina, that the arrhythmia is not just passing palpitations. Aging becomes a painful reality when one has to give up activities one enjoyed pursuing because strength is failing and the stamina is gone. This is the sign of true old age. At such a time a reconciliation with one's aging body, which can no longer perform as it did in the past, is of vital importance. This becomes easier when there are some compensations. The presence of a loving family or friends can dispel loneliness. The ability to maintain or find a hobby nourishes interests. The capacity to accept one's final decline with serenity and tranquility is a rare gift and a sought-after blessing.

Most painful, however, is knowing that a beloved companion or friend is dying. Such a loss, when one is aging, feels and is totally irrevocable. It creates an inner void that only the capacity to evoke a sense of a loving presence can mitigate. Loving memories and reverie may help lessen the pain. Unfortunately, if ambivalence predominated in the relationship, the woman feels abandoned rather than alone, and tends to displace her anger. When this occurs, successful mourning is not possible and there is no solace.

The biblical story of Moses, who could only view the Promised Land but was forbidden to enter it, is a metaphor depicting our fate. When generativity prevails but the joy of doing is no longer possible, what remains is faith in the possibility that the lives we have fostered might have their hopes fulfilled.

11 In Conclusion . . .

I have learned from my analysis, my self-analysis, and especially from my patients about the power of internalized stereotypes and the gripping hold customs and mores have. These are the means by which each society acculturalizes its members and establishes their conformity.

Throughout the centuries delineation of what woman's nature is has been fashioned by what woman is supposed to be as envisioned by men. Men's conscious and unconscious wishes and needs molded their ideas about women. These were expressed in love poetry, ballads, fairy tales, and scientific treatises. Thus the ideal woman was described as passive, pliable, generously available, accommodating, altruistic, selfless, and self-sacrificing, loving and faithful *no matter what*. A woman with all these virtues was the sought-after ideal, loved and cherished. Girls were raised and educated to embody this ideal. The goal was to mold women who wished to be of service for the sake of the family and the future husband. To fulfill these goals girls were taught by all means available not to be assertive and independent; they were discouraged from striving for aims other than those assigned to them by family and society. Girls were imbued with the notion, transmitted from generation to generation, that the female gender is inferior, and women therefore should be subservient to men. It was the superior male's privilege to have at first a mother and then a wife who catered to him in every possible way. At least 95 percent if not all art of this genre depicts a mother with an infant boy, lovingly in her arms. This is especially so for religious, Catholic, and Renaissance art.

However, myths, fairy tales, and world literature inform us that there also were women who did not live up to this stereotype, who rebelled in various ways and who wanted what men had. Such women were looked upon with anger and scorn both by men and by women who had internalized society's norms. Freud epitomized women's dissatisfaction with their lot as "penis envy," the incurable festering wound of a woman's psyche. However, what women yearned for and desired were and are male prerogatives that men made into their birthright and that are symbolized by the phallus. Women wanted and want equal access to men's claims. They also wanted and want the right to be assertive, to pursue their own goals, not to have to be pliable, passive, and at the service of others. Women want the autonomy to respond freely with receptivity and generosity when they so wish.

Thus it is not surprising that little girls whose drive and spunk were not as yet completely squelched, aware of the difference in privilege and treatment between themselves and boys, wanted what they thought accounted for the difference: the penis. The penis symbolized for the little girl what she was lacking in status, privilege, and, most important, loving parental acceptance.

Freud's historic question "What does a woman want?" has a simple answer. To have a chance to develop *freely*, to become and be the woman she is psychobiologically destined to be, and to be able to pursue her own true goals and ego interests. A woman does not want to be *programmed* to be the "servant of society" as up until today she still is in most societies, for instance India, China, other parts of Asia, and especially the Moslem world.

Shakespeare's famous *Taming of the Shrew* presents such a rebellious female character unwilling to submit to her prescribed role. She is therefore regarded as a shrew. The play gives instructions on how to proceed to tame the unruly woman. It is the husband's prerogative to starve her, humiliate her, ignore her until she "comes to her senses" and "learns her place." In other words, as with a bronco, the woman's spirit—if she has one—is to be broken. The woman will then, as a wife should, humble herself before the husband and praise his virtues, acknowledging that he is the master.

In more recent literature, the difficulty some girls have in assuming the submissive second-place role which does not "come naturally," is described by Jo's struggles in *Little Women* (Alcott 1915). Though less stringent means were used, and the author is sympathetic to the heroine, Jo nonetheless eventually had to assume a role considered "proper" for a young lady. In her heart, however, she never gave in. The author's sympathetic attitude indicates her own conflicts. The fate of *Anne of Green Gables* (Montgomery 1908) eventually was similar.

Both these books have remained popular for so many years because the heroines depict and reflect the perpetual conscious and unconscious yearnings and struggles of girls in our society.

Though much has changed since these books were written, the basic disadvantage of girls in comparison to boys remains. This is attested to, among others, by the Association of University Women which points out the continuing differences in attitude and educational opportunities of girls and boys in our coeducational schools, and the disastrous effect this has on the education and self-esteem of girls.

Feminist literature is replete with discussions of this problem, and of the phenomenon of concomitant discrimination against women on all levels of society. The fact that the Equal Rights amendment has not yet been ratified by all states speaks for itself.

The effects sociocultural stereotypic values (Fenichel 1945) have on the formation and shape of a woman's inner world and on her psychic structure is of concern. Girls, like boys, notwithstanding individual differences, are born with zest, aggression (Freud 1933), curiosity, and the impetus for self-fulfillment. In the ensuing process of socialization, different pressures (Freud 1933), different goals, and different expectations are exerted on children of each gender. In our culture, in which girls are allowed relative freedom of choice in the fulfillment of goals, the motto still prevails: "Don't compete with boys, don't show them how smart you are, be demure, if you want him to be your boyfriend and to marry you." It is the rare woman who says: "I did *not* have to compromise intellectually. My lover is my best friend and we support each other's goals even though they may diverge, and I continue with my interests to fulfill my aims."

This all too brief synopsis has been presented to provide a sociopsychological background for one of women's main characterological problems, their conflict between so-called feminine and masculine strivings. This theme is discussed in Chapters 4, 7, and 8. Though we have learned from child observation that assertive strivings are a part of the psychobiological disposition of female and male infants and children, all cultures, including ours, stereotype strident, goal-oriented behavior phallic, that is, masculine, and submissive self-denigrating masochistic behavior as feminine. A clash between these contrasting psychic dispositions, sometimes conscious but frequently unconscious, plagues many women.

Freud put into psychoanalytic language *as facts* what was asserted as "feminine nature" for centuries, namely, that women, in contrast to normal, active men, are *constitutionally passive* (Davis 1993); even their libido—the little of it they have—is passive. Consequently, if girls/women behave contrary to this depiction of normal feminine nature, they were/are considered masculine, wanting to usurp what is not theirs, what is even considered to be alien to their true nature. Society frowns upon such behavior because it was, and is, regarded as contrary to the established norm for girls and women.

Bisexuality was Freud's explanation for women's assertiveness. Child observation points to the significant role played by the normal human biological drive for self-assertion. Analysis of girls and women indicates the important role played by parental internalizations.

In the course of her maturation, the growing girl not only internalizes the parental interactions with each other and with her, she also identifies with each of her parents and internalizes the specificity of this interaction. The girl's feeling of sameness with mother contributes to her identification with mother. The mother's sense of self-worth and her status in the family will be an important factor determining the girl's conscious and unconscious wish to be like mother. When this is not the case, the greater mother's self-devaluation as a woman and the lower her status in the family, the greater usually are her devaluation of daughter and the suppression of daughter's assertive drive. However, the wish to be valued and to value oneself is inherent in everyone, even though it may eventually be destroyed. Under such circumstances, the girl frequently overvalues father's position and attributes. She views her father, in households where he is the master, as having the qualities she longs for. This prompts her conscious and unconscious identification with him. When the conscious enactment is discouraged because such behavior is considered inappropriate for a girl, the frustration may lead to repression and an intensification of unconscious strivings. This may eventuate into various vicissitudes. The intrapsychic conflict between maternally and paternally based identifications may intensify, resulting in behavioral oscillations. However, when both strivings are of equal intensity, the intrapsychic lack of resolution may manifest itself in behavioral paralysis. When suppression predominates, the frustration of the girl's assertive drive often unconsciously turns the aggression against the self, leading to various forms of masochism. Assertive strivings, combined with the enactment of aspects of the paternal identification, may find expression in different forms of rebelliousness. In the Western world, involvement in various forms of proselytizing gave women the possibility to express their assertiveness. They obtained converts to their causes: the feminist movements and reform drives. An outstanding example is the suffragette movement, which established women's right to vote, to inherit, to own property and capital, and to manage it by themselves, enabling them to control their own lives while striving to establish a path that would give all women control of their lives. This autonomy was in stark contrast to women's prescribed submissive roles.

Difficulty with and a lack of psychic integration between feminine and masculine identifications, each of which has a strikingly different structure and goal, brings many women to analysis or therapy. These women suffer because of the lack of intrapsychic cohesion, which leads to conscious and unconscious conflict, behavioral oscillations, and the acting out of one or more identity patterns.

Under optimal conditions the transition of passive-receptive tendencies into active object- and goal-directed behavior occurs in the course of maturation. As a result of selective identifications, a developmental resolution, namely, an integration of female and male identifications, takes place. Combining such internalizations leads to a process of depersonification of male and female aspects included in the ego ideal. As a result, the ego ideal can be regarded as neither female nor male, maternal nor paternal, since the values and ideals it contains no longer have the cathexis of the original objects they stem from. Thus, optimally, the ego ideal is a gender-neutral guidepost of the highest aspirations. Such maturation permits the development in which assertiveness in the attainment of one's wished-for self-image and goals becomes congruent with the superego.

A girl's development does not follow a straight path. For her full maturation into a woman *gratified by her femininity,* wholehearted parental acceptance is necessary. The girl-child's relationship with mother, even under favorable conditions, is ambivalent and conflictual. In spite of that, however, the girl needs mother's affirmation since she must identify with her mother to embrace femininity. The girl also needs the loving, admiring acceptance by father and his encouragement of her striving expanding self to be confident that men will accept her in her totality. Such growth for a girl is possible only when the father–mother relationship has loving *peer* qualities devoid of patriarchal bias, a rare phenomenon indeed.

Contemporary views on female psychosexual development do not question most of Freud's observations. They do, however, differ with his monistic understanding and interpretation of same. Freud's (1933) statement that "a little girl is a little man" (p. 118) and his assertion that penis envy is the "bed-rock" a woman's analysis can reach (Freud 1937) have been the focus of many analytic investigations, as has been his contention that femininity is born from the castration complex.

In the present analytic climate, long-held doctrinaire Freudian views regarding female psychosexual development and sexuality are undergoing reexamination. An open-minded and open-ended approach to analytic child observation provides new developmental data. Female analysands are given a hearing free from interpretations and conclusions that are inferential leaps based on previously established Freudian dogma. The prevalent recognition that the human mind has an almost unlimited capacity for pluralism leads to the acknowledgment that the great variety of fantasies about which we are analytically informed is multidetermined.

The girl's psychosexual development is primarily feminine (Stoller 1968a, 1976). It is enhanced by an early pleasurable body awareness and by pleasurable genital sensations stemming from self-exploration and masturbation. All these bodily sensations are important for the development of a specifically feminine body image and feminine self-representation. When the girl, in spite of her ambivalence, experiences a sense of sameness with mother, perceived as omnipotent, this identification becomes a significant aspect and source of her healthy narcissism. Such development contributes to a girl's attainment of self-realization in spite of the pressure of prevalent stereotypes.

References

Abraham, H., and Freud, E., eds. (1965). *A Psychoanalytic Dialogue. The Letters of Sigmund Freud and Karl Abraham, 1907–1926.* The International Psycho-Analytical Library No. 68. London: Hogarth Press and the Institute of Psycho-Analysis.

Abraham, K. (1920). Manifestations of the female castration complex. In *Selected Papers on Psycho-Analysis,* pp. 335–369. London: Hogarth Press.

Alcott, L. (1915). *Little Women.* Boston: Little, Brown.

Anthony, E. J., and Benedek, T., eds. (1975). *Depression and Human Existence.* Boston: Little, Brown.

Applegarth, A. (1976). Psychopathology of work in women. Paper presented to the Council of Psychoanalytic Psychotherapists. New York, February 24.

Asch, S. (1980). Beating fantasies: symbiosis and child battering. *International Journal of Psychoanalytic Psychotherapy* 8:652–657.

Assaad, M. B. (1980). Female circumcision in Egypt: social implications, current research, and prospects for change. *Studies in Family Planning* 11:5–16.

Bachofen, J. J. (1861). *Myth, Religion, and Mother Right,* trans. R. Manheim. Princeton, NJ: Princeton University Press, 1967.

Bach, S. (1971). Some notes on some imaginary companions. *Psychoanalytic Study of the Child* 25:159–171. New York: International Universities Press.

Balint, M. (1968). *The Basic Fault: Therapeutic Aspects of Regression.* London: Tavistock.

Bardwick, J. M. (1971). *Psychology of Women: A Study of Bio-cultural Conflicts*. New York: Harper & Row.

Barglow, P., and Schaefer, M. (1976). A new female psychology? *Journal of the American Psychoanalytic Association*, Supplement, 24:393–438.

Barker-Benfield, B. (1975). Sexual surgery in late nineteenth century America. *International Journal of Health Services* 5:279–298.

Barnett, M. C. (1966). Vaginal awareness in the infancy and childhood of girls. *Journal of the American Psychoanalytic Association* 14(1):129–141.

Barry, K. (1984). *Female Sexual Slavery*. New York: New York University Press.

Bart, P. B., and Grossman, M. (1978). Menopause. In *The Woman Patient: Medical and Psychological Interfaces*, vol. 1, ed. M. T. Notman and C. C. Nadelson, pp. 337–354. New York: Plenum.

Bemesderfer, S. (1996). Psychoanalytic aspects of menopause. *Journal of the American Psychoanalytic Association* 44(2):631–638.

Benedek, T. (1950). Climacterium: a developmental phase. *Psychoanalytic Quarterly* 19:1–27.

——— (1959). Parenthood as a developmental phase: a contribution to the libido theory. *Journal of the American Psychoanalytic Association* 7:389–417.

Benedek T. and Anthony, E. J., eds. (1970). *Parenthood: Its Psychology and Psychopathology*. Boston: Little, Brown.

Bergmann, M. (1982). The female oedipus complex: its antecedents and evolution. In *Early Female Development: Current Psychoanalytic Views*, ed. D. Mendell, pp. 175–201. Jamaica, NY: Spectrum Publications.

Bettelheim, B. (1954). *Symbolic Wounds. Puberty Rites and the Envious Male*. Glencoe, IL: Free Press.

Bibring, E. (1953). The mechanism of depression. In *Affective Disorders: Psychoanalytic Contribution to Their Study*, ed. P. Greenacre, pp. 13–48. New York: International Universities Press.

Bibring, G. L. (1959). Some considerations of the psychological processes in pregnancy. *Psychoanalytic Study of the Child* 14:113–121. New York: International Universities Press.

Bibring, G. L., Dwyer, T. F., Huntington, D. S., and Valenstein, A. F. (1961). A study of the psychological processes in pregnancy and of the earliest mother–child relationship. *Psychoanalytic Study of the Child* 16:9–72. New York: International Universities Press.

Blum, H. P., ed. (1976). *Female Psychology: Contemporary Psychoanalytic Views.* New York: New York University Press.

——— (1988). Shared fantasy and reciprocal identification, and their role in gender disorders. *Fantasy, Myth, and Reality: Essays in Honor of Jacob A. Arlow, M. D.,* ed. H. P. Blum et al. Madison, CT: International Universities Press.

Bonaparte, M. (1948). Female mutilation among primitive peoples and their psychical parallels in civilization. In *Female Sexuality,* pp. 153–161. New York: International Universities Press, 1953.

——— (1949). *Female Sexuality.* New York: International Universities Press, 1953.

British Medical Journal (1867). The debate of the obstetrical society. April 6, pp. 407–408.

Brunswick, R. M. (1940). The preoedipal phase of the libido development. *Psychoanalytic Quarterly* 9:293–319.

Bychowski, G. (1956). The release of internal images. *International Journal of Psycho-Analysis* 37:331–338.

——— (1958). Struggle against the introjects. *International Journal of Psycho-Analysis* 39:182–187.

Chasseguet-Smirgel, J. (1970). Feminine guilt and the oedipus complex. In *Female Sexuality: New Psychoanalytic Views,* pp. 94–134. Ann Arbor: University of Michigan Press.

——— (1976). Freud and female sexuality: the consideration of some blind spots in the exploration of the "dark continent." *International Journal of Psycho-Analysis* 57:275–305.

Chehrazi, S. (1986). Female psychology: a review. *Journal of the American Psychoanalytic Association* 34:141–162.

Clower, V. L. (1975). Significance of masturbation in female sexual development and function. In *Masturbation from Infancy to Senescence*, ed. I. M. Marcus and J. J. Francis, pp. 107–144. New York: International Universities Press.

Coleman, R. W., Kris, E., and Provence, S. (1953). The study of variations of early parental attitudes: a preliminary report. *Psychoanalytic Study of the Child*, 8:20–47. New York: International Universities Press.

Covarrubias, M. (1974). *Island of Bali*. Kuala Lumpur: Oxford University Press.

Datan, N. (1990). Aging into transitions: cross-cultural perspectives on women at midlife. In *The Meanings of Menopause*, ed. R. Formanek. Hillsdale, NJ: Analytic Press.

Davis, R. H. (1993). Freud's concept of passivity. *Psychological Issues*. Monograph 60. Madison, CT: International Universities Press.

Deutsch, H. (1930). The significance of masochism in the mental life of women. *International Journal of Psycho-Analysis* 11:48–60.

——— (1944). *The Psychology of Women*. New York: Grune & Stratton.

——— (1945). The climacterium. In *The Psychology of Women: A Psychoanalytic Interpretation. Vol. II: Motherhood*, pp. 456–491. New York: Grune & Stratton.

Edgcumbe, R., Lundberg, S., Markowitz, R., and Salo, F. (1976). Some comments on the concept of the negative oedipal phase in girls. *Psychoanalytic Study of the Child* 31:35–61. New Haven, CT: Yale University Press.

Ehrenreich, B., and English, D. (1973). *Complaints and Disorders: The Sexual Politics of Sickness*. New York: Feminist Press.

——— (1978). *For Her Own Good: 150 Years of the Experts' Advice to Women*. Garden City, NY: Anchor/Doubleday.

Erikson, E. H. (1950). *Childhood and Society*. New York: Norton.

——— (1959). *Identity and the Life Cycle*. (*Psychological Issues*, Vol.

1, No. 1, Monogr. 1. New York: International Universities Press.

—— (1968). Reflections on womanhood. *Daedalus* 2:582–606.

—— (1979). Unpublished manuscript, presented at the International Congress on Psychoanalysis, August 3.

Fast, I. (1978). Developments in gender identity: the original matrix. *International Review of Psycho-Analysis* 5:265–273.

—— (1979). Developments in gender identity: gender differentiation in girls. *International Journal of Psycho-Analysis* 60:443–453.

—— (1984). *Gender Identity: A Differentiation Model.* Hillsdale, NJ: Analytic Press.

—— (1990). Aspects of early gender development: toward a reformulation. *Psychoanalytic Psychology*, Suppl., 7:105–117.

Fenichel, O. (1945). *The Psychoanalytic Theory of Neurosis.* New York: Norton.

Ferber, L. (1975). Beating fantasies. In *Masturbation from Infancy to Senescence*, ed. L. M. Marcus and J. J. Francis, pp. 205–222. New York: International Universities Press.

Fessler, L. (1950). The psychopathology of climacteric depression. *Psychoanalytic Quarterly* 19(1):28–43.

Flaste, R. (1979). Research begins to focus on suicide among aged. *New York Times*, January 2, p. C2.

Fliegel, Z. O. (1973). Feminine psychosexual development in Freudian theory: a historical reconstruction. *Psychoanalytic Quarterly* 42(3):385–408.

—— (1982). *Half a Century Later: Current Status of Freud's Controversial Views on Women.* New York: Human Sciences Press.

Formanek, R., ed. (1992). *The Meanings of Menopause: Historical, Medical and Clinical Perspectives.* Analytic Press.

Forrer, G. R. (1959). The mother of a defective child. *Psychoanalytic Quarterly* 28:59–63.

Frenkiel, N. (1993). Family planning baby boy or girl? *The New York Times*, November 11.

Freud, A. (1936). *The Ego and the Mechanism of Defense.* New York: International Universities Press.

——— (1976). Psychopathology seen against the background of normal development. *British Journal of Psychiatry* 129(5):401–406.

Freud, S. (1905). Three essays on the theory of sexuality. *Standard Edition* 7:135–243, 1953.

——— (1912). The dynamics of transference. *Standard Edition* 12:97–108.

——— (1914a). On narcissism: an introduction. *Standard Edition* 14:73–102, 1957.

——— (1914b). Remembering, repeating and working-through. *Standard Edition* 12:145–156.

——— (1915). Observations on transference love. *Standard Edition* 12:157–171.

——— (1917a). Introductory lectures on psycho-analysis. *Standard Edition* 16:243–463, 1963.

——— (1917b). On transformations of instinct as exemplified in anal erotism. *Standard Edition* 17:123–134.

——— (1917c). Mourning and melancholia. *Standard Edition* 14:243–258, 1957.

——— (1919). A child is being beaten. A contribution to the study of the origin of sexual perversions. *Standard Edition* 17:175–204.

——— (1920). The psychogenesis of a case of homosexuality in a woman. *Standard Edition* 18:147–172, 1955.

——— (1923a). The ego and the id. *Standard Edition* 19:20–31.

——— (1923b). The infantile genital organization. *Standard Edition* 19:141–145, 1961.

——— (1924a). The dissolution of the Oedipus complex. *Standard Edition* 19:173–79, 1961.

——— (1924b). The economic problem of masochism. *Standard Edition* 19:157–172.

——— (1925). Some psychical consequences of the anatomical distinction between the sexes. *Standard Edition* 19:248–258, 1961.

———— (1927). Fetishism. *Standard Edition* 21:149–158.

———— (1931). Female sexuality. *Standard Edition* 21:225–43, 1961.

———— (1933). New introductory lectures on psycho-analysis: Femininity. *Standard Edition* 22:112–135, 1964.

———— (1937). Analysis terminable and interminable. *Standard Edition* 23, 216–253.

———— (1940a). An outline of psychoanalysis. *Standard Edition* 23:141–208.

———— (1940b). Splitting of the ego in the process of defence. *Standard Edition* 23:271–278.

Friedan, B. (1995). *The Fountain of Age*. New York: Simon & Schuster.

Galenson, E. (1980). Preoedipal determinants of a beating fantasy. *International Journal of Psychoanalytic Psychotherapy* 8:649–6–52.

Galenson, E., and Roiphe, H. (1976). Some suggested revisions concerning early female development. *Journal of the American Psychoanalytic Association* Suppl., 24:29–57.

Gannon, L. (1990). Endocrinology of menopause. In *The Meaning of Menopause*, pp. 179–224. Hillsdale, NJ: Analytic Press.

Gay, P. (1988). *Freud: A Life for Our Time*. New York: Norton.

Giovacchini, P. L. (1972). The symbiotic phase. In *Tactics and Techniques in Psychoanalytic Therapy*, ed. P. L. Giovacchini, pp. 137–169. New York: Jason Aronson.

Gitelson, M. (1954). Therapeutic problems in the analysis of the "normal" candidate. *International Journal of Psycho-Analysis* 35:174–183.

Glover, L., and Mendell, D. (1982). A suggested developmental sequence for a preoedipal genital phase. In *Early Female Development: Current Psychoanalytic Views*, ed. D. Mendell, pp. 127–174. New York/London: SP Medical & Scientific Books.

Gornick, V., and Moran, B. K., eds. (1972). *Women in Sexist Society*. New York: New American Library.

Greenacre, P. (1950a). Special problems of early female sexual development. *Psychoanalytic Study of the Child* 5:122–138. New York: International Universities Press.

———— (1950b). Development of the body ego. *Psychoanalytic Study of the Child* 5:18–23. New York: International Universities Press.

Greene, J., and Cook, D. (1980). Life stress and symptoms at the climacteric. *British Journal of Psychiatry* 136:486–491.

Grossman, W., and Kaplan, D. (1988). Three commentaries on gender in Freud's thought: a prologue to the psychoanalytic theory of sexuality. In *Fantasy, Myth, and Reality*, ed. H. Blum, Y. Kramer, A. D. Richards, and A. K. Richards, pp. 339–370. Madison, CT: International Universities Press.

Grossman, W. I., and Simon, B. (1969). Anthropomorphism: motive, meaning, and causality in psychoanalytic theory. *Psychoanalytic Study of the Child* 24:78–111. New York: International Universities Press.

Grossman, W., and Stewart, W. (1976). Penis envy: from childhood wish to developmental metaphor. *Journal of the American Psychoanalytic Association* 24:193–215.

Hannett, F. (1949). Transference reactions to an event in the life of the analyst. *Psychoanalytic Review* 36:69–81.

Hartmann, H. (1950). Comments on the psychoanalytic theory of the ego. In *Essays on Ego Psychology*. New York: International Universities Press, 1964.

———— (1958). *Ego Psychology and the Problem of Adaptation*. New York: International Universities Press.

Hartmann, H., and Loewenstein, R. M. (1962). Notes on the superego. *Psychoanalytic Study of the Child* 17:42–81. New York: International Universities Press.

Haspels, A. A., and Musaph, H., eds. (1979). *Psychosomatics in Perimenopause*. Baltimore: University Park Press.

Hoefer, H., ed. (1974). *Guide to Bali*. Singapore: Apa Productions.

Horney, K. (1924). On the genesis of the castration complex in women. *International Journal of Psycho-Analysis* 5:58–65.

———— (1926). The flight from womanhood: the masculinity complex in women, as viewed by men and women. *International Journal of Psycho-Analysis* 7:324–339.

Hosken, F. (1993). Genital and sexual mutilation of females. *The Hoskin Report*, pp. 5–11. Lexington, MA: Women's International Network News.

Isaacs, S. (1927). Penis-feces-child. *International Journal of Psycho-Analysis* 8:74–76.

Jackel, M. M. (1966). Interruptions during psychoanalytic treatment and the wish for a child. *Journal of the American Psychoanalytic Association* 14:730–735.

Jacobson, E. (1937). Ways of female superego formation and the female castration conflict. *Psychoanalytic Quarterly* 45:525–538, 1976.

———— (1954). The self and the object world. *Psychoanalytic Study of the Child*, 9:75–127. New York: International Universities Press.

———— (1964). *The Self and the Object World.* New York: International Universities Press.

———— (1971). *Depression: Comparative Studies of Normal, Neurotic, and Psychotic Conditions.* New York: International Universities Press.

Jones, E. (1922). Notes on Dr. Abraham's article on the female castration complex. *International Journal of Psycho-Analysis* 5:327–328.

———— (1927). The early development of female sexuality. *International Journal of Psycho-Analysis* 8:459–472.

———— (1935). Early female sexuality. *International Journal of Psycho-Analysis* 16:263–273.

Joseph, E. D., ed. (1965). *Beating Fantasies and Regressive Ego Phenomena in Psychoanalysis.* New York: International Universities Press.

Kaplan, D. (1990). Some theoretical and technical aspects of gender and social reality in clinical psychoanalysis. *Psychoanalytic Study of the Child* 45:3–24. New Haven, CT: Yale University Press.

Kaplan, S. M., and Whitman, R. M. (1965). The negative ego-ideal. *International Journal of Psycho-Analysis* 46:183–187.

Karme, L. (1981). A clinical report of penis envy: its multiple meanings and defensive function. *Journal of the American Psychoanalytic Association* 29:427–446.

Kaufert, O., and Syrotuik, J. (1981). Symptom reporting at the menopause. *Social Science and Medicine* 15:173–184.

Kernberg, O. (1966). Structural derivatives of object relationships. *International Journal of Psycho-Analysis* 47:236–253.

——— (1967). Borderline personality organization. *Journal of the American Psychoanalytic Association* 15:641–685.

——— (1971). Prognostic considerations regarding borderline personality organization. *Journal of the American Psychoanalytic Association* 19:595–635.

——— (1975). Normal and pathological narcissism. In *Borderline Conditions and Pathological Narcissism*, pp. 315–343. New York: Jason Aronson.

——— (1976). *Object-Relations Theory and Clinical Psychoanalysis*. New York: Jason Aronson.

——— (1980a). Object relations theory and psychoanalytic technique. In *Internal World and External Reality*, pp. 155–180. New York: Jason Aronson.

——— (1980b). Normal narcissism in middle age. In *Internal World and External Reality: Object Relations Theory Applied*, pp. 121–134. New York: Jason Aronson.

——— (1984). *Severe Personality Disorders and Psychotherapeutic Strategies*. New Haven: Yale University Press.

Kestenberg, J. (1956). On the development of maternal feelings in early childhood: observations and reflections. *Psychoanalytic Study of the Child* 11. New York: International Universities Press.

Kleeman, J. A. (1971). The establishment of core gender identity in normal girls. *Archives of Sexual Behavior* 1:103–129.

——— (1975). Genital self-stimulation in infant and toddler girls. In *Masturbation from Infancy to Senescence*, ed. I. M. Marcus and

J. J. Francis, pp. 77–106. New York: International Universities Press.

——— (1976). Freud's views on early female sexuality in the light of direct child observation. *Journal of the American Psychoanalytic Association* 24(Suppl. 5), 24:3–27.

Klein, M. (1932). *The Pyscho-Analysis of Children.* New York: Norton.

——— (1957). *Envy and Gratitude: A Study of the Unconscious Sources.* New York: Basic Books.

Kohut, H. (1959). Introspection, empathy, and psychoanalysis. *Journal of the American Psychoanalytic Association* 7:459–483.

——— (1966). Forms and transformations of narcissism. *Journal of the American Psychoanalytic Association* 14(2):243–272.

——— (1971). *The Analysis of the Self.* New York: International Universities Press.

Konner, M. (1990). Review of *Prisoners of Reality* by H. L. Klein. *The New York Times Book Review,* April 15, p. 16.

Kronenberg, F., Cote, L., Linkie, D., et al. (1984). Menopausal hot flashes: thermoregulatory, cardiovascular, and circulating catecholamine and LH changes. *Maturitas* 6:31–43.

Kulish, N. M. (1991). The mental representation of the clitoris: the fear of female sexuality. *Psychoanalytic Inquiry* 11:511–536.

Lampl-de Groot, J. (1965). *The Development of the Mind.* New York: International Universities Press.

Laufer, E. (1986). The female Oedipus complex and the relationship to the body. *Psychoanalytic Study of the Child* 41:259–276. New Haven, CT: Yale University Press.

Lax R. (1972). Some aspects of the interaction between mother and impaired child: mother's narcissistic trauma. *International Journal of Psycho-Analysis* 53:339–344.

——— (1977). The role of internalization in the development of certain aspects of female masochism: ego psychological considerations. *International Journal of Psycho-Analysis* 58(3):289–300.

———— (1982). The expectable depressive climacteric reaction. *Bulletin of the Menninger Clinic* 46(2):151–157.

———— (1990). An imaginary brother: his role in the formation of a girl's self image and ego ideal. *Psychoanalytic Study of the Child* 45:257–272. New Haven, CT: Yale University Press.

———— (1994). Aspects of primary and secondary genital feelings and anxieties in girls during the preoedipal and early oedipal phases. *Psychoanalytic Quarterly*, 63:271–296.

———— (1995a). The vicissitudes of boy's envy of mother, and the consequences of his narcissistic mortification. Paper presented at American Psychoanalytic Association Mid-Winter Meetings. To be published in 1997 in *Psychoanalytic Study of the Child.*

———— (1995b). Motives and determinants of girls' penis envy in the negative oedipal phase. *Journal of Clinical Psychoanalysis,* vol. 4, no. 3, pp. 297–314. International Universities Press.

LeBow, M. (1963). Pregnancy of the analyst as a stimulus to the dreams and fantasies of the patient. Paper presented at the 1963 Psychoanalytic Mid-Winter Meeting, American Psychoanalytic Association, New York City.

Lerner, H. E. (1974). Early origins of envy and devaluation of women: implications for sex role stereotypes. *Bulletin of the Menninger Clinic* 38(6):538–553.

———— (1976). Parental mislabeling of female genitals as a determinant of penis envy and learning inhibitions in women. *Journal of the American Psychoanalytic Association* Suppl., 24: 269–283.

Lightfoot-Klein, H. (1989). *Prisoners of Ritual: An Odyssey into Female Genital Circumcision.* New York: Harrington Park Press.

Little, M. (1958). On delusional transference (transference psychosis). *International Journal of Psycho-Analysis* 39:134–138.

———— (1960). Countertransference. *British Journal of Medical Psychology* 33:29–31.

Lussier, A. (1960). The analysis of a boy with a congenital deformity. *Psychoanalytic Study of the Child* 15. New York: International Universities Press.

MacPherson, K. (1981). Menopause as disease: the social construction of a metaphor. *Advances in Nursing Science* 3(2):95–113.

Mahler, M. S. (1966). Notes on the development of basic moods: the depressive affect. In *Psychoanalysis and General Psychology*, ed. R. M. Loewenstein et al., pp. 152–168. New York: International Universities Press.

————— (1968). *On Human Symbiosis and the Vicissitudes of Individuation, vol. 1: Infantile Psychosis.* In collaboration with M. Furer. New York: International Universities Press.

————— (1971). A study of the separation-individuation process and its possible application to borderline phenomena in the psychoanalytic situation. *Psychoanalytic Study of the Child* 26:403–424. New York: International Universities Press.

————— (1974). Symbiosis and individuation: the psychological birth of the human infant. *Psychoanalytic Study of the Child* 29:89–106. New York: International Universities Press.

Mahler, M. S., Pine, F., and Bergman, A. (1975). *The Psychological Birth of the Human Infant: Symbiosis and Individuation.* New York: Basic Books.

Masters, V., and Johnson, W. (1966). *Human Sexual Response.* Boston: Little, Brown.

Masters, V., and Johnson, W. (1970). *Human Sexual Inadequacy.* Boston: Little, Brown.

Mayer, E. (1985). "Everybody must be just like me." Observations on female castration anxiety. *International Journal of Psycho-Analysis* 66, 331–347.

————— (1991). Towers and enclosed spaces: a preliminary report on gender differences in children's reactions to block structures. *Psychoanalytic Inquiry* 11:480–510.

————— (1995). The phallic castration complex and primary femininity: two developmental lines toward female gender identity. *Journal of the American Psychoanalytic Association* 43:17–38.

McCrea, F. (1983). The politics of menopause: the discovery of a deficiency disease. *Social Problems* 13(1):111–123.

McKinlay, S., and Jefferys, M. (1974). The menopause syndrome. *British Journal of Medicine* 28:108–115.

Meissner, W. W. (1971). Notes on identification. *Psychoanalytic Quarterly* 40:277–302.

Menninger, K. A. (1981). A declaration of probable needs. *Menninger Perspective* 12(1), 407. Reprinted from *Kansas Alumni,* 1980, 78, 2–4.

Mikkelsen, A., and Holte, A. (1982). A factor-analytic study of climacteric symptoms. *Psychiatry and Social Science* 2:35–39.

Milrod, D. (1982). The wished-for self-image. *Psychoanalytic Study of the Child* 37:95. New Haven, CT: Yale University Press.

Montgomery, L. M. (1908). *Anne of Green Gables.* New York: Bantam Books.

Moore, B. E. (1964). Frigidity: a review of psychoanalytic literature. *Psychoanalytic Quarterly* 33(3):323–349.

———— (1968). Psychoanalytic reflections on the implications of recent physiological studies of female orgasm. *Journal of the American Psychoanalytic Association* 16(3):569–587.

———— (1976). Freud and female sexuality: a current view. *International Journal of Psycho-Analysis* 57(3):287–305.

Moore, B. E., and Fine, B. D., eds. (1968). *A Glossary of Psychoanalytic Terms and Concepts,* 2nd ed. New York: American Psychoanalytic Association.

———— (1990). *Psychoanalytic Terms and Concepts.* New Haven/London: American Psychoanalytic Association and Yale University Press.

Moulton, R. (1970). A survey and reevaluation of the concept of penis envy. *Psychoanalysis and Women: Contributions to New Theory and Therapy,* pp. 240–258. New York: Brunner/Mazel.

Muller, J. (1932). A contribution to the problem of libidinal development of the genital phase in girls. *International Journal of Psycho-Analysis* 13:361–368.

Mulley, C. and Mitchell, J. (1976). Menopausal flushing: Does estrogen therapy make sense? *Lancet* 1:1398–1399.

Musaph, H. (1979). The trigger function of the menopause. In *Psy-*

chosomatics in Peri-menopause, ed. A. A. Haspels and H. Musaph, pp. 83–100. Baltimore: University Park Press.

Myers, W. (1980). The psychodynamics of a beating fantasy. *International Journal of Psychoanalysis and Psychotherapy* 8:623–648.

Nachtigall, L. (1986). *Estrogen.* 2nd ed. Harper & Row.

Nagera, H. (1969). The imaginary companion. *Psychoanalytic Study of the Child* 24:165–196. New York: International Universities Press.

New York Times. (1990). Puberty rites for girls is bitter issue across Africa. January 15.

——— (1991). Stark data on women: 100 million are missing. November 5, Section C, p. 1.

——— (1992). China revives bias against women. July 28.

——— (1994). Born female—and fettered. February 19, p. 18.

Notman, M. T. (1977). Is there a male menopause? In *The Menopause Book,* ed. L. Rose, pp. 130–143. New York: Hawthorn.

——— (1979). Midlife concerns of women: implications of the menopause. *American Journal of Psychiatry* 136(10):1270–1274.

——— (1995). Reproductive and critical transitions in the lifespan of women patients with focus on menopause. *Depression* 3:99–106. Cambridge, MA: Harvard Medical School.

Novick, J., and Novick, A. (1973). Beating fantasies in children. *International Journal of Psychoanalysis* 53:237–242.

——— (1987). The essence of masochism. *Psychoanalytic Study of the Child,* 48:353–384. New Haven: Yale University Press.

Orr, D. (1954). Transference and countertransference: a historical survey. *Journal of the American Psychoanalytic Association* 2:621–670.

Perlmutter, J. F. (1978). A gynecological approach to menopause. In *The Woman Patient: Medical and Psychological Interfaces,* vol. 1, ed. M. T. Notman and C., C. Nadelson, pp. 323–335. New York: Plenum.

Rangell, L. (1974). A psychoanalytic perspective leading currently to the syndrome of the compromise of integrity. *International Journal of Psycho-Analysis* 55:3–12.

————— (1991). Castration. *Journal of the American Psychoanalytic Association* 39:3–23.

Reich, A. (1940). A contribution to the psychoanalysis of extreme submissiveness in women. *Psychoanalytic Quarterly* 9:470–480.

————— (1953). Narcissistic object choice in women. *Journal of the American Psychoanalytic Association* 1:22–44.

————— (1958). A special variation of technique. In *Annie Reich: Psychoanalytic Contributions*, pp. 236–249. New York: International Universities Press.

Reik, T. (1941). *Masochism in Modern Man.* New York: Farrar, Straus.

Renik, O. (1992). A case of premenstrual distress: bisexual determinants of a woman's fantasy of damage to her genital. *Journal of the American Psychoanalytic Association* 40:195–210.

Richards, A. K. (1992). The influence of sphincter control and genital sensation on body image and gender identity in women. *Psychoanalytic Quarterly* 61:331–351.

Róheim, G. (1942). Transition rites. *Psychoanalytic Quarterly* 11:336–374.

————— (1945). Aphrodite, or the woman with a penis. *Psychoanalytic Quarterly* 14:350, 390.

Roiphe, H., and Galenson, E. (1981). *Infantile Origins of Sexual Identity.* New York: International Universities Press.

Sandler, J., Holder, A., and Meers, D. (1963). The ego ideal and the ideal self. *Psychoanalytic Study of the Child*, 18:139–158. New York: International Universities Press.

Sandler, J., and Rosenblatt, B. (1962). The concept of the representational world. *Psychoanalytic Study of the Child*, 17:128–148. New York: International Universities Press.

Schafer, R. (1960). The loving and beloved superego in Freud's structural theory. *Psychoanalytic Study of the Child* 15:163–190. New York: International Universities Press.

———— (1974). Problems in Freud's psychology of women. *Journal of the American Psychoanalytic Association* (22)459– 485.

———— (1983). Analysis of character. In *The Analytic Attitude*, pp. 134–161. New York: Basic Books.

Schuker, E., and Levinson, N. A., eds. (1991). *Female Psychology: An Annotated Psychoanalytic Bibliography.* Hillsdale, NJ/London: Analytic Press.

Scull, A., and Favreau, D. (1986). The clitoridectomy craze. *Social Research* 53(2):240–258.

Seaman, B., and Seaman, G. (1977). *Women and the Crisis in Sex Hormones.* New York: Rawson Associates.

Severne, L. (1979). Psychosocial aspects of the menopause. In *Psychosomatics of Peri-menopause*, ed. A. A. Haspels and H. Musaph, pp. 101–120. Baltimore: University Park Press.

Shaw, E. (1985). Female circumcision. *American Journal of Nursing* 85:684–687.

Sherfey, M. L. (1966). The evolution and nature of female sexuality in relation to psychoanalytic theory. *Journal of the American Psychoanalytic Association* 14(1):28–128.

Showalter, E. (1985). *The Female Malady: Women, Madness, and English Culture, 1830–1980.* New York: Pantheon Books.

Silverman, D. (1987). What are little girls made of? *Psychoanalytic Psychology* 4:325–334.

Solnit, A. J. and Stark, M. H. (1961). Mourning and the birth of a defective child. *Psychoanalytic Study of the Child* 16. New York: International Universities Press.

Sperling, M. (1950). A contribution to the psychodynamics of depression in women. *Samiksa* 4:86–101.

———— (1970). The clinical effects of parental neurosis on the child. In *Parenthood*, ed. E. J. Anthony and T. Benedek. Boston: Little, Brown.

Sperling, O. (1954). An imaginary companion, representing a prestage of the superego. *Psychoanalytic Study of the Child* 9:252– 258. New York: International Universities Press.

Spitz, R. A. (1949). Autoerotism: some empirical findings and hypotheses on three of its manifestations in the first year of life. *Psychoanalytic Study of the Child* 3/4:85–120. New York: International Universities Press.

———— (1952). Authority and masturbation: some remarks on a bibliographical investigation. In *Masturbation from Infancy to Senescence*, ed. I. M. Marcus and J. J. Francis, pp. 381–409. New York: International Universities Press, 1975.

———— (1962). Autoerotism re-examined: the role of early sexual behavior patterns in personality formation. *Psychoanalytic Study of the Child* 17:283–315. New York: International Universities Press.

Stoller, R. J. (1964). A contribution to the study of gender identity. *International Journal of Psycho-Analysis* 45:220–226.

———— (1968a). The sense of femaleness. *Psychoanalytic Quarterly* 37:42–55.

———— (1968b). *Sex and Gender: On the Development of Masculinity and Femininity.* New York: Science House.

———— (1976). Primary femininity. *Journal of the American Psychoanalytic Association* 24(Suppl. 5), 39–79.

———— (1986). *Observing the Erotic Imagination.* New Haven/London: Yale University Press.

Thompson, C. (1942). Cultural pressures in the psychology of women. *Psychoanalysis and Women: Contributions to New Theory and Therapy*, ed. J. Miller, pp. 49–64. New York: Brunner/Mazel, 1973.

Torok, M. (1970). The significance of penis envy in women. In *Female Sexuality: New Psychoanalytic Views*, ed. J. Chasseguet-Smirgel. Ann Arbor, MI: University of Michigan Press, pp. 135–170.

Torsti, M. (1994). Feminine self and penis envy. *International Journal of Psycho-Analysis* 469–478.

Waelder, R. (1936). The principle of multiple function. *Psychoanalytic Quarterly* 5:45–62.

Wilkinson, S. M. (1991). Penis envy: libidinal metaphor and experimental metonym. *International Journal of Psycho-Analysis* 72:335–346.

Williams, N. (1990). Africa: a ritual of danger. *Time*, Fall Special Issue: Women: the road ahead, p. 39.

Wilson, R. A. (1966). *Feminine Forever.* New York: Evans.

Winnicott, D. W. (1956). Primary maternal preoccupation. In *Collected Papers*, pp. 300–305. New York: Basic Books, 1958.

——— (1960). Ego distortion in terms of true and false self. In *The Maturational Processes and the Facilitating Environment*, pp. 158–165. New York: International Universities Press, 1965.

——— (1962). Providing for the child in health and in crisis. In *The Maturational Processes and the Facilitating Environment*, pp. 64–72. New York: International Universities Press, 1965.

Young-Bruehl, E. (1988). *Anna Freud: A Biography.* New York: Summit Books.

——— (1991). Rereading Freud on female development. *Psychoanalytic Inquiry* 11:427–448.

Zetzel, E. (1970). *The Capacity for Emotional Growth.* New York: International Universities Press.

Credits

The author gratefully acknowledges permission to reprint portions of her own work previously published in the following sources:

Chapter 1: based on "Freud's Views and the Changing Perspective of Femaleness and Femininity: What My Female Analysands Taught Me," in *Psychoanalytic Psychology* 12(3):393–406. Copyright © 1996 Lawrence Erlbaum Associates.

Chapter 2: based on "Some Considerations about Transference and Countertransference Manifestations Evoked by the Analyst's Pregnancy," in *International Journal of Psycho-Analysis* 50:363–372. Copyright © 1969 Institute of Psycho-Analysis.

Chapter 3: based on "Some Aspects of the Interaction between Mother and Impaired Child: Mother's Narcissistic Trauma," in *International Journal of Psycho-Analysis* 53(3):339–344. Copyright © 1972 Institute of Psycho-Analysis.

Chapter 4: based on "The Rotten Core: A Defect in the Formation of the Self during the Rapprochement Subphase," in *Rapprochement: The Critical Subphase of Separation-Individuation*, ed. R. Lax, S. Bach, and A. Burland. Copyright © 1980 Jason Aronson Inc.; and "Maternal Depression and the Development of a 'Rotten Core' in the Child: A Specific Defect in the Formation of the Self during the Rapprochement Subphase," in *The Child and His Family: Preventive Child Psychiatry in an Age of Transition*, copyright © 1980 John Wiley and Sons.

Chapter 5: based on "Aspects of Primary and Secondary Genital Feelings and Anxieties in Girls during the Preoedipal and Early Oedipal Phase," in *Psychoanalytic Quarterly* April 1994, copyright © *Psychoanalytic Quarterly* 1994; and "Motives and Determinants of Girls' Penis Envy in the Negative Oedipal Phase," in *Journal of Clinical Psychoanalysis* 4(3):297–314. Copyright © 1995 International Universities Press.

Chapter 6: based on "A Variation on Freud's Theme in 'A Child is Being Beaten'"—Mother's Role: Some Implications for Superego Development in Women," in *Journal of the American Psychoanalytic Association* 40(2). Copyright © 1992 International Universities Press.

Chapter 7: based on "An Imaginary Brother: His Role in the Formation of a Girl's Self Image and Ego Ideal," in *Psychoanalytic Study of the Child* 45:257–272. Copyright © 1990 Yale University Press.

Chapter 8: based on "The Role of Internalization in the Development of Certain Aspects of Female Masochism: Ego Psychological Considerations," in *International Journal of Psycho-Analysis* 58:289–300. Copyright © 1977 Institute of Psycho-Analysis.

Chapter 9: based on "The Expectable Climacteric Reaction," in *Bulletin of the Menninger Clinic* 46(2):151–167. Copyright © 1982 Guilford Press; and Panel Report: "Psychoanalytic Aspects of the Menopause," in *Journal of the American Psychoanalytic Association* 44(2). Copyright © 1996 International Universities Press.

Chapter 10: based on a presentation at the panel on the Women's Life Cycle, IPA Congress, September 1995; and discussion of Betty Friedan's speech at "Mind, Memories and Metaphor: Psychoanalytic Explorations," The National Membership Committee on Psychoanalysis in Clinical Social Work, October 1995.

Index

Pregnant analyst, 7, 19–45
  analytic literature and, 42
  art and, 42–43
  case examples, 21–37
    female, 21–34
    male, 34–37
    discussed, 37–42
    overview of, 19–21
Primary genital feelings, genital
    anxieties, mutilation, 86–90

Rangell, L., 17, 96, 97
Reich, A., 17, 152, 175
Reik, T., 153
Rejection, impaired child, birth
    of, 56
Renik, O., 86, 97
Richards, A. K., 89
Róheim, G., 95
Roiphe, H., 88, 101
Rosenblatt, B., 180
Rotten core pathology, 63–
    84
  case examples, 69–75
  clinical expression, 66–69
  discussed, 76–84
  mythic expression, 63–66

Sadomasochism, beating
    fantasies, 120. *See also*
    Masochism
Sandler, J., 180
Schaefer, M., 86
Schafer, R., 10, 11, 151, 162
Schuker, E., 97

Scull, A., 93
Seaman, B., 190
Seaman, G., 190
Severne, L., 191, 197
Shakespeare, W., 221
Shaw, E., 93
Sherfey, M. L., 10, 94
Silverman, D., 112
Solnit, A. J., 61
Sperling, M., 61, 146
Spitz, R. A., 89, 93, 95
Stark, M. H., 61
Stereotyping. *See* Gender
    stereotyping
Stewart, W., 111
Stoller, R. J., 10, 86, 87, 97,
    225
Superego, beating fantasies and,
    115–131. *See also* Beating
    fantasies
Syrotuik, J., 197

Thompson, C., 109, 110
Torok, M., 111, 113
Torsti, M., 112

Wilkinson, S. M., 90, 112
Williams, N., 94, 95
Wilson, R. A., 190
Winnicott, D. W., 17, 48, 76, 77,
    81, 169

Young-Bruehl, E., 86, 116

Zetzel, E., 204, 205, 206